The Management of Hotel Operations

The Management of Hotel Operations

PETER JONES, BA (Hons), MBA, FHCIMA

IFCA Chair of Production and Operations Management, School of Management, University of Surrey.

ANDREW LOCKWOOD, BSc (Hons), CertEd, MHCIMA

Professor of Hospitality Management and Deputy Head in the School of Management, University of Surrey.

THOMSON

Australia • Canada • Mexico • Singapore • Spain • United Kingdom • United States

The Management of Hotel Operations

Copyright © Thomson Learning 2004

The Thomson logo is a registered trademark used herein under licence.

For more information, contact Thomson Learning, High Holborn House, 50-51 Bedford Row, London WC1R 4LR or visit us on the World Wide Web at:
http://www.thomsonlearning.co.uk

British Library Cataloguing-in-Publication Data
A catalogue record for this book is available from the British Library

---

ISBN-13: 978-0-82646-294-7
ISBN-10: 0-82646-294-4

First edition published 1989 by Cassell
Reprinted 1990, 1992, 1993, 1994 by Cassell
Reprinted 2002 by Continuum
Reprinted 2004 (twice) and 2005 by Thomson Learning

Printed in the UK by TJ International, Padstow, Cornwall

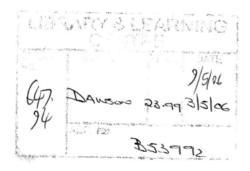

Contents

Preface

Asking hotel managers what they do and looking at what managers are told to do both fail to give a clear indication of how a manager is to be successful and, perhaps more importantly, give no indication of how their performance will be judged. This book concentrates on what it is that managers have to achieve as the framework for improving managerial effectiveness. It is based on the premise that there is little point in looking at the inputs to a job on a day-to-day basis because they may or may not give the right results. The best way to measure effectiveness must be to measure the results or outputs themselves.

It is often the case that management texts present a series of techniques which can be applied to a number of potential problems. This book, however, concentrates on the problems facing managers – getting more customers, reducing costs, getting the best out of staff – and identifies the techniques that might be appropriate for their solution. At the same time, we recognise that the best approach to problem-solving will vary from unit to unit, organisation to organisation and sector to sector. We explore the reasons for this in chapter 1 which looks at the external factors influencing the hotel industry and the special features of the context in which hotels operate. In chapter 2 we consider in more detail the strategic implications of hotel management and explain the task of hotel management as a series of overlapping key result areas.

These key result areas form the focus of chapters 3 to 9. In each of these chapters we examine and review the range of options available to a unit manager in order to maintain satisfactory performance or to take corrective action. A manager will have a great many management tools and techniques available for use but only some of these may be necessary or relevant to a particular problem. The characteristics of each option are explained so that the manager can understand why some are more appropriate for particular units and particular situations than others.

The final chapter attempts to bring all the key result areas together and build a picture of how the hotel manager may be expected to implement successfully an approach based on these guidelines.

This book is intended for students in the final stage of their management qualifications, whether at degree, higher diploma, HCIMA or postgraduate level. It therefore assumes an understanding of the technical side of hotel operations and a basic knowledge of financial, marketing and behavioural areas. We have included examples of current industry practice and case histories where appropriate and each chapter concludes with a list of references to provide further reading and material for analysis. We have attempted to bring together material, not just from the hotel industry, but from the complete range of service industries. We hope that practitioners in the industry will find the book both challenging in the way the ideas and concepts are presented, and rewarding in that it will contribute, in some small way, to the continued success and growth of their unit and the industry.

Acknowledgements

We would like to express our grateful thanks to all those individuals and organisations who have helped in the preparation of this book including:

British Airways, Commonwealth Holiday Inns of Canada (now Commonwealth Hotels International Company), Alfred Crossman, Bernard Davis, Michael Dent, David Eccles, Edwardian Hotels, Paul Gamble, Yvonne Guerrier, Colin Hales, Simon Lake, Jane MacLean, Stephen Mascilo, Richard McKevitt, Paul Merricks, Philip and Harriet Nailon, Mike Nightingale, Mike Riley, Diana Russell, Lynn Shostak, Trusthouse Forte Hotels . . . and our wives and children for their continual love and support.

1 Understanding Hotel Operations

INTRODUCTION

A hotel has been defined as: 'a, usually large, house run for the purposes of giving travellers food, lodging, etc.'[1] This dictionary definition includes some of the characteristics of modern hotels, but fails to do full justice to the complexity and variety of hotel services. Furthermore, it restricts the use of the facility to one specific type of customer – the traveller. In the United States, the hotel industry is more commonly referred to as the lodging industry. This has the advantage that it conveys a key concept, that of providing overnight accommodation to customers, but most hotels do far more than just that. Hotels today are in the business of providing space to customers in which they can eat, drink, sleep, wash, bathe, play, confer, relax, do business and a whole range of other common human activities. Some of these activities are to do with the day-to-day functioning of human existence, that must by their nature be carried out wherever the individual may be. Other activities are related to the choices people make about the way they spend their time, broadly speaking at work or at leisure.

We, therefore, have chosen to define a hotel as: 'an operation that provides accommodation and ancillary services to people away from home.' This definition includes all people who spend time away from home for whatever reason and so it includes the traditional concept of a 'hotel', as well as motels, holiday camps, condominiums, hostels, hospitals and prisons. The inclusion of institutions such as hospitals in our definition is quite deliberate. It is increasingly common to find in larger hospitals a member of the management team with the job title of 'hotel services manager'. His or her responsibilities are in many respects similar to those of the commercial hotel manager, with the exception that the client, i.e. hospital patient, is 'captive' with the impact this has on the marketing role and also that it is a not-for-profit operation with the implications this has for some aspects of financial management. We shall, however, tend to focus on commercial hotel operations as these are the more sophisticated means of providing the accommodation experience both in terms of the service package and business complexity.

1

ORIGINS OF THE HOTEL INDUSTRY

The development of the hotel industry can be traced as far back as the Druids and the Romans who have left the earliest recorded examples of the provision of hospitality. The history of the industry can be traced through the ages from the emergence of the inn, the tavern and the ale house to the first appearance of the 'hôtel garni' in the early 1760s. It was not until the early 1800s, however, that hotels as we know them today began to appear, and even then development was relatively slow until the 1860s.

There are three major influences which historically have affected the development of the industry – transport, social patterns and habits, and the economic climate. Transport has probably had the most important influence on hotels, particularly in respect of their location, as staying away from home inevitably involves some degree of travel and the mode of transport will influence where you may want to stay. The growth of the inns between the sixteenth and nineteenth centuries was influenced by the posting points for the main stage coach routes, and the terminal points of those routes saw the growth of inns able to accommodate over a hundred guests. As transport moved to the railways, so the railway companies built hotels at their terminal stations in competition with their rivals and to accommodate guests whose trains had been delayed. The railways were also responsible to a large extent for the development of seaside resorts like Blackpool and Bournemouth, which only became accessible to the masses when the railways arrived. More recently airport hotels have similarly provided accommodation for travellers as a stopping point before or after their journey, and the dynamic growth in air transport has been mirrored by a similar growth in hotel capacity at airports. In addition, the success of THF's Post House chain has shown the continued importance of transport as the locations of Post House hotels are primarily chosen to catch the motorist – on business or pleasure.

Social patterns and habits have also played their part in shaping the industry. In the Middle Ages travel was very dangerous and was largely restricted to the nobility who tended to stay en route either with their fellow noblemen or in the monasteries. As travel became easier some private houses came to acquire a reputation as a good place to stay, and the dissolution of the monasteries saw the development of these houses into inns. The large hotel capacity at the coast owes its origins to the eighteenth-century passion for sea bathing as a healthy and 'fashionable' pastime. Similarly, hotel developments world-wide have been strongly influenced by the post-war phenomenon of mass tourism on a national and international scale.

The economic climate has influenced hotel development in general, although some specific changes were brought about by two Acts of Parliament. The Limited Liabilities Act 1862 saw the risk of investment in hotels reduced dramatically and many hotel companies were floated in the tide of investment from the wealth generated by Britain's industrial leadership at that time. One of the first was the Langham Hotel Company which opened a hotel in Regent Street. This hotel closed in the 1930s and was taken over by the BBC, but it has recently come back on to the market and Ladbroke's is renovating the property to open it as a hotel once more. The Development of Tourism Act 1969 created the Hotel Development Incentive Scheme which brought about the building of new hotels in London between 1969 and 1976 to cope with a shortfall in accommodation in the capital. Recent reports from Horwath and Horwath[2] would seem to suggest that a similar shortfall will occur in the early 1990s. The overall success of the industry in servicing business needs and in providing tourist accommodation must be influenced by the general economic climate of the country and the world. It can be dramatically influenced by world events as shown by the decrease in American tourists to the UK in the summer of 1986 following the Chernobyl disaster and the bombing of Libya.

THE MODERN UK HOTEL INDUSTRY

Over the period 1970 to 1985 there have been significant changes in the UK hotel industry. The number of hotel units has fallen dramatically by 38.4 per cent whilst the number of rooms available has fallen by only 12.2 per cent. This reflects the trends in the closure of smaller units, the addition of room extensions to existing properties and the opening of more larger units (see table 1.1).

Table 1.1 *Comparison of hotel stock 1971 – 1981.*

Size of unit	Rooms 1971	Rooms 1981	% change	Units 1971	Units 1981	% change	Average unit size 1971	Average unit size 1981	% change
>15 rooms	191,800	96,100	−49.90	20,700	9,500	−54.11	9.27	10.12	9.17
15–50 rooms	223,600	200,000	−10.55	9,600	8,400	−12.50	23.29	23.81	2.22
50–200 rooms	124,200	141,000	13.53	1,550	1,650	6.45	80.13	85.45	6.65
<200 rooms	39,200	70,900	80.87	115	190	65.22	340.87	373.16	9.47
Total	578,800	508,000	−12.23	31,965	19,740	−38.24	18.11	25.73	42.12

Source: *Census of Population 1971/1981*, Office of Population Censuses and Surveys, HMSO.

It is important to note that the reduction in the number of units and rooms available has not been spread evenly throughout the UK. For instance, hotel units in the North-West have decreased by 46 per cent, whereas the reduction in Greater London has been only 13 per cent. In terms of rooms, there has been a decrease in the South-East of England of over 35 per cent but an increase in London of nearly 21 per cent (see table 1.2). The general impact on the regional balance of accommodation available has been a shift towards a larger proportion of the UK's accommodation stock being in London and the major industrial regions with Northumberland, the North-West and the South-East having a smaller proportion of the total. This is largely due to the decrease in the popularity of the UK's traditional seaside resorts, the consequent closure or conversion of many smaller units, and the increasing importance of the business market to hotels in industrial areas. London has also seen a tourist boom and an increase in larger units able to take advantage of economies of scale, particularly following the hotel development incentive scheme in the early 1970s. It is noticeable that Wales, Scotland and the South-West of England, while following the general pattern, have maintained their share of the total hotel stock. This may be in part due to the promotion and support of their respective regional tourist boards.

In addition to the changes in the size, scale and distribution of the industry, there have also been significant changes in the size and scale of the organisations that own and operate hotel units.

There are problems with comparing hotel chains and ranking their relative positions by appropriate criteria. Three main criteria can be used: number of hotels operated, number of bed spaces available and sales turnover. In the early 1970s there were probably only three UK hotel chains of significant size, namely Trusthouse Forte,

Table 1.2 *Comparison of hotel stock 1971–1981 by region.*

Region	Rooms 1971	Rooms 1981	% change	Units 1971	Units 1981	% change	Average unit size 1971	1981	% change	% of total rooms 1971	1981	% change
Northumberland	33,370	22,216	−33.43	1,900	888	−53.26	17.56	25.02	42.45	5.76	4.37	−24.14
Yorkshire & Humberside	22,360	25,638	14.66	1,450	1,113	−23.24	15.42	23.04	49.38	3.86	5.05	30.66
North-West	67,200	52,905	−21.27	4,170	2,235	−46.40	16.12	23.67	46.89	11.61	10.41	−10.29
East Midlands	13,635	13,832	1.44	900	612	−32.00	15.15	22.60	49.18	2.36	2.72	15.60
West Midlands	22,685	20,941	−7.69	1,430	698	−51.19	15.86	30.00	89.12	3.92	4.12	5.19
East Anglia	17,625	15,876	−9.92	1,070	682	−36.26	16.47	23.28	41.32	3.04	3.13	2.64
Greater London	72,845	88,084	20.92	2,495	2,174	−12.87	29.20	40.52	38.77	12.58	17.34	87.79
South-East	121,885	78,467	−35.62	6,740	3,195	−52.60	18.08	24.56	35.81	21.06	15.45	−26.64
South-West	97,915	89,792	−8.30	5,625	4,084	−27.40	17.41	21.99	26.31	16.91	17.68	4.50
Wales	32,605	32,344	−0.80	1,870	1,284	−31.34	17.44	25.19	44.47	5.63	6.37	13.04
Scotland	76,760	67,913	−11.53	4,335	2,727	−37.09	17.71	24.90	40.64	13.26	13.37	0.82
Total	578,885	508,008	−12.24	31,985	19,692	−38.43	18.10	25.80	42.54	100.00	100.00	0.00

Source: *Census of Population 1971/1981*, Office of Population Censuses and Surveys, HMSO

Grand Metropolitan and British Transport Hotels. In the 1980s, the situation is rather different (see table 1.3).

This incredible growth has been achieved both by a policy of acquisition and through substantial hotel building. British Transport Hotels were sold off by British Rail on a piecemeal basis to a number of companies, and Grand Metropolitan sold off its regional properties in a job lot to Queens Moat to concentrate on developing its luxury international hotels, the Intercontinental and Forum chains which it bought from TWA. Mount Charlotte, Thistle and Stakis have tended to grow by acquisition of privately or company owned hotels whereas Crest and Ladbrokes have tended to build new hotels on greenfield sites.

The lack of information in table 1.3 concerning the turnover of hotel groups reflects another aspect of hotel ownership, namely the diversification of business portfolios. There are broadly three types of 'hotel group'. First, there are breweries that have developed their licensed house stock and bought additional hotel units. These groups include Thistle (Scottish and Newcastle), De Vere (Greenall Whitley), Crest (Bass), Embassy (Allied Lyons) and Swallow (Vaux). Secondly, there are leisure based companies, such as Trusthouse Forte, Ladbrokes, Associated Leisure and Kingsmead Hotels, part of MAM, the leisure and entertainment group. Thirdly, there are firms that own hotels primarily as property investments and diversify their business portfolios without any obvious synergy between the hotels and their other activities. Examples of such groups include Rank and Grand Metropolitan.

Table 1.3 *Hotel companies in the UK 1985/6.*

Company	No. of hotels	No. of rooms	Annual turnover £m	Annual turnover/room
Trusthouse Forte (UK)	219	22,156	352	15,900
Queens Moat Houses	68	6,013	74	12,356
Mount Charlotte	58	6,935	58	8,320
Ladbrokes	51	6,530	71	10,903
Crest	45	5,227		
Embassy Hotel	42	2,981		
Swallow	32	3,300	38	11,454
Stakis Hotels & Inns	32	2,993	45	14,934
Thistle	30	4,245	85	19,905
Whitbread Coaching Inns	30	840		
De Vere Hotels	24	2,461	42	17,188
Norfolk Capital	14	1,290	12	8,992
Heritage Hotels	12	1,032		
CHIC	10	2,296	42	18,162
Friendly Hotels	7	993		
Holiday Inns Inc.	6	1,484		

Source: *Hotel Companies in the UK*, Kleinwort Grieveson Securities, spring 1987.

THE EXTERNAL ENVIRONMENT

The changes we have described do not happen in isolation but in the context of the overall environment. We can identify six major environmental forces (see figure 1.1), and each of these six factors has an indirect impact on the hotel organisation. The *legal* environment continues to become more and more complex, both for business in general and the hotel business in particular. Recent changes would include alterations in the VAT regulations and the Business Expansion Scheme, and major changes are forecast in employment and licensing law. The *market* factor is concerned with some of the specific characteristics of the hotel industry's market environment – namely the relationship between provider and consumer, market conditions, and the level of industry concentration. With regard to the *financial* environment, our major concerns are those financial matters that may affect our business objectives or investment decisions, such as interest rates, exchange rates and taxation. The *political* environment is closely related to economic and legal matters and should not be overlooked as a powerful influence on the business environment. *Technology* has made a considerable impact on the industry in recent years and will continue to do so with the increasing use of computer controlled equipment and the growth of information technology in general. *Socio-cultural* aspects are primarily concerned with the consumer, and in particular with changes in attitude and life-style; these changes also relate to the workforce.

These factors cannot be considered in isolation but present an interrelated framework as figure 1.1 illustrates. Within the framework of the environment the business will be further influenced by its 'stakeholders'. These six groups have a much more direct influence on the enterprise as they may require management to act in a particular way, although their relative degree of influence will change from time to time. The six groups are financial backers, competitors, customers, employees, central and local government and suppliers. Each of these groups makes a contribution to the business and expects something in return.

Financial backers contribute the capital needed to allow the business to develop and grow. In return for this they expect growth in the investment's value and an adequate rate of return. It is easy to overlook the business's relationship to its *competitors*. Often there are unwritten rules about pricing, for example, and in certain market

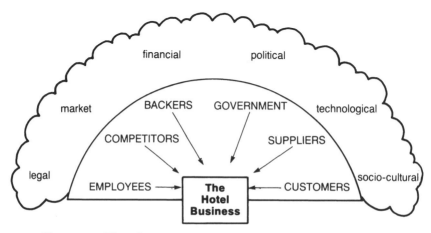

Figure 1.1   *The influence of stakeholders and the external environment.*

situations – such as the small seaside town – the hotelier who breaks the unwritten rules about price maintenance by undercutting may reduce the profitability of not only his own business, but in the long run everyone else's as well. *Customer expectations* cover a wide area but are likely to include 'value for money'. The cash which they contribute to the business is dependent on the product meeting their own personal requirements. Managers must therefore be concerned with ways of monitoring how well their product meets their customer's expectations. *Employees* also have expectations, primarily about the quality of working life. There is a noticeable shift towards, and increased desire for, participation in decision-making and better conditions of employment. *Central and local government* provide a range of essential business services ranging from sewage disposal to job centres. In return a business must fulfil a number of statutory obligations including rates, taxation, health and safety standards, employment standards and so on. *Government* may also be concerned with the generation of trade for hotel businesses through national and local initiatives to increase tourism. The last group of people who have an influence over the hotel business are the *suppliers*. Hotels require a wide variety of commodities, frequently purchased in relatively small quantities. Hotel managers must maintain an effective supply – the right material at the right time in the right quantity at the right price. The complexity of this management task will depend on the numbers and types of suppliers encountered.

As an example, consider a typical district hospital with about 500 beds. What are the particular characteristics of the stakeholders which affect the management of this business? The financial backers of a hospital operation are the local health authority. Most hospitals have traditionally had little or no competition. Residents require the 'hotel services' as a subsidiary to their health treatment. Employees in the health sector are likely to belong to a trade union which constitutes a distinctive feature of this sector not necessarily found to the same extent in other sectors. The influence of the government is through direct action and indirectly through economic constraints, although legislation concerning organisation and management structure has also had a major impact. Suppliers to hospitals are usually nominated suppliers to the local health authority from a list prepared by the DHSS. This results in managers not being concerned with supplier selection but simply with purchasing administration.

CLASSIFYING BUSINESS ACTIVITY

Effective management responds proactively to these environmental influences and the potentially conflicting needs of the respective stakeholders. Service management is becoming an increasingly significant part of the total industrial mix of most developed economies. This is illustrated in table 1.4.

Table 1.4 *Employees in employment in UK (000s).*

	1979	1980	1981	1982	1983
All industries	23,200	23,000	21,900	21,500	21,200
Service industries	13,600	13,700	13,400	13,500	13,500
Hotel and catering	950	980	950	980	970

Source: *Annual Abstract of Statistics 1985*, HMSO.

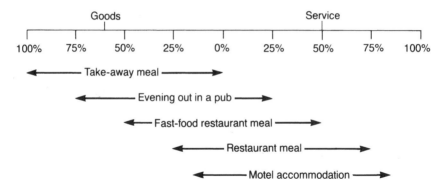

Figure 1.2   *Comparison of goods and services packages in the hospitality industry.* Adapted from *Management of Service Operations,* Sasser, Olsen and Wyckoff.

There are two main approaches to identifying the distinguishing features of service industries. Sasser, Olsen and Wyckoff[3] have suggested the continuum approach, with manufactured products at one end and pure services at the other (see figure 1.2). This illustrates the idea that most services are not 'pure' services but a combination of service and product. For example, the 'service' of a restaurant meal can easily be seen to include a sizeable 'product' element, and indeed some products that appear to be largely tangible can also have a high service component.

The second approach is that developed by Wild[4] whose classification has four groupings. In addition to manufacturing and services, he has added transport and supply. Each of these has a different 'utility' or value to the consumer. Manufacturing involves the physical transformation of raw materials into goods, i.e. changes in the *form* of materials, to provide utility for the consumer. As well as the typical examples of mass-produced fast moving consumer goods, a hotel based example is the transformation of raw food into meals. Services relate to the situation where a customer or something belonging to the customer is treated in some way and is affected by that treatment, i.e. there is a change in the *state* of the customer or his or her possessions. For instance, a hotel provides overnight accommodation so that tired guests can be refreshed; during their stay it is also possible that guests may use the hotel's laundry service to clean and press their clothes. Transportation is where customers or their belongings are moved from one place to another, i.e. no physical change occurs, it is simply a change of *place*. Clearly airlines, bus companies, taxi drivers and so on are examples of this type of business, although airport hotels are regularly involved in providing transport to and from airport terminals. Finally, supply is the change in the possession of goods from the supplier to the customer, i.e. a change in *ownership*. The retail industry is the most obvious example of this activity.

However, attempting to classify business into one of these four groupings is very difficult, for the same reason as identified in discussing the Sasser *et al.* model, namely that all activities can be seen to include elements of two or more of these categories. For instance, railways do not only provide transport but also provide elements of service; retail businesses are mainly supply, but can include elements of service and transport; restaurants are manufacturers, suppliers and service providers; hotels could be seen to include all four.

This approach has led to the idea of the 'operations tetrahedron' illustrated in figure 1.3, developed by Armistead and Killeya.[5] In this analytical framework, hotel opera-

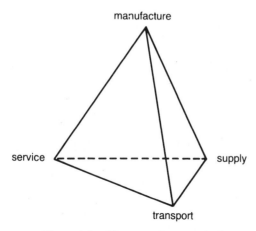

Figure 1.3 *The operations tetrahedron.*

tions are largely services, with some elements of supply and manufacture and the possibility of transport. The service component is largely to do with the change in state of the consumer through the provision of accommodation, food and drink, and space in which to conduct business or relax. The supply component is the provision of meals and drinks through the hotel's food-service departments and the supply of information through front-office departments. The manufacturing component is the change in form of raw food into meals and dirty bedrooms into clean ones. The implication of this approach is that the four groupings each have different operational performance characteristics and hence require different approaches for their effective management.

The analyses just described cannot be accepted without question. In particular the continuum approach, which suggests a dichotomy of products and services, has been severely criticised. Foxall[6] argues that 'those who argue for clear-cut distinctions between services and products have actually demonstrated no more than that if some "services" are located at or near one end of various continua, then some "products" can be logically located at or near the opposing poles'. In looking at the characteristics that distinguish services, we shall temper these distinctions with some reservations about the extent to which they are relevant or meaningful.

Levitt[7] argues that the distinction between goods and services is of limited value and that instead we should consider 'tangibles' and 'intangibles'. Tangible products have tangible elements – things that can be directly experienced, seen, touched, smelled, tasted and tested, probably in advance of purchase. Intangible products on the other hand cannot be tried out in advance. It can be seen, however, that even the most tangible of products will have some intangible elements, some features which it is not possible to test in advance of purchase. It is the degree of this intangibility which makes some products more difficult to manage, not whether they can be classified as goods or services.

Another approach which includes the concept of 'tangibles' and 'intangibles' is that put forward by Shostack.[8] She proposes a molecular model of an enterprise as being made up of a tangible or intangible nucleus surrounded by additional tangible or intangible elements. In this way the enterprise can be seen to be either tangible- or intangible-dominant but it stresses that a business is made up of a mixture of discrete

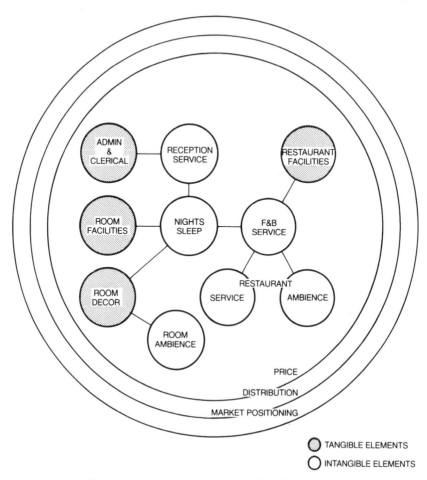

Figure 1.4   *A molecular model of hotel operations.*

elements that need not be of the same type. The overall characteristics of the business are made up of the nature of the core plus the nature of each of the separate elements. This is illustrated in figure 1.4.

The molecular model relates well to the nature of the hotel product since it too comprises a collection of separate but interrelated elements such as the room facilities, the room decor, the food in the restaurant, the service received from the staff, the overall ambience of the establishment and so on, built around the intangible core of a night's stay away from home. One conclusion from the molecular approach is that intangible-dominant enterprises should stress the tangible features of their operation to counteract the abstract nature of the intangible features. In this way it is suggested that hotels should pay particular attention to the people who work in contact with the guest, the decor of the establishment, the correspondence with the guest, and any other tangible evidence for that particular operation.

THE CHARACTERISTICS OF SERVICES

Despite the difficulty in agreeing on a way of classifying service business activity and the fact that hotels cannot in any case be described as a 'pure' service, they nevertheless display many of the general characteristics of other services.

First, services are *perishable*. A hotel room which is unsold on one day cannot be 'stored' until a later date. Thus, during troughs in demand, the high incidence of fixed costs which still need to be met will have a detrimental effect on profitability, whilst peaks may be much greater than the hotel is capable of handling. Management is unable to take advantage of this excess demand by using previously inventoried surpluses as is possible in a manufacturing situation.

Secondly, services are *intangible*. It is often difficult to pinpoint the benefits of visiting a particular hotel. The benefits may be associated with the personality of the staff, the establishment's image or the attraction of associating with other customers. In these circumstances identifying, gaining and prompting a competitive advantage is a difficult and complex task.

Services are thirdly also *heterogeneous*. The service given to one customer may differ from the service given to the customer in the next room. This may be deliberate, perhaps because one customer is attending a conference, whereas another is on a speciality weekend break package, while yet another is a private business customer. It may also be because staff favour serving one type of customer over other types. It is therefore more difficult to establish and monitor quality standards for service than for manufactured products.

Fourthly, services are *contact dependent*. Unlike manufacturing where the producer and the consumer may never come into contact, it is impossible for the customer to experience the hotel's services unless there is physical interaction between the two. In the same way the customer must initially make choices about which hotel to stay at prior to experiencing the hotel's facilities, unlike manufactured goods which can be described, photographed, measured and even tested before purchase.

Finally, the purchase of a service does not give the consumer *ownership* of whatever it is that has been purchased. All the physical attributes necessary for the provision of accommodation remain the property of the hotelier. In effect, customers are hiring these facilities for the time that they are staying in the hotel. Thus the relationship between the hotelier and his customers is very different to that between the manufacturer or supplier and his customers.

THE OPERATIONAL CHARACTERISTICS OF HOTELS

In this section we will go on to analyse in more detail the operational characteristics of hotel provision by using a framework established by Lovelock.[9] We will begin by considering the traditional model of the independently owned and managed hotel operation, placing it in the context of service industries in general. From this will emerge some key result areas that the independent hotelier will need to manage. We will then continue by exploring the ways in which the management of a chain hotel, hostel accommodation and hospital accommodation differ from this traditional model and hence how the relative importance of the same key result areas has been affected. It is our contention that while the priority and scale of these key result areas may be different they are common to all types of hotel management.

An independent hotel: its service context

The starting point for our analysis is the traditional hotel which is independently owned and managed and operates with commercial objectives. We shall analyse the nature of this type of hotel using a framework based on a wide range of approaches to the classification of services such as those proposed by Lovelock,[10] Shostack,[11] Sasser,[12] and Chase.[13] There are four key questions. In answering these questions differences in services are identified according to two dimensions, thereby locating different service sectors into the quadrants of the matrices illustrated in figures 1.5 to 1.8, which were developed from the ideas proposed by Lovelock.[14]

The first question relates to the *nature of the service act*. It is suggested that the two dimensions along which services can be differentiated are who or what is the direct recipient of the service and how tangible is the service act. Recipients can be either people or things, so for instance air transportation can move both passengers and freight. Clearly a hotel directs its services at people. The second factor of tangibility is more subjective. Tangible actions can be thought of as being directed at peoples' bodies whereas the intangibles are directed at their minds. It is interesting to note that in applying this analysis Lovelock does not identify where hotels fit into such a matrix (see figure 1.5). A restaurant is identified as being tangible since it presumably is

Recipient of the service

	People	Things
Tangible	Directed at people's bodies hotel?	Directed at physical goods, e.g. laundry.
Intangible	Directed at people's minds, e.g. theatre.	Directed at 'assets', e.g. banking.

Figure 1.5 *Understanding the nature of the service act.*

directed at satisfying hunger, so that on the same line of argument a hotel provides a tangible service since it satisfies the consumers' physiological need for sleep. However, there is a strong argument to be made out for the idea that hotels also meet the consumer's psychological needs for comfort and security.[15]

The second question is concerned with the *service organisation's relationship with its customers*. This can be either continuous or discrete and can be directed at 'members' or 'non-members' (customers with no formal relationship with the organisation). Once again there are conceptual problems with identifying the location of hotels along these dimensions (see figure 1.6). With regard to the time span of service delivery certain types of transaction can clearly be identified as discrete, for instance an individual one-night stay. Other transactions are clearly continuous, for instance it is not unusual for hotels to have permanent residents. The provision of accommodation to the business traveller does not easily fit either of these categories since the firms requiring accommodation for their staff will tend to have a continuous relationship whereas the individual bookings will be discrete. Similar problems of analysis relate to the membership criterion. Customers of hotel services are not members of the orga-

Level of 'membership'

	Member	Non-member
Continuous	E.g. motoring organisation.	E.g. radio station.
Discrete	E.g. train season ticket.	Hotel?

Time frame of transactions

Figure 1.6 *Relationship with customer.*

nisation in the same way as you can become a member of a motoring organisation. However, in many respects hotel customers feel and behave as if they are 'members', particularly if they stay in a hotel for any length of time. This sense of membership is of advantage in a service industry as it creates customer loyalty, it facilitates effective identification of market segments, and often has implications for pricing policy.

The level of *customisation and judgement in service delivery* is the third factor to be analysed. Services can be categorised as having either high or low levels of customisation, and the role of service personnel can be similarly categorised in terms of the extent to which such personnel in contact with customers exercise judgement in meeting individual customer needs (see figure 1.7). In this case Lovelock does use a hotel

Level of customisation

	High	Low
High judgement	E.g. legal services.	?
Low judgement	Hotel	E.g. fast food.

Role of services personnel

Figure 1.7 *Customisation and the role of service personnel.*

as an example of a service with high customisation but low judgement by service contact personnel. In effect a hotel customer customises the level of service for himself in that once he has checked in he can come and go as he pleases and utilise a wide range of hotel facilities as and when he wants. Hotel staff meet these needs but do so in the role of order-taker or operator of a fairly well regulated system. It is the range of products available rather than the service personnel's discretion that creates the customisation. There has been in the hotel industry an ongoing debate over whether or not hotel rooms should be identical or individual. The question is one of the extent to which customers require customisation as opposed to familiarity and security.

Lovelock's fourth question examines the *nature of demand and supply* (see figure

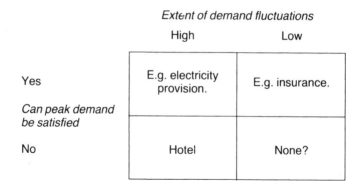

Figure 1.8 *Supply and demand.*

1.8). In terms of demand, hotels generally have wide fluctuations in demand and peaks which exceed capacity. Customers have to interact with the hotel in order for them to receive the benefits of the service package, so production and consumption are more or less simultaneous. This means that hotels are unable to store capacity to meet peak demand. This is not a problem if demand is reasonably stable over time but, like many service industries, the demand for hotel accommodation has wide variations. Such fluctuations are both short term, for instance more demand during the week than at weekends, and longer term such as the seasonal trends experienced by London hotels where average occupancy in winter months is typically around 60 per cent whereas in the summer months it can peak to over 90 per cent.[16] The perishable nature of the hotel 'product' therefore makes marginal sales extremely valuable.

In addition to the problems of demand, hotel managers also have problems of supply. First, the unit has a fixed location so that it is impossible to respond to shifts in demand by moving the unit to more preferred locations. Secondly, the physical capacity of the hotel is limited to the number of bedrooms available. Thirdly, whilst it is possible to change the capacity of each bedroom, by putting in extra beds for instance, this is largely limited by consumer resistance to sleeping with strangers! These three factors combine to place constraints upon the manager with regards to his ability to respond to the fluctuations in demand identified above.

IMPLICATIONS OF THE SERVICE CONTEXT

The insights and implications provided by answering the questions in the previous section enable us to identify a number of important factors. First, the customer needs to be physically present throughout the service experience. This applies at least to the core service, that of providing overnight accommodation. It does not apply to some of the peripheral services that a hotel offers, such as providing information. For instance, the role of the concierge or receptionist often includes supplying guests with information about the hotel, the locality and other aspects of the customer's stay. However, this information could be provided by telephone or by television and does not necessarily require the customer's physical presence in the unit. Likewise, if in addition to providing a good night's sleep, the customer also receives the more intangible benefits of comfort and security, some of this 'service' can also be supplied before the customer ever arrives at the hotel, by assuring the customer of accommodation through the reservation system.

Secondly, it was suggested in figure 1.4 that the service provided by a hotel is tangible, since it affects people's bodies. This is not necessarily an accurate assessment. Whilst the physical act of resting may be tangible, the perception of this act by the customer is much less so. Sleep after all is hardly a commodity that most people would be prepared to pay a lot of money for unless they thought they were getting far more than a good night's rest. The modification to the consumer's body/mind that takes place during the service act is largely one of 'restoration' rather than 'improvement'. Earlier in this chapter we suggested that services provide a change in the 'state' of something (see page 9). Some services change the state by enhancing it and modifying it so that it is clearly changed in some way, for instance a hair-cut. Other services restore from a state of decline to the original state, such as a night's rest. We would suggest that people can easily measure the benefits of service acts that result in some tangible improvement, such as the new hairstyle, but they are much less aware of services that simply restore them to a 'normal' state. It is partly this fact that makes the perception of what a hotel does intangible, in that consumers are unable to identify any concrete benefit from the experience, although they will quickly be aware of any impediment to the effective provision of this service. A customer will quickly complain if they are unable to sleep due to too much noise in the hotel but will not think it out of the ordinary to have slept well. This perception applies not only to the core service, but to most of the peripheral services a hotel offers, such as the provision of food and drink, laundry and information.

Thirdly, for the independent hotel, it is likely that most transactions are discrete. This creates many of the features of the typical hotel. Customers have to be encouraged to come to the unit, and be welcomed upon their arrival. So the discrete nature of the provision is the reason why hotels need a marketing department, advance reservations and reception desk. The impact of this discreteness can be seen by looking at the effects of differing lengths of guest stay. A seaside hotel where guests are traditionally resident for a week or a number of weeks at a time will have much less need for reception and reservations services than a city centre hotel catering mainly for one-night stay business travellers.

Almost by definition, the discrete nature of the transactions means that individual customers are not 'members' of the organisation. This is certainly true in a technical sense, in that they have almost certainly not paid a subscription in the same way as the telephone service is available to subscribers. In a practical sense, however, the customer has all the benefits of 'membership' without the need for a subscription. That is to say that the hotel's services are available to anyone who requires them unless the hotel is actually fully booked. Indeed the hotelier has a statutory duty to provide accommodation to travellers. What does not exist in most cases is the consumer's perception of this sense of membership, which would have the benefit to the hotelier of customer loyalty. Independent hotels do have a more continuous relationship with the organisations that use them rather than with individuals. Such organisations may be firms who send their staff to stay on a regular basis or travel agents or tour operators who book tourists into the unit. Tour operators may indeed have block bookings for rooms for the whole of the holiday season and the hotelier has to be careful to weigh up the advantages of such continuous relationships (see page 83).

Furthermore, many service industries attempt to persuade their customers to 'join' their organisation by completing an application form. This gives the firm access to information about their customers, including names and addresses, and this provides an ideal way of contacting their target market. In the hotel business, this is made possible simply by the fact that customers are required by law to provide the hotel with their name and address. Most hotels attempt to enhance the quality of this market information by asking for the name of the organisation for which the customer works, or the number of their car (to identify how many customers travel to the hotel by road).

A fifth factor, derived from figure 1.7, is the level of customisation a hotel provides. This customisation derives from the wide range of services available. The reason why a five-star hotel is more expensive than a three-star one is that this range is wider and available over a longer period of time. For instance, the five-star unit must provide 24-hour room-service. There is a high degree of customisation about the experience, because in essence each customer creates a unique set of experiences according to his own specific needs. It is therefore the physical plant of the unit and the mix of services built into the fabric of the building that make such customisation possible.

One of the problems with the emphasis on the physical environment is that it is largely fixed and not easily or cheaply adapted. In effect, then, management have only a high degree of control over the staff, who constitute potentially the most responsive and flexible component in the hotel. But as figure 1.7 also shows, in a hotel such staff have usually little or no judgement to exercise over the level of service provided. Most hotel staff are in operative positions, with relatively low levels of skill, pay and responsibility. There is no doubt that they can have an important influence on the quality of the customer's experience, but they cannot make up for any deficiencies there may be in provision due to shortcomings of the physical environment.

A seventh factor to consider is the impact of fixed capacity and its responsiveness to demand. Hotels are nearly all in a position of having to 'chase demand', that is to say seek custom to fill troughs in demand. It was suggested earlier that peaks cannot be met by hotels, but there are some circumstances where hotels were built and designed in the first place to meet such peak demand. For instance, an island with an exact number of flights each week can only have a certain number of tourists requiring accommodation. Therefore the total possible demand is known and can be met. There still remains the problem of maintaining demand at this peak level throughout the year, since many such island locations have seasonal demand patterns. This need also places an important emphasis on the marketing and front-office functions. At the same time, the manager's response to troughs takes the same form as above. Unable to make rooms disappear or move them to a location where there is demand, the manager does what he can to maintain profitability by modifying the staff component, usually by laying off staff recruited for the peak season, or sometimes by closing the hotel altogether.

CHAIN HOTELS: THEIR SERVICE CONTEXT

So far we have only considered the model of an independently owned and operated hotel. But as we saw earlier, there is a growing concentration in the industry and the grouping together of several hotels either within one firm or as some form of consortium. This adds another factor, namely the impact of providing a more or less similar service on a number of sites in a variety of different locations.

Lovelock[17] has also considered this point and looks at the method of service delivery. In the case of an independent hotel, its outlet is definitely a single site which necessitates the customer going to that particular location. Many service businesses are attempting to transact their service provision at arm's length by post or electronic communication, for instance mail-order catalogues and home banking. It is clear from what we have seen so far that this can never be the case in the hotel business. Customers will always have to go to the hotel. But hotel chain operations overcome the constraint of fixed location by providing their service on a number of sites located where there is expected to be customer demand. Furthermore, they benefit from being able to generate referral business.

This spread of sites also has implications for some of the factors that we identified earlier, principally the time span of transactions, the concept of membership, the level of customisation and the management of demand. With regard to the time span of transactions a hotel chain can create far more continuity with its customers than can potentially an independent hotel. This is particularly true for business travellers whom we have identified as typically having short-term discrete transactions with a hotel. These transactions are no longer discrete if the businessman moves from one unit operated by a chain to another. Whilst chain hotels maintain the same continuous relationships with outside organisations as do independent hotels they are also able to foster a much greater sense of membership to individual customers than can be generated by independent hotels. The concept of membership is being actively marketed to customers by many hotel chains, as illustrated in case example 1.1.

Case example 1.1   Holiday Inn – Club Europe

In 1986 Holiday Inn introduced the idea of 'Club Europe'. For a membership fee of £15.00 business travellers can receive special facilities and an improved level of service. This includes a room equipped specifically for the business traveller, secretarial support, extended check-out time, priority for an extended stay and preferential handling of reservations. (See figure 1.9.)

Whilst chain hotels cannot be more customised than independent hotels, by offering a range of different types of hotel in different locations, the chain does in effect provide a more customised service to its clientele. Associated with this, chain operations are also able to manage demand more effectively than independent hoteliers for a variety of reasons. Their market information is much greater; through membership they can create high levels of customer loyalty; they can achieve economies of scale in marketing; they can afford to discount during low periods in some units whilst maintaining overall cash flow by maintaining tariffs in other units serving different market segments; and they can transfer demand from one hotel to another, through a centralised reservations system or even upon the arrival of guests if overbooked.

In other respects, however, chain hotels are similar in their characteristics to independent hotels. The customer needs to be present during the service experience; the service provided is tangible in the sense defined above; the role of service personnel is limited; and customisation within the unit is dependent upon the facilities available.

HOSTELS AND HOSPITALS: THEIR SERVICE CONTEXT

Since our definition of a hotel includes those operations in the welfare or institutional sector, we must also consider the service context of these units. These types of 'hotel' vary in almost every respect from the traditional model developed above. It is still the case that the customer must be physically present, but there has to be a much greater emphasis on just the tangible aspects of the stay in a hospital and hostel than on the

Holiday Inn Club Europe,
CPA House,
350A King Street,
Hammersmith,
London,
W6 0RX,
ENGLAND

Holiday Inn CLUB EUROPE

TURNING REGULAR BUSINESS TRAVELLERS INTO VERY SPECIAL GUESTS

1986

Holiday Inn® hotels have become the world's largest hotel chain, because we put you first. That's why we've introduced Holiday Inn Club Europe, developed especially with your needs in mind.

A VIP WELCOME

Present your membership card on check-in and you will receive a special welcome. Your luggage will be taken to your room and a member of staff will telephone to ensure you are comfortable. In addition, your room key will have a Holiday Inn Club Europe tag to identify you as a VIP guest during your stay.

A ROOM EQUIPPED FOR THE BUSINESS TRAVELLER

The very best rooms have been set aside at every Holiday Inn hotel in Europe. Not only do they offer our well known standards, but in addition every Holiday Inn Club Europe room has a trouser press, hair dryer, larger, thicker, towels and a bathrobe for your extra comfort and convenience. A luxury range of toiletries is also provided with your needs in mind. And to keep you up to date with current events, a specially selected newspaper and magazine will be provided.

BUSINESS SERVICES ON CALL

To help you make last minute arrangements, or prepare for an urgent meeting when you are away from your office, secretarial support including

typing, telex, copying facilities, and flight confirmation, will be available during normal office hours.

EXTENDED CHECK-OUT TIME

If your business takes longer than expected, you may extend your check-out time to 5.00 p.m. Simply make the request by 9.00 a.m. through Reception.

PRIORITY FOR AN EXTENDED STAY

And if business makes it necessary to extend your stay, just inform Reception by 9.00 a.m. and priority will be given to your request, even when the hotel is fully booked.

SPECIAL CHEQUE CASHING PRIVILEGES

For unforeseen expenses, you may cash a personal cheque for up to U.S. $50.00 per stay, or the equivalent in local currency, with a valid banker's card. Subject to local currency regulations.

PREFERENTIAL HANDLING OF RESERVATIONS

To reserve a room at any of the 64 Holiday Inn hotels in Europe, just call our reservations office, or your local Holiday Inn hotel. Simply quote your unique identity number and we'll check availability. At most hotels we can confirm your Holiday Inn Club Europe room, in seconds.

MEMBERSHIP APPLICATION FORM

Please type or print

50093

Figure 1.9 *Holiday Inn – Club Europe.*

intangible aspects. Increasingly, there is a much greater recognition of the psychological impact of staying in hospital, which is being addressed by improvements in the peripheral services available, particularly in private health care.

Transactions are also predominantly continuous in these sectors. For instance, a student may stay in the same hostel for two or three years, and the average length of stay in acute patient hospitals is three or four days. There is a consequent increase in the level of association with the service provider and a real sense of 'membership'.

The different business context in which these units operate, usually not for profit, also reduces the level of customisation. Likewise there is potentially even less service personnel contact since such units may have non-hotel staff to carry out some functions, such as nurses in hospitals, or may necessitate the consumer himself to carry out some of these functions, such as students being responsible for the daily servicing of their own rooms.

Finally, the longer length of stay and the relatively captive market of such operations also create very different conditions of demand. Hostels and hospitals very often do operate at peak for long periods of time, although hostels in academic institutions do have very clearly identifiable troughs during the vacation periods. The trend for universities and colleges to maximise the occupancy of their hostel accommodation illustrates the difficulties of attempting to draw discrete boundaries around types of operation. As the universities seek to fill hostels they increasingly market themselves as conference centres and are hence in direct competition with hotels, and at least during these periods must modify their service package to offer traditional hotel-type services to their customers.

SUMMARY

We defined a hotel as 'an operation that provides accommodation and ancillary services to people away from home'. Whilst this includes both commercial and welfare sectors, we have concentrated our analysis of the industry on the commercial sector. This analysis has identified important trends in the development and present position of the industry as regards the size and location of operating units, the concentration of ownership and their increasing diversification. These changes take place in an environmental context that is continually shifting and developing. One such major shift has been the growing importance of the service sector within the UK economy.

We have considered a number of approaches to the nature of service industries and identified the distinctive service characteristics of perishability, intangibility, heterogeneity, contact dependency and lack of ownership. These approaches raise key issues for the manager regarding the specific operational characteristics of service businesses in general.

We then went on to analyse the specific nature of hotel provision using a framework suggested by Lovelock. The key questions are the nature of the service act, the service organisation's relationship with its customers, the level of customisation and contact personnel's judgement, and the nature of demand and supply. The model of the traditional, independent hotel was established and seven factors emerged as important:

- Customers need to be physically present to receive the core service.

- This core service is tangible, although there are also some intangible elements of provision.

- Transactions are typically discrete with individual customers, but more continuous with organisations.

- Customers are not subscribing members of the hotel organisation, but there is a trend towards encouraging this idea.

- The level of customisation is largely derived from the facilities available within the unit.

- Service personnel can influence the quality of provision, but have little or no discretion over the type and style of service.

- Finally, hotels have to chase demand in an effort to fill troughs.

This traditional model was then compared with chain hotel operations, hostels and hospitals. In many respects there were major differences in the nature or importance of the seven factors. As we shall see in the next chapter, these differences have major implications for what unit managers in these different types of unit have to do.

REFERENCES

1. *Chambers English Dictionary*.

2. *London's Tourist Accommodation in the 1990's*, Horwath and Horwath London Prospects Report, 1986.

3. Sasser, W. E., Olsen, R. P., and Wyckoff, D. D., *The Management of Service Operations*, Allyn and Bacon, 1978.

4. Wild, R., *Production and Operations Management*, Holt, Rinehart and Winston, 1971.

5. Armistead, C. G., and Killeya, J. C., 'Transfer of concepts between manufacture and service', *International Journal of Hospitality Management* vol. 3 no. 3, 1984.

6. Foxall, G., 'Marketing is service marketing', *Service Industries Journal* vol. 4 no. 3, pp. 1–6.

7. Levitt, T., 'Marketing intangible products and product intangibles', *Harvard Business Review*, May/June 1981.

8. Shostack, G. L., 'Breaking free from product marketing', *Journal of Marketing* vol. 41, pp. 73–80, April 1977.

9. Lovelock, C. H., 'Classifying services to gain strategic marketing insights', *Journal of Marketing*, vol. 47, pp. 9–22, Summer 1983.

10 Lovelock, C. H., 'Towards a classification of services', in Lamb, C. W., and Dunne, W. R. (eds), *Theoretical Developments in Marketing*, American Marketing Association, 1980.

11. Shostack, G. L. *op. cit.*

12. Sasser, W. E., 'Match supply and demand in service industries', *Harvard Business Review* vol. 54, November/December 1976.

13. Chase, R. B., 'Where does the customer fit in a service operation?' *Harvard Business Review* vol. 1, pp. 137–142, April 1978.

14. Lovelock, C. H., *op. cit.* (1983).

15. Nailon, P., 'Theory in hospitality management', *International Journal of Hospitality Management* vol. 1 no. 3, pp. 135–143, 1982.

16. 'Outlook in the hotel and tourism industries', *London Trends* (1986 edn.), Pannell Kerr Forster Associates.

17. Lovelock, C. H., *op. cit.* (1983).

2 Managing in the Hotel Business

INTRODUCTION

In chapter 1 we defined a 'hotel' and placed this in the context of service businesses. We also identified the variables that distinguish the independent hotel, the chain hotel, the hospital and the hostel. In this chapter we go on to explore the roles and responsibilities of the hotel manager. In order to do this it is first necessary to identify the nature of the hotel operations over which the manager has charge and the extent to which he or she has control over the business enterprise.

COMMERCIAL HOTEL OPERATIONS

As well as considering the characteristics of services in general, the hotel manager must also be aware of their implications in the running of a successful business. For the moment, we shall only consider the commercial sector of the hotel industry as previously defined. The hospital and hostel sectors have very different stakeholders and very different criteria for success.

In the commercial sector, service characteristics have particular implications for the strategic issues of *creating and maintaining a competitive advantage*. In service industries such an advantage is difficult to achieve. First, services cannot easily be protected by patent so they are readily available to be copied. Secondly, for those services that are people-based there are low barriers to entry due to low initial capital investment costs. Thomas[1] believes that service businesses also differ from product-oriented businesses in their approach to achieving higher levels of productivity, to establishing prices and to developing new services.

As we saw in chapter 1, in many respects hotels have some of the characteristics of typical services, but they also have a high degree of product orientation. Hotels are not wholly people-based services; they are largely equipment-based. Whilst hotel customers have a high level of contact with the operation, most of this interaction is with the physical plant of the operation rather than with its service personnel. For instance, a guest may spend five minutes registering at reception, two minutes talking to the porter about the location of a restaurant in the town and then five minutes the next morning at the cash desk with the cashier out of a total time of several hours that are spent in the hotel. This places a great emphasis on getting the physical surroundings right in the first place. This is not to say that the nature of the human interaction that takes place between the customer and staff must not also be of the highest quality, as they have to create the best response in a short contact time.

The reliance on the physical plant of the hotel to provide the service results in a lack of flexibility. If a customer dislikes the colour scheme of the room or the view from the window, it may be possible to move him to another room but, if the hotel is full, it would not be possible to redecorate the room or change its outlook to meet his specific requirements. This lack of flexibility does make the hotel susceptible to competition, unless money is invested in maintaining the level of decor and interior design. The physical construction of the property requires considerable additional investment should it require alteration to meet with new market conditions. For instance, many seaside hotels had extensive banqueting suites and ballrooms but were unable to compete for the conference market without adding the sophisticated facilities expected by the present-day conference organiser. They have had to invest heavily in upgrading their facilities to include such things as air-conditioning, centrally controlled lighting and public address systems, manoeuvrable staging, audio visual aids and recent demands for leisure facilities for conference delegates.

This level of product orientation, rather than service focus, means that there are considerable barriers for competitors wishing to enter the market. A hotel is a major investment. Holiday Inns and Sheraton are reported to be spending over £40,000 per bedroom on new constructions, and the renovation of the Piccadilly Hotel carried out by Gleneagles PLC was estimated at £17.5 million. Whilst these are very much at the top end of the market, even budget hotels and motel concepts are costing £17,000 per room to build.[2] Since few modern hotels are built with less than 100 rooms, the investment cost for a hotel of this size ranges from £2 million up to £5 million, and could go much higher as land prices and building costs continue to rise rapidly. This places a heavy responsibility on the unit manager to achieve the levels of return that justify such an investment by making crucial decisions such as those about tariff structures and marketing policy.

In addition to the lack of flexibility in operating the unit there is another sense in which the hotel is inflexible – it occupies a fixed location around which the environment may change. For instance, many large hotels were constructed in the seaside resorts during the nineteenth century. As the nature of national and international tourism has changed, so these locations have decreased in popularity. Seaside hotels must therefore search for new markets as demand from holidaymakers has declined. The Grand Hotel in Scarborough, for example, was one of the most luxurious of its day when it was first built but has now been converted by the Rank Organisation to a Butlin's Family Holiday hotel. However, whereas a seaside location was an advantage in terms of the holiday customer, it holds no great locational advantage for conference organisers, particularly in the winter when most conferences are held.

The nature of the premises and plant of the hotel also has consequences for the cost structure of the business. Hotels are subject to high fixed costs as a proportion of their total operating costs as far as the provision of accommodation is concerned. They are therefore susceptible to fluctuations in profit performance under unstable demand conditions. There was widespread concern amongst hoteliers in early 1986 following the Chernobyl nuclear accident and terrorist activities, since there was a dramatic decrease in tourist demand from America. Concern was so great that the British Tourist Authority launched a very expensive promotional campaign in the USA in order to win back some of the lost business. Hotels in London laid off staff on a widespread basis in an effort to reduce those costs over which they had some control. In competitive terms this means that hotels would prefer to compete on aspects of their operations other than price (see chapter 5).

One solution to the need to differentiate from competitors and also to tackle the intangibility of services is to create a strong brand image. However, the nature of hotel provision is extremely difficult to portray in terms of identifying images that customers can relate to. Hotel firms have used a variety of images – smiling staff, individuality of units, concern for quality, value for money, and so on – but few of these address what it is that hotels provide for their customers. Arguably intangible feelings such as comfort, security and homeliness are what attracts customers to use hotels.

Organisations require branding not only to differentiate themselves from their competitors, but also to generate referral business from one unit to another. This requires that hotel organisations create a culture that ensures that the behaviour and attitudes of staff are similar across all their units, so that the quality of provision conforms to customer expectations. This is problematic due to the physical isolation of one hotel from another and the need to rely on the recruitment of local staff who may have very real attitudinal differences from one part of the country to another, or indeed between different countries. The hotel's culture will also be significantly affected by the particular approach and style of different unit managers, whose backgrounds may also be quite diverse.

Another facet of the hotel business is that, unlike many services, customers cannot generally shift their purchases to a different time because their need for a bedroom relates to their need for accommodation at that location at a time specified by business circumstances or holiday periods. This results in a time horizon covering up to two or three years ahead. Whilst this can facilitate long-range planning, it can also introduce inflexibility into the system making it difficult to respond to shorter-term problems such as the last minute cancellation of rooms.

NOT-FOR-PROFIT HOTEL OPERATIONS

For managers in the institutional sector, many of these business characteristics do not seem to be important, but in fact there are trends that suggest that many of these operations will have to face very similar problems. Rice *et al.*[3] have identified several characteristics that indicate that hotels and hospitals in particular have many similar issues to face. These include:

- the product is overnight occupancy of beds;

- high investment cost;

- operating costs are labour intensive.

- physical plant is a major focus of attention;

- reservations are often made through intermediaries (travel agents for hotels and doctors for hospitals);

- markets are becoming more competitive (NHS hospitals face increasing competition from private health care).

They also show similarities in terms operating conditions:

- average unit sizes of both hospitals and hotels have increased;
- there is a tendency towards the grouping together of units either as hotel chains, consortia, regional health authorities, or private hospital chains;
- occupancy rates are high in both sectors.

Rice *et al.* go on to argue that many of the factors that affect the guest experience in hotels are identical to those that affect the patient in a hospital. These include the building design, signing, reception staff, cleanliness, bed size and quality, decor, view from the window, amenities and so on.

A distinctive feature of the not-for-profit sector is the tendency for these operations to become more commercial in their outlook. Hospitals now market their catering facilities more aggressively. For instance, the Eastbourne District General undertakes functions, buffets and wedding receptions in its staff restaurants at the weekends. Likewise many hostels, particularly on university or college campuses, now sell their facilities to tour organisers such as SAGA or develop conference business, such as at Sussex University. Even the YMCA has submitted plans to convert its Tottenham Court Road hostel into a budget hotel.

IMPLICATIONS FOR HOTEL UNIT MANAGERS

We would argue that the characteristics we have discussed so far – those of services in general, service businesses, and the hotel business specifically – make the hotel unit manager not only responsible for operations but also responsible for strategic issues. Strategy is concerned with the setting of long-term goals and making long-term plans for a business, and determining policies and procedures designed to meet those strategic aims.

As service organisations grow and expand they greatly increase in complexity. Most hotel companies begin with one or two hotels, often in relatively close proximity, serving very similar markets. For instance, Mount Charlotte Hotels in the late 1970s comprised five seaside hotels all clearly aimed at satisfying the family holiday market. As the organisation expands three things tend to happen: the number of sites increases, the range of services offered is widened, and the number of markets served increases. Thus Mount Charlotte now has over 30 hotels throughout the UK, having purchased four central London hotels from Trusthouse Forte for £19 million in 1983 and two hotels from Grand Metropolitan for £21.5 million. It has divisions of luxury city centre hotels, city centre hotels, country hotels, family holiday hotels and budget hotels. This growth results in what has been called the 'Bermuda Triangle' of service businesses[4] which is illustrated in figure 2.1 below. To put it simply, 'The complexity kills you!'[5]

There are two possible approaches to the strategic management of large-scale hotel chains or so called 'multi-site operations'. Either they can be controlled from the centre or control can be devolved down to the site or unit manager. In the past there has been a tendency for hotel firms to adopt the former strategy. Centralised control tends to result in rigid, hierarchical control systems, a large head office supposedly taking advantage of economies of scale, a strongly branded product and a high level of standardisation. The second response is to attempt to reduce one of the dimensions of the complexity. In the hotel business one way to do this is to reduce effectively the

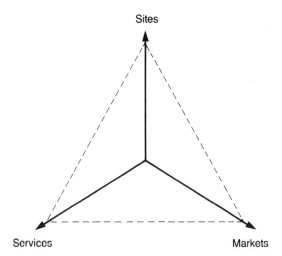

Figure 2.1   *The 'Bermuda Triangle' of service businesses.*

impact of having many sites by delegating much of the decision-making and responsibility to unit level, as is being attempted by CHIC. Another response is to reduce the number of market segments by subdividing the organisation into divisions each with responsibility for specific segments, such as Trusthouse Forte's Inns, Post House or Family divisions.

Independent hoteliers have always needed to be strategic as well as operational managers. Managers in hotel companies have less strategic responsibility, although this varies widely according to the organisation's level of centralisation. There appears to be plenty of evidence to show that in those organisations that have attempted to exercise rigorous central control, unit performance has not achieved the levels expected and management turnover has been high. On the other hand, Schaffer[6] believes that a 'decentralised management system . . . appears to have made an important difference and helped Hyatt in its climb to recognition as one of the lodging industry's top innovators and performers.' This is also supported by Ley's study[7] of company-owned Holiday Inns which concluded that the role of 'entrepreneur' was the most significant in determining the success of the unit.

If hotel managers are strategists and entrepreneurs, what sort of responsibilities will they have? Merricks and Jones[8] identified some major policy option areas which can be used as a checklist against which those areas that a hotel manager would typically have control over can be listed (see table 2.1).

MODELS OF HOTEL MANAGEMENT

The checklist given in table 2.1 shows that hotel managers must have knowledge and skills covering a wide range of issues. From the discussion above it is clear that the management of a hotel is highly complex, and operates in a relatively competitive and turbulent environment. It is not therefore surprising to find that there have been a number of studies carried out to research and develop insights into the hotel manager's role.

This research interest has attempted to provide a conceptual framework through

Table 2.1 *Strategic policy areas in hotel management.*

	Level of decision-making		
	N/a	Low	High
Geographic coverage:			
– local		×	
– regional	×		
– national	×		
Markets:			
– nature			×
– development			×
Product design			×
Production process		×	
Pricing			×
Credit sales			×
Promotion:			
– media		×	
– coverage			×
Staffing			×
Industrial relations			×
Finance:			
– source		×	
– growth		×	
Organisation:			
– rewards			×
– structure of unit			×
– delegation			×
– leadership			×

which evidence of what hotel managers do may be organised. Such models should make it easier to understand what hotel managers do, provide a framework for further research or analysis, identify how to measure the performance of managers, and focus attention on those areas which are most important to successful management.

Broadly, three types of model have been developed in the hospitality industry:

1. *Contextual models* – these identify the context in which management is carried out, for instance those of Nailon[9] and Reuland, Choudry and Fagel.[10]

2. *Activity models* – these evaluate what role managers play by looking at the activities they engage in, for instance those of Ley[11] and Arnaldo.[12]

3. *Expectations models* – these analyse what managers are expected to do, for instance that of Hales and Nightingale.[13]

The principal advantage of the contextual models is their relative simplicity. Thus Nailon's model identified four components which the hospitality manager must manage: the external environment, the human resources, the technical infrastructure and the management information system. He states that traditionally hospitality management has been seen as a series of more or less discrete disciplines, as in the development of the *Corpus of Knowledge* prepared for the HCIMA by Dr Paul Johnson.[14]

He, however, sees hospitality management as the balancing and co-ordination of the four systems identified above, stressing therefore the need for the integration of the separate disciplines such as finance, marketing and personnel to deal with the problems arising in each of the four systems. He also emphasises the need to consider the areas of overlap between those systems.

Reuland, Choudry and Fagel have produced a model which is more complex and focuses on the provision of hospitality as a process for which the manager is responsible and which can be described in mathematical terms. Whilst these models identify *broadly* what has to be managed, they do not provide any guidance as to the results managers could be expected to achieve, nor do they identify how the manager should go about managing.

The activity models have largely been developed from the framework provided by Mintzberg.[15] Following a review of existing literature and his own study of five top American chief executives, he suggested that there were three main roles; interpersonal, informational and decisional. Arising directly from the manager's formal authority and status, the manager's interpersonal roles involve his basic interpersonal relationships. His position as the focus of interpersonal contacts makes him the centre for the collection and processing of information and this information provides the basis for decision-making. These three main roles were subdivided into a total of ten roles. The interpersonal roles involved acting as a figurehead and a leader and providing the necessary liaison between individuals and functions. The informational roles were monitoring the environment for information, disseminating this information to the right people in the organisation and acting as the spokesman for the organisation. The decisional roles included acting as an entrepreneur, dealing with problems as they arise, allocating resources and negotiating between internal and external environments.

This basic framework has been applied to the job of the hotel manager in two recent studies. Arnaldo surveyed 194 hotel general managers in the United States and asked them to indicate the amount of time and the importance they attached to each of the ten roles. The role of leader was the most time-consuming and the most important interpersonal role, being the manager's responsibility for the work of the people of the unit. This involves the selection, training, motivation and encouragement of employees and the reconciling of individual needs to organisational goals. From the informational roles, monitoring – scanning the environment for information, talking to outside contacts and subordinates, maintaining a network of personal contacts – and disseminating – passing on some of the collected information to subordinates who need the data and who would otherwise have no access to it – were both seen as time-consuming and important. But, surprisingly, acting as a spokesman, which did not take up much time, was not seen as less important. All the decisional roles took up about the same amount of time but the entrepreneurial role – seeking to improve the unit's performance and to adapt it to the changing conditions of the environment through new developments and projects – was seen as the most important, although the degree of importance attached to it (55.2 per cent of the respondents saw it as most important) was not matched by the time spent on it (only 35.6 per cent spent most time on it).

Ley's study attempted to correlate the general manager's effectiveness with the time spent on different managerial roles. His research on seven managers of Holiday Inns, although limited in scope, did show that effective managers seem to allocate their time between the roles differently in comparison with less effective managers. He found that managers who allocated a lot of time to the entrepreneurial role were seen by head office as effective managers but that those who concentrated on the leadership role were seen as less effective.

This approach has provided a good framework for identifying the activities that managers carry out and again stresses the multi-faceted and integrated nature of the manager's work. It also suggests that some aspects of the manager's job are more appropriate for effective management, although no precise indication of which roles are more important and in which circumstances can be made.

The approach which does address the issue of what managers should do to meet what is expected of them is that developed by Hales and Nightingale. They identified the 'role set' – that set of people with whom the manager comes into contact – of managers across a wide range of establishments in the hospitality industry. Each member of the role set was then asked to identify their demands, expectations and requirements of the manager forming the subject of that study. These responses were then recorded on a managerial wheel as illustrated in figure 2.2.

When the 'wheels' of all the members of the role set are collected together it should be possible to identify what the key unit management activities are. Overall they found the unit manager's job to be subject to many conflicting and competing demands from a wide variety of sources, both inside and outside the organisation itself. They identified a common core of tasks and activities relating to standards, customers, costs and stock control and human resource management but with additional expectations subject to variation both between different sectors, particularly between public and private sectors, and between different members of the role set.

The Hales and Nightingale approach therefore identified very clearly what managers are expected to do. Unfortunately the wealth of detail it provides makes it difficult to apply in general terms to the features of hotel management, but it provides some indication of the core activities to be included.

We wish to provide a model that incorporates the elegance and simplicity of the Nailon model, with the implications of the Mintzberg approach and the relevance and applicability of the Hales and Nightingale framework.

KEY RESULT AREAS IN HOTEL MANAGEMENT

A recent study conducted on the attitudes of management and staff in a large international hotel chain[16] has shown that a major component of all managers' jobs is 'getting things done' – a common orientation to activity and results. This was reinforced by Lord Forte in his autobiography – 'success rests first and foremost on the activities of the manager on the spot.' In ensuring the success of the unit, the manager is not interested in marketing, finance and personnel as disciplines in their own right; he is interested in using these techniques to achieve the results required of the unit at that time. He is concerned with using techniques in an integrated way to apply to the problems facing the unit and the organisation. Similarly his success as a manager will be determined by the results he achieves judged against the results that were expected of him. Results are not only a target but also a measure of success.

The results that a manager is concerned with must be derived from the three major components of the hotel operation:

- the customers;
- the workforce;
- the assets.

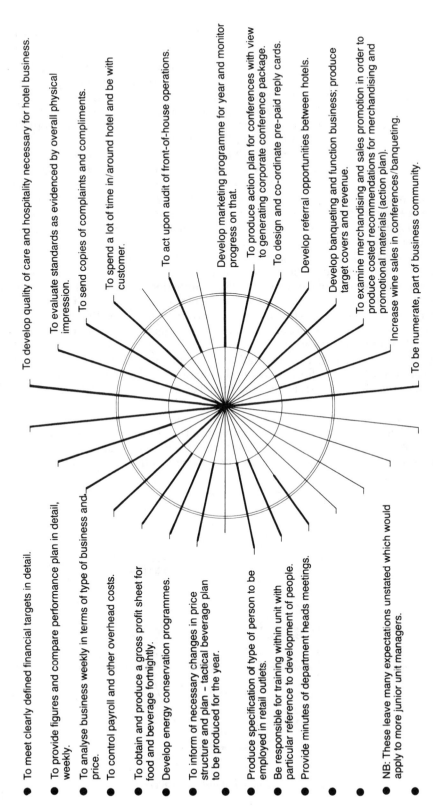

- To develop quality of care and hospitality necessary for hotel business.

- To evaluate standards as evidenced by overall physical impression.

- To send copies of complaints and compliments.

- To spend a lot of time in/around hotel and be with customer.

- To act upon audit of front-of-house operations.

- Develop marketing programme for year and monitor progress on that.

- To produce action plan for conferences with view to generating corporate conference package.

- To design and co-ordinate pre-paid reply cards.

- Develop referral opportunities between hotels.

- Develop banqueting and function business; produce target covers and revenue.

- To examine merchandising and sales promotion in order to produce costed recommendations for merchandising and promotional materials (action plan).

- Increase wine sales in conferences/banqueting.

- To be numerate, part of business community.

- To meet clearly defined financial targets in detail.

- To provide figures and compare performance plan in detail, weekly.

- To analyse business weekly in terms of type of business and price.

- To control payroll and other overhead costs.

- To obtain and produce a gross profit sheet for food and beverage fortnightly.

- Develop energy conservation programmes.

- To inform of necessary changes in price structure and plan – tactical beverage plan to be produced for the year.

- Produce specification of type of person to be employed in retail outlets.

- Be responsible for training within unit with particular reference to development of people.

- Provide minutes of department heads meetings.

- NB: These leave many expectations unstated which would apply to more junior unit managers.

Figure 2.2 *Expectations of unit manager in hotel chain by line superior – Director City Centre Hotels. Reproduced with permission.*

These three components represent the core elements identified in the Hales and Nightingale study over which the manager is meant to exert his or her expertise. This combination of components is meant to *fit*. The assets exist to satisfy the needs of its customers through the skills of its workforce. In practice, many management problems are derived from a lack of 'fit'. A major theme running through this book is the idea of 'fit', and we shall return to in nearly every chapter.

It is now possible to identify *key result areas* that are derived from managing the three components so far identified. A key result area can be defined as an area of activity that must be successfully managed in order to ensure the continued existence and the ultimate success of the operation. Thus the key result area derived from the customer is *ensuring customer satisfaction*; the key result area derived from the workforce is *maintaining employee performance*; and that from considering the assets is *protecting them from threat*.

But the manager does not manage these components in isolation from each other. They interact and overlap. Where each component interacts with one of the other two, a new key result area is evident. The interaction of the workforce and the customer highlights the key result area of *managing customer service*. The workforce/ asset interface is concerned with *maximising productivity*. And the interaction between the customer and the assets focuses the manager's attention on *maximising income and profit contribution*.

Finally, the combined interaction of all three components focuses on the key result area of *managing quality*. This is illustrated in figure 2.3. The model shown in figure 2.3 identifies the key result areas that the manager must consider but, as has already been stated, there will be variations in the requirements of different sectors of the industry, and of the same sector at different times and when facing different market conditions. The focus of attention or relative priority of each of the key result areas will vary across sectors and with time within sectors. For instance, commercial hotels may focus largely on occupancy rate and profit contribution, where hostels may be

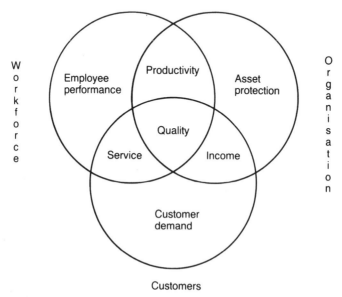

Figure 2.3 *A model of hotel management.*

more concerned with occupancy and productivity. Within a sector, during the off-peak season, hotel managers may be concerned with occupancy whereas during the peak they may focus on quality.

The model can be applied and modified to suit this wide variety of different requirements. For instance, a hospital in the public sector, which would be largely unconcerned with income and profit contribution, but should be relatively more concerned with productivity, asset protection and customer service, can be modeled as in figure 2.4.

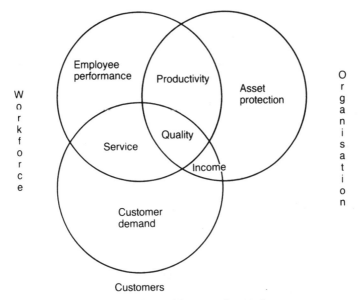

Figure 2.4 *A model of public sector hospital management.*

Implicit in this model is the idea that the tactics or techniques for achieving successful performance in any particular key result area will vary according to context. For example, the approach to quality management in a five-star hotel is likely to be very different from that in a small guest-house. In order for any approach to be effective it must be appropriate to the particular circumstances of the organisation. Indeed the results that the manager can achieve may be constrained by the directives of the organisation's senior management. General managers often complain that they would take certain courses of action to improve the performance of their unit were it not for head office 'flavour of the month' policies which change on a regular basis. The successful manager, however, is still the one who is constantly seeking to improve the unit's performance in the appropriate key result areas and responding to the changing conditions faced by the business.

SUMMARY

This chapter identifies the features of the hotel environment. It illustrates the extent to which the hotel, hostel and hospital sectors are similar. We argue that these features make the managers of hotels responsible for both the strategy and the operation and go on to explore models of hotel management.

We advocate a model of hotel management based on the concept of key result areas. The key characteristics of this model are:

1. Successful managers are concerned with achieving results in certain key areas of the business.

2. The relative importance of each of these will be different from one sector to another and will vary over time.

3. The key result areas do not exist in isolation one from the other. Management action in one area will affect others.

4. There is a wide range of options for successfully managing each key result area. The application of the most appropriate procedure, system, technique or approach will depend on the analysis of the specific nature of each operation at that moment in time.

5. Key result areas should not be considered as discrete in time – you do not consider one today and another tomorrow. Although one result area may require more activity at one particular moment, all result areas must be monitored and acted upon together.

Over the next seven chapters each of the seven key result areas will be discussed in detail and the range of appropriate procedures, systems, techniques and approaches identified.

REFERENCES

1. Thomas, D. R. E., 'Strategy is different in service businesses', *Harvard Business Review*, July/August 1978.

2. O'Connor, J. (ed.), *The British Hotel Industry*, Jordan and Sons (Surveys) Ltd, 1986.

3. Rice, J. A., Slack, R. S., and Garside, P. A., 'Hospitals can learn valuable marketing strategies from hotels', *Hospitals* vol. 55, no. 22, Nov. 16, American Hospital Publishing Inc., 1981.

4. Sasser, W. E., and Morgan, I. P., 'The Bermuda Triangle of food service chains', *Cornell HRA Quarterly*, pp. 56–61, February 1977.

5. Bateson, J., in conversation.

6. Schaffer, J. D., 'Strategy, organisation structure and success in the lodging industry', *International Journal Of Hospitality Management* vol. 3, no. 4, pp. 159–165, 1985.

7. Ley, D. A., *An empirical examination of selected work activity correlates of managerial effectiveness in the hotel industry using a structured observation approach*. Unpublished PhD Dissertation, Michigan State University, 1978.

8. Merricks, P., and Jones, P., *The Management of Catering Operations*, Holt, Rinehart and Winston Cassell, 1986.

9. Nailon, P., 'Theory in hospitality management', *International Journal of Hospitality Management* vol. 1, no. 3, 1982.

10. Reuland, R., Choudry, J., and Fagel, A., 'Research in the field of hospitality', *International Journal of Hospitality Management* vol. 4, no. 4, pp. 141–146, 1985.

11. Ley, D. A., *op. cit.*

12. Arnaldo, M. J., 'Hotel general managers: a profile', *Cornell HRA Quarterly*, pp. 53–56, November 1981.

13. Hales, C., and Nightingale, M., 'What are unit managers supposed to do? A contingent methodology for investigating managerial role requirements', *International Journal of Hospitality Management* vol. 5, no. 1, pp. 3–11, 1986.

14. Johnson, P., *The Corpus of Knowledge*, HCIMA, London, 1977.

15. Mintzberg, H., *The Nature of Managerial Work*, Harper and Row, 1973.

16. Guerrier, Y., and Lockwood, A., unpublished.

3 Protecting Assets

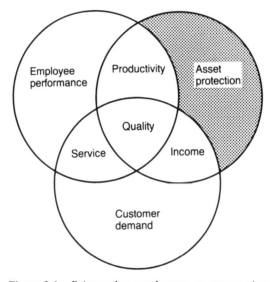

Figure 3.1 *Primary key result area: asset protection.*

INTRODUCTION

Of the three primary key result areas (see figure 3.1), the assets of the hotel represent all those aspects of the operation that are the property of or in the care of the hotel's owners. The assets obviously include the hotel premises, its plant and equipment, fixtures and fittings, and stocks of consumables and non-consumables. But it also includes two categories of 'asset' that are not so obvious. The first is the capital invested in the business and the subsequent stream of revenues generated by the business. The second 'asset' is not the property of the hotel's owners, but it is something over which the hotelier has temporary care, that is, the hotel's guest and his or her belongings. Thus 'assets' cover all aspects of the business that require 'protecting' to ensure that no unnecessary loss results, either through malpractice, poor security, mis-storage or whatever.

This chapter is largely concerned with best practices – those routines, procedures and approaches adopted by hotels to ensure the effective and secure use of all the operation's 'assets'. Assets contribute towards the success of the unit largely as a result of their original conceptualisation and design. The hotel's location, vistas, building design, interior design, decor and so on have been created to provide the right kind of experience for the expected market segment. In protecting these assets, the manager has the role of ensuring that they continue to be effective in meeting customer's expectations and needs.

Nonetheless, the manager in focusing on this key result area is concerned less with generating extra income but rather with minimising cost. If these things are not done, or not done well, losses may result directly, or indirectly, from lost future customers. But if they are done well, it is extremely unlikely that the hotel guest is even aware of them. For instance, a hotel fire both can directly damage assets and indirectly may put off future reservations. But a hotel that has not had a fire does not attract customers because of this.

A central feature of understanding how to manage the hotel's assets is to recognise the essential paradox derived from the fact that measures taken to secure the hotel from one type of threat may increase the danger from another type. For instance, by ensuring the security of the hotel from intruders and potential theft, the hotel may be more difficult to evacuate in the event of a fire. Thus this key result area requires the hotel manager to make high quality value judgements about the most desirable courses of action.

HOTEL DESIGN

The environment created by the hotel building is fundamental to the nature of the hotel experience. Clearly it is the responsibility of the manager to manage this environment well. Such management entails not only physical security and safety, but also the psychological safety and comfort needs of guests. In designing hotel properties it is necessary not only to consider the physical aspects in ergonomic terms by looking at lighting levels, noise levels and accessibility, but also the psychological effects of the environment on the guest in terms of stress. If guests are unable to identify where they should be going in the hotel, or how the system works, this will result in disorientation. Guests will have a negative response to the environment, which could lead to dissatisfaction with the service experience.

A major area of concern for hoteliers has been hotel lobbies. This environment creates the customers' first impressions of the hotel, but at the same time is a major centre of activity and a high traffic area. The layout and design of the lobby should vary according to the nature of the usage. For instance, it may be necessary to provide separate check-in facilities for individual customers and large groups. There is also a trend towards making lobby areas more effective by reducing the level of lounge-type casual seating. At the Sheraton Hong Kong, for example, this area was crowded by a large number of non-buying visitors, so that customers wishing to register had difficulty finding and getting to the registration desk. In conjunction with this, such space is being made more welcoming by providing bar or food service facilities. This has the added advantage of increasing the revenue-earning potential of this area. Lobby bars are increasingly being incorporated into four- and five-star hotels. In Las Vegas, the revenue potential of this space is fully exploited by filling it with opportunities to gamble on fruit machines, blackjack tables, and so on. In this extreme example, hotels make very much more money out of gambling revenues than room sales, so that hotel accommodation is among the cheapest in the USA.

The extent to which the manager is able to manage the environment depends largely on the original design of the building and the capital available to invest in it. The Grand Hotel in Brighton is an example of how a hotel can be transformed as a result of investment. Before it was bombed, the Grand was a typical seafront hotel built in the 1910s. It was in need of renovation, slightly run down, and operating a four-star service. After the bombing, extensive work has restored the building to its former glory, improved the standard of facilities and raised it to five-star status. Such refurbishment is being carried on throughout the world, as at the Carlton in Cannes and the Grand in Paris.

THE DESIGN OF HOTEL BEDROOMS

As the part of the hotel in which guests are likely to spend the majority of their stay, the design and decoration of the hotel bedroom will have a significant impact on the guests' perceptions and enjoyment of that stay. The decoration and furnishing of bedrooms seem to follow a pattern across hotels. In the early 1970s, there was a trend to the 'modern' look with bright colours and hard surfaces. The late 1980s are characterised by much softer lines and colours with an emphasis on floral prints. Comparing the decor of, for example, four-star hotels in central London reveals a remarkable similarity in design, such that it is often difficult to distinguish between hotels on decor alone.

Examining the impact of decor and furnishing on the customer is not easy. A study was recently conducted by the authors with the help of Dr Yvonne Guerrier on the perceptions of a group of hotel and catering managers attending a short course. They were shown a set of nine photographs of hotel bedrooms from four-star London hotels. Using a simplified version of a repertory grid interview, they then examined their perceptions of those bedrooms individually. These individual responses were combined to get an overall impression from the group. The survey generated some interesting results:

- There were significant differences in the descriptions used by individuals in the survey, suggesting that they looked at the rooms in quite different ways. However, in overall terms, there was considerable agreement between those rooms that were liked and those that were disliked.

- There was little correlation between the perceptions of the cost of the room as cheap or expensive and the actual price of the room.

- Perhaps not surprisingly, those rooms that were seen as expensive were also those that were liked best.

- The factors which contributed most to the liking of the room were the lightness of the room, the availability of natural and artificial light and whether or not the lights were turned on. These factors were closely linked to feelings of spaciousness and expensiveness. In general rooms that were light, airy and spacious, had their lights turned on and looked expensive were those that were liked best on first impressions.

This survey suggests that, as well as considering the physical facilities provided in the room, hotel designers should be aware of the psychological impact of decor and furnishings on the customers' satisfaction with their room and their stay.

ASSET AUDIT

The possible 'threats' to the hotel's assets range widely from deliberate acts of malevolence to negligence and accidental occurrences, some of which could be prevented and others which are in effect so-called 'acts of God'. These include fire, physical damage, theft, pilferage, breakdown, and the provision of below standard service. As a framework for deciding how to approach the effective protection of assets the manager should undertake an 'asset audit' to find out the full extent of *all* the assets he or she is responsible for, and then determine whether or not to institute procedures or activities designed to control or assure against the possible 'threats'.

The extent to which an 'asset audit' is common practice varies widely. For most hotel operations only certain types of assets will be analysed and recorded. Such assets are typically the consumable stocks, such as foodstuffs, liquor stocks, cleaning materials, linen and guest supplies. The recording of these is carried out by the responsible storeperson, and monitored by departmental heads. Hotels may also keep effective records of non-consumable stocks, particularly small items such as kitchen and restaurant equipment, cleaning equipment, and so on. Such records and checks are likely to be much less frequently made than the stock control of consumables. Even less frequently, hotels may make a check on the larger items of capital equipment that they might well take for granted, such as beds, carpets and TV sets. There is the apocryphal story of the large London hotel that had a splendid Persian carpet in its lobby worth many thousands of pounds. One day two men in overalls walked in, told the reception manager they had come to collect the carpet for cleaning, rolled it up and walked out with it. Not only was the carpet never seen again, but it was several weeks before the management of the hotel even realised what had happened!

This concept of an asset audit can also be extended to those assets of the hotel that are not typically checked or monitored, particularly the premises, fixtures and fittings. Some hotels, particularly the larger ones, do this in effect by having planned maintenance programmes. As regards cash – which we have said should also be thought of as an asset – the audit approach involves the identification of levels of cash held and the measurement of cash flows.

CONTROL v. ASSURANCE

The audit should identify the full range of assets that need to be protected. Such protection can basically be instituted in two ways. One way is to adopt a 'control' strategy which is designed to monitor closely all the assets as frequently as necessary. This approach is 'curative' in that if losses are found to be occurring action will be taken to put things right. The second approach is the 'assurance' strategy which is an ongoing and continuous range of activities aimed at preventing loss or damage of assets.

The strategy adopted is largely determined by the characteristics of the asset itself and the level of possible threat. For instance, a fire could affect the entire hotel; it is therefore a high-level threat to a major asset and clearly the strategy to adopt is the

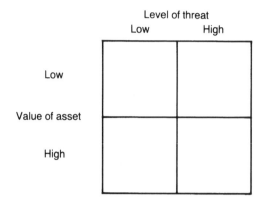

Figure 3.2 *Determining factors in asset protection strategies.*

'assurance' one. However, the theft of a towel by a room-maid is a low-level threat to a low-cost asset, and would be subject to a 'control' strategy. This is illustrated by figure 3.2.

The assets that are definitely in the category of high asset value are the hotel premises and the hotel guest. In both cases the manager would want to ensure that nothing detrimental happens to either of these. With regards to other assets such as plant, equipment, stocks and guest belongings, the value of the asset can largely be based on the financial value placed on the item by either its original cost, current value, replacement cost or level of insured cost, all of which may be different.

The threats that are typically high level are those of fire, both accidental and deliberate acts of arson, bombings and other terrorist activity, and major structural damage resulting from negligent maintenance. Low-level threats include minor accidents, petty pilferage and wastage.

The categorisation of assets and threats into high or low level, will be influenced by the type of hotel, the markets it serves, and its location. For instance, hotels in Belfast and Beirut have to adopt entirely different approaches and be concerned with issues quite different to those facing hotels in Bradford and Burton-on-Trent. Likewise, a hospital faces different problems to a hotel since many of its 'guests' are unable to help themselves in the event of a major threat such as a fire, so the prevention measures and emergency procedures instituted will be more comprehensive.

Another factor influencing the decision about whether a control or assurance strategy should be adopted is the cost of implementation compared with the benefits derived. This is illustrated in table 3.1.

Wyckoff identified four cost components in adopting either a control or assurance approach. We have applied these to asset protection as follows:

1. *Prevention costs* – those expenses associated with creating performance standards, i.e. staff training in relation to asset protection, preparing operating procedures.

2. *Assurance costs* – expenses of inspection, measurement, and data collection and analysis.

3. *Internal failure* – expenses due to the occurrence of low-level threats.

4. *External failure* – expenses relating to the occurrence of high-level threats, including loss of repeat business.

Table 3.1 *Cost comparison of approaches to asset protection.*

Cost component	Cost factor	Approach Control £	Assurance £
Prevention	Cost of premium	n/a	high
	Employee training	low	high
Assurance	Materials inspection	n/a	low
	Supervisor's inspection	high	low
Internal failure	Occurrence of threat	high	low
External failure	Occurrence of threat	high	low
	Placating customer	high	low

Adapted from table 'Hypothetical comparison of two cost control strategies', in Wyckoff, D. D.[1]

The assurance approach spends much more time, effort and investment on the prevention element than the control approach, in the belief that this will give rise to major savings in the other three areas.

THE PLAYERS ON THE SCENE

Before we go on to examine the control strategy and assurance strategy in more detail we need to analyse the 'players' involved. Whilst assets may be threatened or lost due entirely to 'non-human' intervention – so-called acts of God – by far the greatest number of threats and losses will result from human error or activity. In any case, the manager has no control over 'acts of God' and can only hope that the hotel's insurance policy covers such occurrences.

There are four sets of players. First, there are the *bona fide residential guests* of the hotel. In the main their activities are likely to be no threat to the hotel's or their own assets. However, there is the possibility that such residents may be involved in activities that are a threat. For instance, the terrorist who placed the bomb in the Grand Hotel in Brighton was a 'bona fide' guest some months previously. Secondly, there are the *bona fide visitors* to the hotel. This category includes non-residential guests using restaurant, bar, banqueting or conference facilities; persons making deliveries to the hotel; and contractors working in the establishment, such as contract cleaners, plumbers and so on. These too are likely to be engaged on legitimate activities, but it may be difficult to distinguish them from unwelcome visitors, such as thieves or prostitutes. Such unwelcome visitors are categorised as *non-bona fide visitors*. Almost certainly such visitors are present for nefarious purposes which may well threaten the range of assets we have identified. Finally, one of the most important categories of player is the *employees* of the hotel. These too should be engaged in activities that are non-threatening, but this is not always the case. Employees may pose a threat due to their negligence or by their deliberate actions. A serious hotel fire in the Philippines in 1986 was thought to have been started deliberately by a disgruntled employee.

Curtis[2] has suggested that there are signs that staff may be a security threat and that there is a danger in 'employee contamination', that is to say one dishonest member of staff can result in more staff members acting dishonestly. Such problems tend to occur in organisations with authoritarian management styles, that use punishment and threats of punishment as controlling mechanisms. This can be compounded by poor morale, which as we shall see in chapter 4 may be due to a variety of factors. Theft is also more likely in larger organisations, which may be perceived as 'being able to afford it', especially if the remuneration package of staff is perceived as being relatively poor. Finally, a dishonest member of staff can promulgate theft in an attempt to gain peer recognition and status.

Powers[3] has suggested that potentially dishonest staff members have a particular employee profile. Based on experience with people who have been proven guilty of theft or pilferage, the characteristics of dishonest employees are:

- resentment of criticism;

- financial difficulties, asking for advances in wages, borrowing from other members of staff;

- air of dissatisfaction with someone or something;

- no identification with the hotel which is referred to as 'they' rather than 'we';

- lack of respect for people or property, allowing high level of breakage or waste, poorly dressed;

- refusal of responsibility.

Many of the approaches and ideas put forward in subsequent chapters on employees, productivity and service address the issue of how to get the best out of staff. They are equally relevent to the idea of ensuring staff are honest and safety conscious. Specific approaches to this problem adopted by hotels include effective employee selection procedures, using identification badges for personnel, theft awareness training, application and monitoring of standards of performance, and security training.

CONTROL STRATEGIES FOR ASSET PROTECTION

We have argued that this strategy will tend to be used for the protection of low value assets against low-level threats. It is therefore not worth the cost of an assurance programme to protect them. Typically used in hotels are 'standard operating procedures', inventory control systems and 'subroutines'. Clearly these have a role other than just to protect the assets; they are also fundamental in the provision of service quality and essential to effective cost and revenue control. However, we choose to concentrate here on their 'protective' role, especially since this is an aspect that is not recognised or is quite often ignored.

Standard operating procedures (SOPs) are usually found in chain hotel operations. Typically they comprise a simple statement of policy, followed by paragraphs indicating directives, procedures, explanation of forms, records to be kept, positional responsibilities and co-ordinating relationships. They can apply to all departments of the hotel, but we shall concentrate here on those relating to the provision of accommodation.

SOPs are applied to activities which occur frequently, are usually delegated to operating personnel, can be communicated in written form and require some standard to be achieved for quality or security purposes. In the housekeeping department,

SOPs can be set for key control, lost property, stock control, linen handling, use of
chemicals, guest loans, staff performance standards, and so on. An example of a SOP
for key control is illustrated in figure 3.3.

As well as standard operating procedures, many of the everyday operational activities of the housekeeping department, known as subroutines, provide additional security for the hotel's assets. Subroutines can cover a wide range of activities such as room
supplies, stock-taking, room inspections, maintenance work requests, public area

---

HOUSEKEEPING PROCEDURES

SUBJECT	DATE	NUMBER
KEY CONTROLS	9.1.81	200.01

Key security is of critical importance to the hotel's guests and employees. Severe
penalties can be paid by the hotel responsible for thefts or assaults directly
related to poor key controls. Access to guest rooms can be gained by taking
advantage of careless supervision of master and submaster keys. Therefore, to
protect guests and employees from criminal actions, careful attention must be paid
to preventing the loss or theft of master and submaster keys.

Coding
- Code all master and submaster keys.

Issuing Keys
- Make sure all keys are issued by and turned in to the housekeeping office.
- Make sure the following information is record-ed on a key control sheet:
  (1) Current date
  (2) Key code
  (3) Name of person to whom key will be issued
  (4) Signature of person to whom key is issued
  (5) Time that the key is issued
  (6) Initials of person issuing keys

Custody of Keys
- Do not allow employees to loan their assigned keys to one another. Such loans increase the chances of keys being lost or stolen and make it harder to trace missing keys.
- Make sure that room attendants keep their keys with them at all times. Keys must never be left on a cart or laid down in a room; room attendants should keep keys affixed to their person by a leather strap or some other means.
- Whenever employees leave the property, even for meal breaks, have them sign the keys in on the key control sheet.

Figure 3.3 *Example of standard operating procedure.*

cleaning and so on. Room inspection is a good example of an operational necessity that provides a check on assets.

Room inspection in the UK is usually carried out by supervisory staff, such as floor housekeepers. Some American chains use inspectresses whose only role is to check on rooms. Whoever checks the room can do so using a highly detailed checklist or simple standards of performance. Inspection can be systematic or spot-checks. A survey in the United States[4] found that hotels with well maintained and very clean rooms were those that were spot-checked by supervisory staff. It would seem that the high level of control imposed by detailed checklists and inspectresses resulted in lower levels of performance from chambermaids due to the demotivating impact of this approach. It is also suggested that senior personnel, such as the executive housekeeper or general manager, should also be identified with the inspection process, on a regular 'inspection day'. This has positive results on performance and motivation.

Likewise routine maintenance can be carried out through the use of regular inspections, utilising a checklist as illustrated in figure 3.4. However, in large hotels, such weekly routine inspections may be inadequate. Often the staff involved are too familiar with the property or not skilled enough to notice potentially serious defects. To ensure the protection of assets, some hotel chains use 'total property inspections'. This involves the allocation of every square foot of the property as the responsibility of a senior manager in the management team. For instance, the food and beverage manager may be responsible for the bars, restaurants, kitchens and food stores, or the chief engineer may be responsible for the heating plant and hotel exterior, including car parks, gardens and boundaries. These managers are then required to check systematically on their designated areas to ensure proper maintenance, cleanliness and safety.

In addition, 'zone inspection programmes' provide a regular check of parts of the hotel.

Case example 3.1   Tropicana, Las Vegas

The Tropicana Hotel's zone inspection programme divided the hotel into six zones of approximately equal size. Since Zone 1 comprised all the guest rooms, a random sample of fourteen rooms was checked. It was the hotel's policy to inspect the entire hotel by zone every two weeks. Eight chief zone inspectors were appointed comprising the eight most senior management personnel other than the general manager. Each chief zone inspector was assigned several assistant inspectors, usually along organisational lines. The eight inspectors were to carry out an inspection by rota of any of the six areas. They could delegate the actual inspection to one of their assistants, but they were nonetheless held accountable. There would be three inspections in one week, and three in the next, held at any time between the end of the weekly staff meeting on Wednesdays and 4.00 pm on Thursday. The Zone 2 inspection report is illustrated in figure 3.5.

ASSURANCE STRATEGIES FOR ASSET PROTECTION

Assurance strategies are required to protect high-value assets from high-level threats. This means protecting the hotel building and its occupants from threats such as flood, fire, typhoon, earthquake, civil disturbance and bombing. Most hotel companies do not explicitly differentiate policies aimed at low-level security from high-level security.

MAINTENANCE CHECKLIST

☐ **CHECKED**　　☐ **NEEDS REPAIR**　■ **REPAIR COMPLETED**
Room No. _____

AIR CONDITIONERS

☐ 1. Switches/controls/valves—
   check operation
☐ 2. Thermostat dial positioned,
   works correctly
☐ 3. Thermostat probe secure,
   calibrated, working
☐ 4. Filter—clean
☐ 5. Fan & fan motor—clean, lubricated, secure
☐ 6. Evaporator and condenser—
   clean
☐ 7. Condensation pan & drain—
   clean
☐ 8. Exterior grill—clean, maintained
   to complement building exterior
☐ 9. Compressor—clean
☐ 10. Check for leaks in refrigeration
   system
☐ 11. Check electric plug, recepta-
   cles, cord
☐ 12. Heating unit, clean & operating
   correctly

ELECTRICAL

☐ 13. Lamp switches on/off-3 way
   working correctly
☐ 14. Lamp sockets & swivels, tight,
   in good repair
☐ 15. Lamp shades, clean, no holes,
   secure
☐ 16. Light bulb—replace burned,
   check wattage
☐ 17. Plugs, cords & connections,
   repair as needed
☐ 18. Lamp base/body in good repair
☐ 19. Light switches on/off—working and in good repair

☐ 20. Switch & outlet wallplates—
   good repair and match in color
☐ 21. Wall sockets/receptacles
   operate, no shorts
☐ 22. Timer switches work correctly,
   knob secure
☐ 23. Heat lamps, correct wattage,
   clean, good repair
☐ 24. All light fixtures are clean, dust
   free, complementary to room
   decor

TELEVISION

☐ 25. Audio—clear (radio and television)
☐ 26. Visual—in focus (check each
   station)
☐ 27. Knobs—replace, if necessary
☐ 28. Fine tune—color contrast,
   horizontal, vertical
☐ 29. Antenna—cable connections
   secure
☐ 30. Chassis/screen—clean, dust-
   free, no apparent damage—
   security mounts secure

TELEPHONE

☐ 31. Overall appearance & condi-
   tion—clean, good repair
☐ 32. Dialing instructions—replace
   if faded
☐ 33. Defects (good connections,
   audio good, bell works, etc.)
   report to telephone company

FURNITURE

☐ 34. Drawer handles, knobs tight,
   good repair and drawer guides
   lubricated

Figure 3.4 *Example of maintenance checklist.*

TROPICANA

ZONE INSPECTION REPORT

Zone 5

BUILDING EXTERIOR AND GROUNDS

Accountable Manager <u>GROUNDS SUPERINTENDENT/COUNTRY</u>
<u>CLUB MANAGER/CHIEF ENGINEER</u>

Inspected by _____ Date/time _____

Inspection to be completed no later than Thursday (4:00 P M) on weeks
scheduled. Make two copies. Original and one copy is to be forwarded to the
Executive Secretary by 4:00 P M on Thursday. Second copy to be delivered
to the Accountable Manager for this zone. Discuss as necessary. The Accountable Manager will indicate corrective action taken in accordance with
corrective code (see basic procedure). Follow-up copy to be forwarded to
the executive office no later than the following Tuesday.

Space	Sat.	NI	Unsat.	Comment	ACC. MGR. Corrective Action
Grounds policing					
Front entrance					
Parking lot lighting					
Grounds lighting					
Pool area					
Outdoor tennis area					
General signage					
Tennis Pavilion: inside					
Tennis Pavilion: outside					
Employee parking lot					
Entrance #1					
Entrance #2					
Entrance #3					
Entrance #4					
C/C bldg.					
Golf course					
C/C parking					
C/C lighting					
Flags and poles					

Figure 3.5 *Tropicana zone inspection form.*

However, they do recognise differences between the two. For instance, Holiday Inns
Inc. differentiated between housekeeping procedures covering key controls, day-to-
day safety and security procedures and handling do-not-disturb signs, and a highly
sophisticated major security strategy called the 'Emergency Organisation Plan'.

The first step in an assurance programme is taken when the hotel is first designed. One of the criteria for the architect or designer must be the security of the building, both in terms of it not falling or burning down, and in terms of protecting the people and artefacts inside. We have identified that the average size of hotels is increasing and most new hotels that are being built are quite large. This requires, particularly in tall buildings, that hotels are structurally designed to withstand both natural and man-made threats and as much as possible localise them to one part of the building. So if a fire starts or a bomb goes off the damage and threat to people is contained in the immediate vicinity of the fire or explosion.

The second step is actually to ensure that the detailed daily controls discussed on page 40 are adhered to. Although they have the role of protecting low-value assets from low-level threats, they contribute greatly to assuring the safety of higher value assets. The continual movement of staff around the building in the course of their work assists in the identification of fires before they get out of control, suspicious persons and suspect packages.

The third step is a contingency programme that details exactly what course of action to take in the event a serious threat occurs. It is the nature of such threats that they are not easily predicted nor controllable by the unit management.

The most important part of such contingency planning is the allocation of responsibilities to appropriate staff. In the case of some threats the allocation is along organisational lines. For instance, in hotels facing a hurricane warning the general manager will have responsibility for guest liaison, directing operations and monitoring radio and television broadcasts; the engineer will be responsible for installing protective shutters, preparing sandbags, and setting up a secure store of tools; the food and beverage manager may take charge of storing three days' supply of canned goods in a secure place, along with disposables, candles and cooking utensils and equipment; and so on.

In the case of other types of serious threat, the contingency planning may allocate responsibilities on the basis of expertise rather than position in the organisation. For instance, in the case of a fire the general manager, although responsible, is likely to hand over control of the operation to a member of staff designated as fire chief, who has had appropriate training and experience in this field. Reporting to the fire chief will be a variety of personnel drawn from across the hotel and allocated specific responsibilities during a fire. These include:

- *a fire squad* whose job it is to fight the fire until the fire brigade arrives;

- *communications person*, usually a senior telephonist, whose role it is to carry out all the necessary communications with the fire service, other emergency services and internal communications, both by telephone and over the public address system;

- *an engineer* whose role it is to ensure the effective operation of all appropriate fire-fighting and fire-prevention equipment such as hoses, sprinklers and shut-off systems on gas and electrical supplies;

- *a fire liaison officer* whose role it is to direct both the internal fire squad and the fire service on its arrival to the fire.

In many cases, serious threats involve the evacuation of the building. As part of the assurance programme, clear evacuation procedures should be laid down. Such procedures detail the level of response, the approach to informing guests over the public address system or by telephoning each room, the allocation of staff to emergency stairs and exits to supervise guests leaving and prevent unauthorised persons from entering, the location of assembly areas, the shut-down of energy supply systems, the securing of cash and stock, and so on. Due to the size of many modern hotels, particularly those with many storeys, it is less common for the level of response to be total evacuation. Partial evacuation of the floor on which the threat occurs (e.g. fire or bomb) and two floors above and below that floor are quite common in order to avoid panic and congestion. Of course if the threat becomes more serious a full evacuation will be ordered. An example of an evacuation procedure is illustrated in figure 3.6.

EVACUATION PROCEDURES

These procedural guidelines can be used when the decision is made to evacuate any part of a building for any reason. At all times, the personal safety of the guests and employees should have priority.

In a large building that is structurally sound, authorities may not wish to evacuate all floors even if a bomb is found, because of the risk of panic. Normally initial evacuation would include the floor on which the bomb is found, and the two floors above and below that floor.

A record of chronological activity should be established.

Before an evacuation is put into effect, personnel should be dispatched to the stairwell entrances on each floor to direct and reassure the guests. Elevators, initially, may not be used, and should be returned to the main floor.

In a calm voice, the general manager should make an announcement over the public address system, similar to the following example, and repeat the message at least once:

'Attention please – Attention please – the management requests that all guests and visitors evacuate the hotel (or evacuate specific floors) as a precaution. Please leave the building by the nearest exit. Walk, do not run, please.'

In fire evacuation the message should instruct guests to close room windows and doors. In bomb threat evacuation, the message shoud instruct guests to leave windows open.

DO NOT MENTION THE REASON FOR EVACUATION.

When directed by the general manager, the switchboard operator should systematically begin to ring the rooms, indicating to the guests the following:

'I am sorry to disturb you, but the management has asked that all guests in your area vacate their rooms, immediately, for security reasons. Please use the stairwell at the ends of the corridors.'

Figure 3.6 *Example of a hotel evacuation procedure.*

SUMMARY

One of the major key result areas for a hotel manager is the protection of the hotel's assets. These assets may be valued at many millions of pounds. The manager must protect a wide range of different types of assets, such as the premises, equipment, people and their belongings, from a wide range of threats, such as pilferage, fire and natural disaster. Much of the activity undertaken in the hotel has the role of protecting assets, but it is rarely identified as having such a role. In order to provide a framework for understanding how to operationalise the management of this key result area, we have suggested two broad approaches.

The *control strategy* includes procedures, systems and control mechanisms designed to prohibit minor losses through negligence or deliberate acts. Most of the cost of such a strategy is spent on putting things right after the event. The *assurance strategy*, however, is designed to ensure things do not go wrong, so most of its costs are spent on preventive measures, particularly those incorporated into the building itself, such as smoke detectors, fire-escapes, etc.

REFERENCES

1. Wyckoff, D. D., 'New tools for achieving service quality', *Cornell HRA Quarterly*, pp. 78–91, November 1984.

2. Curtis, R., 'Tips on keeping employees honest', *Nation's Restaurant News*, September 1979.

3. Powers, B., 'Crime shouldn't pay; curbing employee theft', *Lodging*, p. 31, May 1983.

4. Martin, R. J., *Professional Management of Housekeeping Operations*, Wiley, 1985.

4 Improving Employee Performance

Figure 4.1 *Primary key result area: employee performance.*

INTRODUCTION

This chapter is concerned with the primary key result area that relates to the manager's responsibility for the workforce – improving employee performance (see figure 4.1). It is the manager's task to ensure that the organisation's most valuable resource – its employees – are used as effectively as possible. Recent surveys by Horwath and Horwath[1] have shown that the average of its sample of 266 hotels throughout the UK gives a figure for payroll and related expenses as a percentage of total sales of 29 per cent, ranging between 27 per cent in London and 31 per cent in Scotland. When nearly a third of all sales revenue is being used to pay employee wages, it is essential that employee performance is at an optimum level.

Employee performance is a difficult concept to define but is principally to do with the application of effective effort. In the first place employees must be putting the right amount of effort into their work. This effort will be ineffective, however, if the employee does not have the skills and abilities to carry out the task to the standard required, i.e. *the right person*; if the job has not been correctly designed to be efficient or the standards expected have not been communicated, i.e. *the right job*; if the organisation is not arranged to provide support to the individual and avoid conflict, i.e. *the right atmosphere*; if employees are not scheduled to cope with peaks and troughs of demand, i.e. *the right place at the right time*. Performance, then, is the right person applying the right effort to the right job in the right atmosphere in the right place at the right time.

In broad terms there are two main areas for concern – the performance of individual members of staff, and the collective performance of the staff as members of a team. It is often assumed that achieving the best from an individual will improve the operation's performance, but it might not, whilst it is equally questionable that good team-work is a result of maximising each individual's performance. In reality this distinction is very difficult to see and hence to manage.

Hotel managers should be concerned about employee performance for a number of reasons. First, poor performance will have a direct influence on the overall performance of the unit as measured both by management in financial terms and by customers in terms of service. Secondly, it will have consequences for the performance of the team, particularly with respect to morale. Thirdly, it is time consuming for the manager to correct through counselling, disciplinary interviews, tribunals, training and the recruitment and selection of replacement staff. Poor team performance is also a serious problem with major consequences for the operation's effectiveness. The manager of a poorly performing team is not really 'managing' at all. A fundamental part of management responsibility is to achieve results through others – through the management of the team.

This chapter will provide a framework for the analysis and solution of problems related to poor employee performance. It will examine the nature of the performance results that should be achieved and how they can be brought about through motivation, job design, individual and group abilities, creating the right environment and proper labour scheduling.

EMPLOYEE PERFORMANCE AS A KEY RESULT AREA

Although it is simple to identify the problems caused by poor employee performance, it is more difficult to adopt the alternative approach of positive indicators. Similarly, while it is relatively straightforward to consider the consequences for the organisation, it is less obvious what the results will be for the individual or the group. Successful employee performance must be a mutually beneficial relationship; it should not only result in the fulfilment of the organisation's expectations but also provide satisfaction of the individual's needs. The two sets of expectations must *fit*. Mumford[2] has developed an approach which looks for results in five areas.

1. *Knowledge*: The organisation requires its employees to have a certain level of skills and knowledge to operate effectively, whereas the employee wants the

organisation to use and develop the skills and knowledge which he brings to the job.

2. *Psychological expectations*: The organisation needs employees who are motivated to look after the interests of the organisation, whereas the employee looks to satisfy his own personal needs. A fit exists when employees satisfy these private needs through the satisfaction of company interests.

3. *Efficiency*: The organisation is looking for a reward system related to output and standards of performance, whereas employees are looking for a reward which they feel is equitable for the amount of effort they put in. This area also relates to the amount and method of control imposed on the employee.

4. *Task structure*: The organisation needs employees who will carry out the task as defined bearing in mind technical and other constraints, whereas the employees are looking for a job which will give the variety, interest, targets, feedback, task identity and autonomy they require.

5. *Values*: The organisation needs employees who will accept and adopt its own ethics and values, whereas employees are looking for an organisation whose values do not contravene their own.

ANALYSING EMPLOYEE PERFORMANCE

Performance has previously been described as 'effective effort'. The factors affecting the amount of effort that an employee will apply to work, and the conversion of that effort into effective performance with beneficial results for both the individual and the organisation, based on the areas identified in the previous section, are illustrated in figure 4.2.

The amount of effort that an employee will apply to his work will depend on the motivational force, i.e. expectation that the application of effort will result in performance and that performance will result in some form of reward which will be of valuc to him. However, the effectiveness of the effort will in turn be affected by the interaction of the skills and abilities of the individual and his work group, the design of the work itself, the climate of the organisation as a whole and the scheduling of the workforce to meet expected customer demand. The actual level of performance will generate rewards both for the employee and the organisation – for the employee in terms of pay, bonuses, recognition, achievement, etc., and for the organisation in terms of income, customer satisfaction or productivity. The value of the reward to the organisation will be assessed against company objectives and any mismatch will result in corrective action and will influence future decisions about recruitment, pay scales, management style and so on. The value of the reward to the employee will complete the loop to motivation and consequent effort on the job. The model also identifies that there should be a fit between the needs and consequent motivation of the employee and the needs and objectives of the organisation.

Two key features of this model should be noted. First, the five factors directly affecting performance are all closely interlinked and changing one will automatically influence the others. Of these five factors, management has direct control over four, effort being outside direct influence but subject to indirect influence through the other factors. Secondly, there should be a fit between individual rewards and reward to the organisation; reward to one party should not be at the cost of reward to the other. For

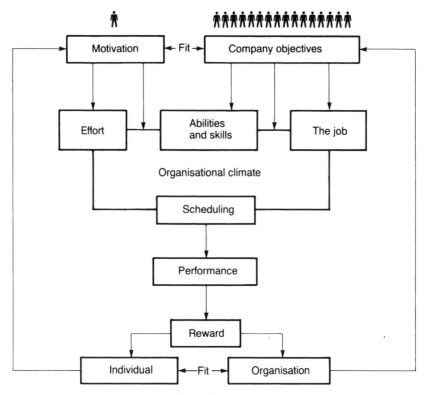

Figure 4.2 *A model for analysing employee performance.*

example, the common practice of using floor housekeepers to clean rooms on a regular basis so that the number of chambermaids can be kept to an absolute minimum will have beneficial effects for the organisation in terms of controlling costs and maintaining cleaning standards, but for the floor housekeepers, whose satisfaction from the job may result from the supervision of the task and not from doing it themselves, the financial reward of being paid a supervisor's salary may not compensate for the effort involved in cleaning rooms.

THE MOTIVATION CALCULUS

The expectancy theory of motivation, based on Vroom's expectancy-instrumentality theory[3] and developed by Porter and Lawler,[4] suggests that the effort an employee applies to his work is a function of the perceived value of the reward and the perceived effort-reward probability – the motivation calculus.

The rewards for effort can be extrinsic or intrinsic and should be seen as equitable. Extrinsic rewards are the physical rewards the organisation can give such as pay, promotion, status, security, free weekend breaks. Except in the case of some simple incentive bonus schemes the link between extrinsic rewards and performance are rather weak and difficult to see. An assistant manager who wants promotion to deputy manager may spend very long hours at work on the understanding that the organisation will reward his effort by the extrinsic reward of promotion but the actual link may not be so direct.

Intrinsic rewards are internal to the individual and include feelings of accomplishing something worthwhile, a sense of achievement, feelings that skills and abilities are being fully used and developed. These rewards have a more direct and immediate relationship to actual performance because they are the rewards the employee gives himself!

The value of the rewards both intrinsic and extrinsic will be affected by the perceived equity of those rewards – was it fair? Comparisons of fairness will be made with what the employee expected the reward to be and what the employee sees other people getting in a similar situation or should be getting in a particular position. For example, it may be company policy for sales managers to be given company cars but not their subordinates, the sales executives. This could be seen as a fair policy giving the manager the additional perk associated with such a position. However, when the sales executives are expected to make sales calls to outside companies on an almost daily basis for which they must use their own private car, and when some sales executives in the company have a company car because their units are too small to justify a full time sales manager, then the policy may not be seen as quite so equitable.

It is also important to recognise that the value of the reward is as perceived by the individual and therefore that what is rewarding for one employee may not be rewarding for another. The value of the reward will also be affected by the satisfaction that those rewards have given in the past. For example, most employees would see the reward of a free weekend break at one of the other properties in the chain as having high value, but if one employee has previously had a bad experience on one of these packages for whatever reason (a row with the boyfriend, a strained ankle in the leisure complex, a delay on the train journey home) they will not see the reward as having such high value.

The overall probability that rewards depend on effort can be further subdivided into the expectation that rewards depend on the performance generated and that the performance generated will result from the application of effort. For example, a house manager may wish to be promoted to general manager but may believe that only food and beverage managers stand a chance. In similar circumstances the house manager may see promotion as directly related to performance but may feel unable to improve the performance of the hotel because of an ineffective sales team, the isolated location of the property, or its general need for refurbishment or updated facilities.

The motivation calculus, as described above, is dependent on the individual perceptions of the employee and therefore difficult to predict in any but the most general terms but will be related to that employee's overall orientation to work. Three basic orientations to work have been identified: expressive, instrumental and alienative. An *expressive orientation* to work involves a positive attitude to work with the main interest being in the intrinsic rewards of the job deriving from the nature of the work itself and fellow workers. Within this expressive orientation, employees can either have a positive (solidaristic) or negative (bureaucratic) attitude to management. An *instrumental orientation* also displays a positive attitude to work but with an interest in the extrinsic rewards, mainly economic returns and security. This implies that a positive decision has been taken to maximise earnings at the expense of intrinsic job satisfaction as the money and security provide a degree of satisfaction despite the dissatisfying nature of the work itself. An *alienative orientation* implies a negative attitude to work which is seen simply as a means to an end, employees displaying no interest in the work at all. This type of alienation has been seen to be due to the following feelings:

- *powerlessness* – a lack of control over the work process;
- *meaninglessness* – only seeing a small part of the total process;
- *isolation* – a lack of a socially integrated work organisation;
- *self-estrangement* – a conscious decision to keep outside the organisation.

The implication of work orientation to the motivation of employees is that employees will see work in different ways, and although some techniques to encourage effort will work on some employees, it is unlikely that they will work on all of them or indeed on the same employees at different times.

A further aspect of motivation highlighted by a study of car workers[5] is that while certain aspects of a job may attract people to it and explain their attachment to it, there may be a different set of factors that contribute to the employees' satisfaction with the work they do. There will be different factors affecting a person's motivation to apply for a job ('I will apply for this job rather than that one because the pay is better'); to come to work ('I will not go in to work today because all my friends are on a day off'); and to work hard once on the job ('I am going to work hard today because the head receptionist said what a good job I did yesterday').

It can be seen from the above discussion that the process of motivation is both complicated and highly individualistic. However, although an individual's needs and orientations may be different, the *process* of motivation will remain constant. The hotel manager must be aware of this process of motivation calculus → effort → performance → reward → feedback, if attempts are to be made to influence the amount of effort a member of staff applies to the job.

THE JOB

The conversion of effort into performance will be influenced by the way in which the job the employee does is designed, and in turn the design of the job will either encourage or discourage effort. Approaches to job design have concentrated recently on the motivational aspects of job design, the so-called QWL or quality of working life approach, through the following techniques:

- *job enlargement* – expanding the job content horizontally through the addition of one or more related tasks;
- *job rotation* – moving employees from one job to another to provide variety and challenge;
- *job enrichment* – the vertical expansion of the job through the addition of different types of tasks and increased involvement and participation.

It must be recognised, however, that the organisation, as well as looking for motivation in job design, will also be looking for the efficient completion of the task at a reasonable cost. This implies a balance between individual and organisational expectations in a number of dimensions.

A well designed job will fit the needs of the organisation in terms of providing the appropriate quality of performance, quantity of performance, flexibility and cost. The job should also fit the needs of the job holder in terms of providing appropriate intrinsic and extrinsic rewards. It is similarly important that the employees understand exactly what the job involves and the standards expected of them in the tasks they have to perform. It should be noted that quality and quantity of performance need to form an acceptable balance. If staff are motivated to provide high quality service, this may conflict with a desire for high quantity. Similarly a desire for cost reduction and a high speed of service may result in a deterioration of quality standards with staff not having time to give the standard of service they feel the customer expects. It is, however, a management decision.

In designing jobs to balance the organisational and individual needs the dimensions of content, context, contact, control and communication should all be considered.

Content

The dimension of job content relates to the nature of the tasks the job involves. From the organisation's perspective the technical content of the job must be efficient. In designing the job of a chambermaid, for example, due consideration needs to be given to the number of different types of room that a chambermaid can clean in a certain time. In addition, time should be allowed for cleaning corridors, dealing with linen, carrying out special cleaning, talking to the guests and so on.

The technology that is to be used must also be taken into account. The job of a receptionist will obviously be very different if the front office operates on a fully integrated computer system than if it relies on manual systems and billing machines.

From the motivational perspective three aspects should be considered. Does the job provide for the employee to use a variety of different skills? Does the job have task identity (the degree to which it involves doing a 'whole' piece of work)? Does the job have task significance (is it possible to see the impact the job has on others)? These three aspects should increase the employee's perceptions of the meaningfulness of the work to be done and so improve intrinsic rewards assuming that they fit with his work orientation.[6]

Context

The job context relates to the conditions of work which provide the extrinsic rewards. The employee will be concerned about the pay structure, incentive or bonus schemes, uniforms, hours of work, job security, promotion prospects, etc. The organisation must also consider the conditions of work in relation to the ergonomics of the work-place design: Where should the VDU be sited for best viewing? Where will the keyboard be? Will there be enough room for documents? A seat? A printer?

The environment in which the work takes place is also important, although in front-of-house jobs at least the environment provided for the guest should already be pleasant. Aspects of lighting, noise, temperature and ventilation must be taken into account.

Contact

Most jobs will involve a degree of social contact either with guests or with work colleagues. In general some element of social contact is desirable and should be planned for. This is particularly true when rearranging present jobs which may result in the breakdown of established social interactions. For example, the reorganisation of lunch breaks may interfere with an established pattern of interaction in the staff canteen.

Contact with customers should also be planned for so that it can be as effective as possible. For service employees, a major reason for the choice of a job in a hotel will be the desire to come into contact with other people. This desire to give service should be encouraged in the design of the job, for example by providing time for the waitress to chat to the customer.

For back-of-house staff, however, the prospect of guest contact can be a demotivator, although many chefs have found the need to serve the customer in the restaurant due to the introduction of carvery style restaurant operations has been an enjoyable experience which they now see as a fundamental part of their job. Similarly, chambermaids may find delivering room-service orders a rewarding experience, but the prospect of serving in the restaurant a nightmare!

Control

Control systems are essential in any work organisation. However, the degree of control exercised by the manager should be balanced against the motivational force of giving employees greater autonomy in the job, allowing them to use discretion, having less detailed controls over them and conferring on them more responsibility for the final output of their work. Approaches involving giving authority and responsibility for an identifiable section of the work to a group of people who have specific targets and standards to meet but are left to organise themselves have proved very successful in manufacturing industry and could be appropriate in many hotels.

There is, however, a direct balance between trust and control. Trust is that which the employee feels his manager has in him, and control that which the manager imposes on his subordinate. Any increase in the control exercised by the manager decreases the amount of trust. Any desire on the manager's part to display trust in the employee by giving additional responsibility etc. must be accompanied by a reduction in the amount of control. Controls are costly to introduce and maintain but trust involves an element of risk that the task will not be completed correctly.

Communication

Communication in job design has two elements. First, it is important to establish exactly what a particular job entails and what the expected standards of performance are, and to ensure that the employee knows and understands both aspects. Secondly, it is important to give feedback on how well tasks are being carried out and the standards of performance being achieved. This will not only ensure that the job is carried out as planned, but it will also reduce the employee's role ambiguity – not knowing exactly what is expected of him – and knowledge of the actual results of work activity has been seen to have a high motivational effect.

The above description of the job can be seen to include the personnel management techniques of job analysis, job description, job clarification and appraisal, combined with the operational management disciplines of work study, work-site design and control mechanisms.

Case example 4.1   Redesigning the chambermaid's job

The Ambassador Hotel is a 250 bedroom, four-star unit catering mainly for the business and conference market. Occupancy levels can vary considerably from week to week and day to day and are difficult to predict exactly.

The head housekeeper is in her fifties. She has worked in the hotel for ten years and been in her present job for five. She has no vocational qualifications and has never worked in any department other than housekeeping. The aspects of her work that she likes the most are 'looking after her staff and dealing with staff problems'. She is less confident about the budgeting, control and paperwork aspects of her job.

All the chambermaids work full time. They are expected to clean 16 rooms each day and are paid per room. Each room is checked by a supervisor who is responsible for returning rooms to reception. If the hotel is full or one or two maids ring in sick, supervisors have to clean rooms. On the other hand, if occupancy levels are lower than forecast and the department is overstaffed, the head housekeeper will try to meet her staffing budget by encouraging staff to take holidays or go on training courses. At these times maids may only be required to clean 14 rooms, but even though this means losing money, maids don't seem to mind, as they find it extremely tiring to clean 16.

It is difficult to attract and retain maids because the hotel is situated close to an airport where much better paid cleaning jobs are available. Staff working in other areas of the hotel are unwilling to help out if the department is short staffed and would anyway not be sufficiently trained to do so as it takes one month to train a maid to the required standard.

The Berkeley Hotel is in the same chain as the Ambassador. It is slightly smaller but has a similar market. The head housekeeper is in her twenties, has catering college qualifications and ambitions to become a general manager.

Only eight of the chambermaids in the hotel are full time. The rest are part time; they work two days a week and agree to wait by the phone on other days up to 10 am in case they are required. Labour turnover is low. Staff and supervisors do not mind changing jobs and opportunities are provided for those interested to move to other jobs for variety and to improve their long-term job prospects.

As an experiment, the chambermaids have been given more control and responsibility for their work. They now check their own rooms and return them to reception. The full-time maids have been allocated a block of rooms on a particular floor as 'their' rooms. Supervisors now carry out rigorous inspections against a detailed checklist on a random sample basis. The current success rate is over 90 per cent.

SKILLS AND ABILITIES

Having established the nature of the job to be done, the next consideration is to find members of staff with the right blend of personality, skills and abilities to fit into the organisation. The techniques used by personnel management to achieve this aim start with the preparation of a personnel specification (sometimes called a person specification or a job specification). The person specification is a highly detailed description of the type of person who would perform a particular job successfully. It outlines in precise fashion the characteristics of such a person using some form of profile and some form of grading system with minimum and desirable levels identified so as to allow a relatively objective assessment of the suitability of applicants to be carried out. The standard profile would include characteristics such as physical attributes, mental attributes, education and qualifications, experience, training and skills, personality and special or family circumstances. This profile is usually based on a previously prepared job description following a detailed job analysis.

Job analysis is based on the need to identify the personal characteristics needed in relation to the job and may be carried out by the personnel department in isolation from the actual place of work. Trusthouse Forte, for example, in the late 1970s developed and published for circulation to all units and all teaching establishments a person specification for their ideal hotel receptionist, implying that there is just one type of person who would be suitable for all of THF's very different properties. It is obviously more sensible to bear in mind the particular circumstances of the particular job in a particular establishment. In addition to the job characteristics, it is also important to consider the characteristics of the work group that the job holder will be placed in and the characteristics of the workplace itself. It could indeed be more important to consider how well a person would fit into the establishment than concentrate on the technical content of the job. Technical skills and knowledge can be developed in a relatively short period of time but it may be impossible to change a person's personality characteristics, work orientations and attitudes.

When the characteristics of the person required have been identified then recruitment can follow the standard process of advertisement, application, shortlist, selection and appointment. At all stages in this process it is necessary to consider the circumstances and characteristics of the people you are trying to recruit so that, for instance, you select the right advertising media, or write appropriate advertising copy, or design the right sort of application form for that particular job to elicit the type of information you need to be able to make a shortlist decision.

It must also be remembered that recruitment is part of the image the hotel presents to the outside world and dealings with potential applicants or candidates for interview should be seen in this light. A badly designed job advert in the local paper can also affect customers' perceptions of the establishment. The common practice of putting a long list of jobs in one advertisement with limited space for details not only provides little to attract applicants but also can give the impression to recruits that conditions of work cannot be all that good if so many people have left recently. It can also communicate to customers that the hotel is short staffed and so service standards are likely to be suffering. It is perhaps not surprising that many hotel managers complain that they get little response from advertisement in the local press.

Once the appointment has been made, the training and development process can begin. Induction training is important to socialise the new recruit into the establishment. This should be followed by a training programme designed to make the trainee aware of the procedures and policies of your establishment. The emphasis in much training is on technical knowledge and skills but, particularly for service contact personnel, interpersonal skills may be a more important focus. After this initial programme, training has three other functions. First, it can be used to correct substandard performance identified during performance reviews. Secondly, it can be used to prepare for change, for example for the introduction of new technology or new working systems. Finally, it can be used to provide development for the individual as a form of reward, although as discussed earlier some members of staff would look favourably on a week away on a course whereas others would see it as a punishment.

From the organisation's point of view training can provide major benefits in improving performance through increasing knowledge and skills, clarifying the work role and through motivation. However, training involves cost to the organisation. Management time and effort must be spent on planning and implementing training strategies for all members of staff. There will be a financial commitment to training materials, premises and staff. There will also be a time commitment in providing the opportunity for training to take place. A common complaint of heads of departments is that they are expected to train their staff but are not given the time resources to carry it out. Especially when staffing levels are being strictly controlled, training will assume a low priority. Training must have the commitment of senior management to allow it to be conducted properly and to generate the extensive benefits which can result.

ORGANISATIONAL CLIMATE

The climate for a geographical region is described as the prevailing atmospheric conditions of temperature, rainfall, humidity, wind, etc. The climate for an establishment can also be seen as the prevailing atmosphere of the unit in terms of warmth, policies and procedures, management style and overall orientation, being the expression of the culture of the organisation as a whole. The detailed discussion of organisational culture has been left to chapter 7 but some examples will illustrate the role climate plays in determining performance.

Schneider[7] conducted some interesting research on the effect of organisational climate in banks. He found that customers' perceptions of the effectiveness of service in the bank were very similar to those of the banks' employees, and that effectiveness was higher in those establishments with a positive service orientation which was derived in the main from the orientation of management in that unit. Managers were typified as being either service bureaucrats or service enthusiasts. Service bureaucrats were measured by the constraints they put on giving good service, such as a stress on rules, procedures and maintaining the system, the routine performance of the job expected, and the use only of established methods of solving customers problems. Service enthusiasts on the other hand showed a flexible and personal involvement with the customers and the encouragement of a sense of 'family' among employees, and were interested in the involvement of the unit in the local community and in giving customers service in new and creative ways.

Another feature emerging from this research was the importance of support systems in generating good performance. Support came in the form of the 'right' personnel and the availability of up-to-date information, in the importance of marketing in preparing staff and customers for new product developments, and in the critical area of equipment and supplies. Many employees have a genuine desire to give good performance but feel frustrated by 'the system' setting up obstacles to giving the standard of service they feel they should be giving. This can range from the waitress who does not have time to talk to customers as she would like because the restaurant is constantly short of staff due to a management directive to cut costs, to the head housekeeper who is depressed by the standard of cleanliness and finish of her linen following the switch from in-unit to a centralised laundry.

Management style not only has an effect on customer and staff perceptions of service but can have a very real impact on the organisational structure of the unit. A general manager whose philosophy involves the development of potential in his subordinates may create new positions in his organisation to allow this to happen. This policy, although admirable in its intentions, may not create the best atmosphere for performance improvement.

Scanlan[8] has proposed a four-point plan for encouraging a climate of achievement. His first requirement is the presence of explicit goals that are definite, challenging and achievable. The second necessity is a system for feedback and positive reinforcement. The feedback should be given as soon as possible after completion of a task and should try to cover all the elements of the employee's job that are under his direct control. Positive reinforcement is encouraged when employees display the correct behaviour or make a move in the right direction. The basis of positive reinforcement is that the motivational effect of a series of small successes is greater encouragement than a series of small criticisms is discouragement. If hotel receptionists are not balancing their floats correctly, positive reinforcement would be to concentrate on the days that they got it right rather than criticise them for the days it went wrong. The third element is an emphasis on individual responsibility and accountability. Participation and involvement are a major part of this strategy, although it is suggested that informal involvement through talking to individuals and soliciting their opinions may be just as effective, and probably more so, than formal group meetings. The final element is the linking of rewards to results. Although the obvious way to bring this about is through financial 'merit' awards, these awards can lead to perceived inequalities between staff if they are not fully documented and explained, and do not appeal to the desire for intrinsic rewards which are by their nature more difficult to identify.

The organisational climate is difficult to pin down but has a very real effect on encouraging high performance. Creating the right climate involves a realisation that all management activity, from the design of systems and procedures to the way the manager handles interpersonal interactions with customers and staff, will contribute to the overall atmosphere of the workplace. The manager is a role model that staff will follow.

SCHEDULING

At this stage of the model proposed earlier in the chapter (see figure 4.2), we have an employee who has the requisite skills and abilities to do a well defined job which contributes to the organisational objectives, and that employee, operating in a supportive climate which encourages performance, will be willing to expend effort in carrying out his duties. But unless that employee is available to do those duties at the appropriate time then performance will still not be optimised.

The work of the hotel receptionist, for example, is subject to many peaks and troughs of activity. There will be a peak of activity at morning check-out when queues are likely to develop. Later in the morning activity will be at a normal to quiet level with plenty of supporting staff available such as telephonists, reservations clerks and sales staff. There will be a small peak of activity in the early afternoon as the cash is balanced in preparation for shift change-over. In the middle of the afternoon, when both shifts may be on duty, there will be very little activity but this will change in the early evening as the bulk of guests check in, and once again queues may form. Activity through the evening will be steady as charges are posted to accounts but will tail off towards the end of the shift. This pattern will also be influenced by the occupancy level for that day of the week or that time of year.

The scheduling problem, then, is to match as closely as possible the available supply of labour to the demands of customers. Two main approaches are available: alter the supply of labour, or modify customer demand. In practice both approaches will be used at once but it is beneficial to separate the two into demand management (dealt with in chapter 5) and workforce scheduling.

Before attempting to schedule the workforce a standard has to be set for the amount of work someone employed in a particular position should be able to do. For some positions this is reasonably straightforward. In Holiday Inns, for example, room-maids are expected to clean 16 rooms per day, casual banqueting waitresses are generally expected to silver serve between 10 and 15 covers. For other departments it is not so easy. For example, there is no simple linear relationship between occupancy and the number of receptionists, and in any case do you use the occupancy of the departing guests or the occupancy of the arriving guests – or both! It is possible to establish a relationship between occupancy and reception staffing, based on a minimum staffing level without which the department could not operate plus additional staff for additional bands of occupancy, e.g. one extra member of staff for each 10 per cent extra bed occupancy. This approach will cope with the seasonal and weekly patterns of variation in demand but cannot cope with variation in demand patterns over the day which have to be dealt with in a different way. This approach can also identify the number of chambermaids you need on any one day but does not solve the problems of queues at reception.

The second requirement is an accurate forecast of customer demand within the hotel. Again this is not a simple problem. Demand generated by hotel accommodation as identified in chapter 5 follows three main cycles: daily, weekly and annually. Each of the different market segments that the hotel caters for will follow different patterns around those cycles. There will be regular events (like Farnborough Air Show) or irregular events (like Chernobyl) which will upset the pattern once more. Given the growth in computer technology in the industry and sufficient past records it should be possible to build a forecasting model using quantitative techniques such as time series forecasting or multiple regression analysis. However, there is little evidence that such models are being developed.[9] In the meantime the industry relies on the skills and experience of its management to make predictions.

These predictions can be very accurate. In the mid 1970s, the head receptionist in the Viking Hotel, York, was able to make predictions of guest count a week in advance for the following week, i.e. up to 14 days in advance, which were invariably accurate to + or − 5 per cent. Forecasting guest count or occupancy is not the total picture, however, as attention must also be given to demand for food and beverage facilities from inside the hotel and from chance customers, usage of banqueting and conference suites, and demands generated by local members of the leisure club.

Based on the standards set and the forecast of demand it should now be possible to prepare rotas to have the right number of staff on duty at the right time. This may seem a simple manpower planning exercise, but it is one which must consider the behavioural requirements of the staff as well as the functional requirements of the organisation. The problem is further complicated by the daily variations in customer demand over the hotel. The tendency is to staff for the peaks and occupy staff on other duties during the troughs. Over the whole hotel this can lead to considerable wastage of labour resources. The solution would seem to be to improve the flexibility of hotel employees.

Flexible working is not new; hotels have been making use of overtime hours, part-time and temporary workers and multi-skilled general helpers, etc., for years. The IMS studies[10] define four different types of flexibility:

1. *functional flexibility* concerned with the versatility of employees and their ability to handle different tasks and move between jobs;

2. *numerical flexibility* concerned with the ability to adjust the number of workers or the number of hours worked in response to changes in demands;

3. *pay flexibility* concerned with financial reward systems that encourage functional flexibility and reward scarce skills or individual performance;

4. *'distancing' strategies* which involve contracting out operations to shift the burden of risk and uncertainty elsewhere.

Table 4.1 shows the variety of flexibility methods available within these broad categories.

Table 4.1 *Methods of work flexibility.*

Functional:	Numerical:
• Multi-skilling	• Part time
• Horizontal job enlargement	• Temporary
• Vertical job enlargement – up	• Job sharing
• Vertical job enlargement – down	• Overtime
• Job rotation	• Sabbaticals etc.
• Career development	• Flexible daily hours
• Task group approaches	• Flexible weekly hours
• Total retraining	• Compressed working week
	• Annual hours contracts
	• Committed hours schemes
	• Shift-work systems
Distancing:	• Short-term contracts
• Agency staff	**Pay**:
• Subcontracting	• Incentive schemes
• Home working	• Rare skills payments
• Computer terminal systems	• Multi-skill payments
• Government subsidised trainees	• Pay/performance links

The methods of job flexibility given in table 4.1 are increasingly in evidence in manufacturing industry but are still rare in hotel operations, although the following examples all came from one chain operated hotel:

- a relatively small number of full-time chambermaids, supplemented by 'on-call' maids who could be brought into the establishment at short notice to match as closely as possible the occupancy levels achieved (it is easy to see how this could be extended to other areas of hotel operation);

- arrangements for service staff in restaurant, bar and room-service areas to be moved between areas as demand requires and to allow for a change of environment;

- in-house trainees who have experience in a number of operational areas providing a pool of flexible staff, particularly for special or exceptional occasions;

- negative examples of flexibility also in evidence, for instance the use of leisure club staff to carry out the duties of front-hall porters but who are inappropriately dressed, and using supervisors to clean rooms on a regular basis.

As well as the identification of work standards and the development of computer technology to allow informed decisions to be made about staffing levels, job flexibility in hotel operations will also require management development to prepare for a change in management culture in an approach to a 'holistic' view. This means seeing the hotel as one operation and not as a collection of separate departments. Workforce development will also be required to prepare them for changing attitudes to flexibility, greater skill acquisition and training for multi-skilling.

Job flexibility does not only contribute to coping with peaks and troughs of customer demand. Different methods can also be used for the following strategies:

- *Workforce development* – this strategy concentrates on developing the skills and abilities of the existing workforce in order to upgrade that workforce and to improve its performance.

- *Job satisfaction/motivation* – the aim of this strategy is to improve job satisfaction and performance by increasing the intrinsic interest and reward deriving from the job itself.

- *Attraction/retention of staff* – this strategy looks to solve the problems of staff turnover and recruitment difficulties.

- *Economy* – this is largely about reducing short-term costs.

- *Concentration of effort* – this strategy identifies that a contributing factor to the success of any organisation is its ability to concentrate its efforts on the things that it does best without being distracted by peripheral activities.

- *Risk avoidance* – this strategy aims to avoid the inherent risks of economic activity by displacing that risk to third parties; high-risk activities will therefore impinge less on the organisation.

The scheduling of the workforce is an important area that has received relatively little attention but which makes a significant impact on employee performance as a whole. Job flexibility provides opportunities for coping with the unpredictable demand fluctuations experienced by the industry, and although some of the methods may not be seen as acceptable for use in a hotel context, the idea of moving staff between certain departments and the fostering of interdepartmental co-operation do seem desirable goals.

TEAM EFFECTIVENESS

So far this chapter has concentrated on the individual, but the problems of improving team effectiveness must also be considered. There are two main perspectives: getting the best from the team, and reducing conflict between teams. Work groups usually result from a deliberate organisational decision to place workers together to meet operational needs. This is traditionally based on the functional nature of the task to be performed by the group. The hotel industry is largely divided into two sorts of groups – front-of-house staff who come into contact with the guest, e.g. reception, and back-of-house staff who are mainly responsible for the production side of the operation, e.g. housekeeping. It is often at the interface between these teams that conflict arises which diverts effort away from working together to achieve organisational aims. Ever since Whyte's study[11] attention has been given to the social interactions at the interface between these two groups and how they can be made to work effectively.

Within the organisation it is possible to identify two types of group. The formal group is that set up by the organisation to carry out specific tasks and satisfy strategic aims. The informal group, on the other hand, arises from the social interaction between individuals who develop an affinity for each other. The aims of the informal group can contribute to the goals of the organisation but can also be in conflict with the formal structure, as in Elton Mayo's Hawthorne study. Where mismatches occur the problems identified in table 4.2 may arise.

Table 4.2 *The consequences of formal and informal goal mismatch.*

	Purpose	Structure	Process
Formal	Financial return for effort and investment	Jobs, roles, accountability, delegation	Policies, tasks and procedures
Informal	Satisfaction of personal social needs	Influence based on knowledge, social skills and friendships	Interpersonal, intergroup, group
Mismatch problems	Low productivity, poor standards	Authority without power	Red tape, finger pointing, buck passing

Many attempts have been made to identify the characteristics of an effective team. The consensus of opinion identifies the following:

- members depend on one another to achieve the organisation's formal goals;
- members trust each other;
- members have common objectives;
- members make decisions by consensus;
- members are strongly committed to the group;
- members solve conflict by working through the problem;
- communication is a key factor by which group feelings can be expressed freely;
- members will be open with one another and will listen to one another.

It is also possible to identify the signals which indicate poor team work:[12]

- low productivity;
- poor service quality;
- a decrease in customer satisfaction levels;
- hostility and conflict among team members;
- an increase in the number of requests for transfers;
- poor co-operation between management and staff;
- high levels of absenteeism, poor timekeeping or labour turnover;
- blaming others for poor performance.

Although teams do perform badly due to formal, work-oriented reasons, it is more common for the problem to be an informal one.

Managers must accept responsibility for the teams under their control and take positive steps to improve their performance. This may involve generating a group support climate through stressing the importance of groups in policies and procedures, but in more general terms this can be seen as the management of three areas; achieving the task, developing the individual, and building and maintaining the team.[13]

Despite efforts to build and maintain the team, optimum performance will still not be achieved if effort is expended on dealing with intergroup or interdepartmental conflict. Four main sources of interdepartmental conflict have been suggested:[14]

(a)   the interdependence between departments;

(b)   the nature of the hotel environment;

(c)   the reward structure; and

(d)   perceptions of status or stigma.

Interdependence between departments can cause conflict for two main reasons. First, there is a desire for independence but a need for interdependence, a sense of having to rely on somebody else – the kitchen has to rely on the restaurant to present its food properly, reception has to rely on housekeeping to get the rooms back on time. This can be tinged with feelings of unfair treatment: 'We managed to get all the rooms for the tour group back by three o'clock but not a word of thanks.' Secondly, it is possible to identify different goals between the parties who place different demands upon the same situation. For example, the goals of many leisure club staff are primarily aimed at the sport side of the business, perhaps concentrating on local club members, whereas staff serving food or drink in these areas will retain the traditional hotel values of service and deference.

The hotel environment provides many sources of stress and conflict. There is an obvious source of conflict between those groups who come into contact with guests and those that do not. Staff in direct customer contact adapt their attitudes and working patterns to cope with their position, and this may result in what a non-contact group would see as inappropriate behaviour. The speed of operations also causes pressure on groups where a large number of quick decisions are needed to cope with unplanned situations as they arise. The receptionist who rings the housekeeper to ask for an extra bed or a bed board or for luggage to be moved from one room to another is often viewed as a trouble-maker, not someone responding to a legitimate customer request.

The reward structure can cause conflict where it is seen to be inequitable. This issue is often complicated by the question of tips which is likely to lead to a distorted view of differentials. It is not only the pay system that is of concern; the unauthorised rewards of institutionalised fiddling can be a source of conflict, as can differences in the allocation of scarce resources such as funding for the purchase of new equipment, staff uniforms, additional staffing and so on.

Perceptions of status differentials are potential problem areas as some groups of workers see themselves as of traditionally higher status than others. Reception staff have always seen themselves as being one of the highest status groups within the hotel. This status differential can be extended to include differences between groups of different national or religious background or even between men and women.

SUMMARY

This chapter has considered the task of improving employee performance and has proposed a model to aid in the identification of the possible obstructions to optimum effectiveness. It was assumed that motivation arises out of a desire to fulfil the individual's needs but that these needs are difficult to identify and therefore difficult to manage. The emphasis of the chapter has therefore been on the process of motivation and the generation of effort through the motivation calculus. Having established effort the other barriers to effective performance – the nature of the job, the skills and abilities of the employee, the organisational climate, the scheduling of the workforce, the development of team effectiveness and the avoidance of conflict – have been examined.

It is possible to extract from these areas a checklist of *the* things to do to manage motivation such as that proposed by Cook:[15] clarify the task role, provide positive feedback, personalise the causes of performance, make apparent the personal gains, personalise pride in accomplishment, encourage personal goal clarification, match the job with personal motives, remove supervisory blocks, remove organisational blocks. This sort of approach does not, however, explain the reasons for this sort of behaviour and seems to miss one fundamental feature – the creation within the unit of a culture of support and concern for staff and the job that they do.

Another key aspect of the chapter has been to identify the interdependence of the various approaches and techniques. It should be apparent that anything which happens to alter one aspect of the equation will automatically affect the others. It is necessary to be aware of this interdependence to be able to predict the outcome of the techniques used to try to bring about the correct balance between the achievement of the goals of the individual and those of the organisation.

REFERENCES

1. *United Kingdom Hotel Industry 1986*, Horwath and Horwath (UK) Ltd, 1986.

2. Mumford, E. *Values, Technology and Work*, Martinus Nijhoff, 1981.

3. Vroom, V. H. *Work and Motivation*, Wiley, 1964.

4. Porter, L. L., and Lawler, E. E., *Managerial Attitudes and Performance*, Irwin, 1968.

5. Goldthorpe, J., Lockwood, D., Bechhofer, F., and Platt, J., *The Affluent Worker in the Class Structure*, Cambridge University Press, 1969.

6. Hackman, J. R., and Oldham, G. R., 'Motivation through the design of work: test of a theory', *Organisational Behaviour and Human Performance*, vol. 16, 1976.

7. Schneider, B., 'The service organization: climate is crucial', *Organizational Dynamics*, pp. 52–65, Autumn 1980.

8. Scanlan, B. K., 'Creating a climate for achievement', *Business Horizons*, April 1980.

9. Gamble, P., and Smith, G., 'Expert front office management by computer', *International Journal of Hospitality Management* vol. 5, no. 3, pp. 109–114, 1986.

10. Atkinson, J., 'Flexibility, Uncertainty and Manpower Management', *Institute of Manpower Studies*, Brighton, 1985.

11. Whyte, W. F., *Human Relations in the Restaurant Industry*, Wiley, 1948.

12. Berger, F., and Venger, R., 'Building your hospitality team', *Cornell HRA Quarterly*, pp. 82–88, February 1986.

13. Adair, J., *Effective Leadership*, p. 44, Pan, 1983.

14. Dann, D., and Hornsey, T. 'Towards a theory of interdepartmental conflict in hotels', *International Journal of Hospitality Management* vol. 5, no. 1, pp. 23–28, 1986.

15. Cook, D., 'Guidelines for managing motivation', *Business Horizons*, pp. 61–69, April 1980.

5 Managing Demand and Supply

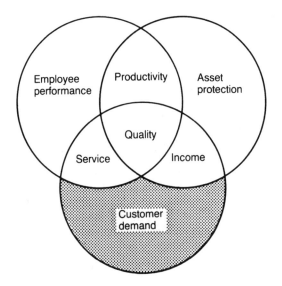

Figure 5.1 *Primary key result area: customer demand.*

INTRODUCTION

In chapter 2, we identified seven key result areas for managers to monitor and act upon. Two of these were managing capacity and improving income. Both of these depend largely upon ideas, approaches and techniques usually derived from the concept of marketing. All too often, however, marketing is applied in an *ad hoc* way to hotels so that it is unsuitable for the characteristics of hotels and indiscriminate in its effects. By clearly separating out the two key result areas, that of attracting people to the hotel in the first place (see figure 5.1) and then maximising income from these sales (see figure 6.1), we hope to provide managers with much more precise control over the complex marketing function and fit this much more closely to the specific needs of different types of unit.

The key marketing issue for all hotels is that the 'product' is perishable, that is to say it has a very short shelf-life, in effect twenty-four hours. A hotel room that remains empty is a sale lost. All products and services have some degree of shelf-life. For most consumer durables the shelf-life is considerably longer than just one or two days. But eventually a television set that has not sold will become too out of date or unfashionable to be sold. For most products, too, there is a second-hand or discount market for obsolete or unsold stock. The brevity of the hotel room's shelf-life makes such alternative sales outlets virtually non-existent and thus marginal consumption is valuable. It is for this reason that managing capacity effectively is a central issue for the hotel manager.

The impact that contact dependency and intangibility have on capacity management are that they both make the marketing effort required to manage capacity and attract marginal consumption much harder than for product marketing. The fact that the consumer must physically be in the hotel in order to enjoy its services means that the manufactured goods approach is impossible (i.e. production disconnected from consumption, usually in both time and space, so that the functions of the factory and marketing are autonomous). For hotels, the provision of the service and its marketing must be contiguous. In addition, the intangible nature of the hotel experience presents major problems in terms of the pricing, promotion and advertising of the hotel.

THE MARKETING PLANNING PROCESS

Partly because of the differences outlined above, Bell[1] has argued that the planning process for services marketing should be considered as different to that for goods marketing. The goods marketing planning process (see figure 5.2(a)) can be divided into three stages: pre-consumption, consumption and post-consumption. For goods marketing, marketing planning largely takes place in stage 1, prior to the consumption of the product by the consumer. In addition, with the exception of such things as point-of-sale merchandising and personal selling, much of the implementation of these marketing plans is also carried out during stage 1. During stage 2, the actual consumption of the product, the marketing system has relatively little impact upon the consumer's satisfaction with the product. Finally, in stage 3, marketing receive feedback from consumers which reports on the level of satisfaction and hence may influence future approaches to marketing the product.

Bell goes on to argue that this sequence of events and the relative level of activity in the marketing planning process is quite different for services (see figure 5.2(b)). The scope of marketing and production in stage 1 is much less. Much of the 'production' cannot take place until stage 2 since, as we have seen, services are contact dependent. In addition, much of the tactics of marketing are carried out in stage 2, in the sense that product modifications can be made, pricing levels changed, and so on. Bell calls this 'remixing'. These modifications are made possible by observing the consumer during the 'consuming process' and hence receiving immediate feedback. The result of this is that the need to receive feedback in stage 3, whilst still of relevance, is of less importance than in goods marketing.

This proposal emphasises a key point from chapter 2, namely that hotel managers tend to have a 'strategic' role in operating their units. They are required to make

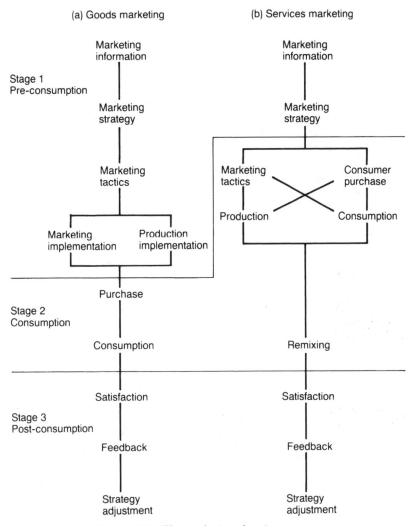

Figure 5.2 *The marketing planning process.*

decisions about the marketing mix that are normally made at corporate level in other types of business activity.

THE MARKETING MIX

The analysis of the marketing planning process adds to the complexity of marketing services and further illustrates the interrelationship between strategy and tactics identified in chapter 2, but it does little to address the issues raised in the introduction to this chapter. The basic marketing approach is to consider the four Ps of Product, Place (distribution), Price and Promotion proposed by McCarthy.[2]

There are a variety of views on the validity of this approach. As we have seen in chapter 1, there are those like Foxall who argue that the marketing of services is not significantly different to the marketing of products. Levitt,[3] for instance, suggests that it is only a question of the level of intangibility. Shostack[4] too rejects the product/service dichotomy, but advocates an entirely new conceptual model such that 'service marketing to be effective and successful requires a mirror-opposite view of conventional product practices'. Both of these views, however, accept the fundamental marketing concept of the four Ps. Booms and Bitner[5] modify the four Ps for service firms by adding an additional three Ps to the existing four: People, Physical evidence and Process (see below). Gronroos[6] rejects the traditional marketing mix entirely, regarding it as being of little value to service managers, whilst a third viewpoint is expressed by Renaghan,[7] who suggests that for the hospitality industry specifically there should be an entirely different marketing mix.

The Booms and Bitner model is illustrated in table 5.1. Buttle[8] has argued that the addition of people, physical evidence and process is unnecessary, as the first two should be regarded as part of the 'product', and the process is part of the 'place'. However, the test of any model is its value to the user. If hotel managers find that by expanding the marketing mix into seven components helps them to understand and implement effective marketing then the model has at least limited validity. In our view the heightened emphasis on people, environment and processes is insightful and useful.

Table 5.1 *Booms and Bitner's marketing mix for services.*

Product:	People:
• range	• personnel:
• quality	– training
• level	– commitment
• brand name	– appearance
• warranty	– incentives
• after-sales service	– social skills
	• attitudes
Place:	• other customers
• location	
• channels of distribution	**Physical evidence:**
• coverage	• environment:
• accessibility	– colour
	– layout
Price:	– furnishing
• level	• facilitating goods
• discounts	• tangible clues
• terms	
• differentiation	**Process:**
	• policies
Promotion:	• procedures
• advertising	• mechanisation
• selling	• employee discretion
• sales promotion	• customer involvement
• public relations	• flow of activities
• publicity	• customer direction
• merchandising	

Gronroos argues that the four Ps model was designed to facilitate marketing planning in product-based industries by allowing the separation of the marketing task into four separate sub-mixes. These four elements of product, price, place and promotion can then be combined into a total marketing mix. This approach requires the tangible core of a product to be successful for, without this core, as in service-based industries, it is not possible to plan each element in isolation. The intangible nature of service requires an integrated marketing approach. He suggests that there are three major components to consider – accessibility, personal market communication and auxiliary services. He also points out that the consumer is a fourth, relatively uncontrollable element of the service provided. He concludes that service organisations in their marketing planning process cannot separate these new elements of the marketing mix as they are so inextricably linked to the provision of the service itself.

Renaghan's model has been developed specifically for the hospitality industry. His suggested marketing mix is made up of three major sub-mixes:

1. *the product/service mix* – the products and services aimed at satisfying the target market;

2. *the presentation mix* – designed to make the product/service more tangible at the point of sale;

3. *the communication mix* – all the media used to persuade customers to buy, heighten product/service tangibility and monitor satisfaction.

It can be argued that this is a rebundling of the same components that make up the original four Ps, but that it has no greater value than the original concept.

Having compared and contrasted these alternative approaches, the key point is that, whichever conceptual framework is adopted, the *fit* between the component parts of the mix is fundamental to achieving effective performance. None of the approaches or frameworks will be successful if the mix is not a fully integrated whole. Furthermore, there is a consensus view that what service managers must do is make the intangibles tangible. Berry calls this managing the 'evidence', Levitt the 'tangible clues' and Shostack the 'surrogates'.

UNDERSTANDING THE NATURE OF DEMAND

In an ideal situation the hotel manager would be able to match exactly the capacity of the unit with the demand for that accommodation. Any deviation from this maximum utilisation of resources will result in a reduction in the overall profitability of the hotel, and due to the high incidence of fixed costs even small shortfalls in utilisation can result in significant loss of profits against their maximum potential. The success of the hotel in the maximum use of its resources will therefore depend on two factors – the nature of the demand and its planned capacity.

The nature of demand for hotel accommodation and associated services is, however, very difficult to predict and suffers from wide variations in volume and type. A number of different patterns of demand can be identified.

Daily variation in demand

The level of demand for different hotel services can be seen to change on a daily basis. In the case of reception two major peaks of activity can be identified. In the morning between approximately 7.00 am and 10.00 am will be the peak time for guests to check out and it is common for large hotels to have queues form during this period. A similar situation arises during the late afternoon and early evening as guests arrive to check in. Other times of high activity in this department of the hotel will occur when the business for the day is being brought together and balanced and when large batches of charges come through from the restaurant or bars for posting to guest accounts.

For the housekeeping department the morning is usually the busiest time for the chambermaids; floor housekeepers, on the other hand, will only be able to check rooms after they have been serviced and therefore they have a different activity pattern. Throughout the hotel each department and group of employees within the department will be faced with different peaks of demand for their services. Different types of hotel will also face different types of activity pattern. For instance, the demands on the housekeeping department of an airport hotel with guest check-ins and check-outs happening at any time during a twenty-four hour period will be very different to a resort hotel with mainly long-stay guests.

Weekly variation in demand

A commonly used classification of the weekly demand pattern for hotel accommodation is into the 'four-day market' and the 'three-day market'. As business tourism is largely concentrated on Monday to Thursday nights (the four-day market), hotels catering mainly for this segment could suffer a severe drop in occupancy at the weekends. Hotels concentrating on the short-holiday market (the three-day market) will show a weekend peak as most of these are taken over the weekend period or around national holidays. This weekly distribution of demand is not stable and could change considerably over the year.

Seasonal variation in demand

Variations in hotel occupancy can also be identified on an annual basis and can be split into off-season, on-season and shoulder periods as demand moves from peak to trough. The specific nature of the annual cycle will depend on the type of hotel, its location and the markets it attracts. A seaside resort hotel may operate at almost 100 per cent occupancy during the summer months but may well be completely closed during the winter, apart possibly from opening over the Christmas period. London hotels, on the other hand, are often at their quietest during July and August, due to the lack of business customers, and likewise at Christmas.

A recent study[9] based on occupancy data collected by the Yorkshire and Humberside Tourist Board has classified hotels into categories based on a combination of weekly and annual patterns. Group A hotels show a pronounced midweek peak with little variation over the year. These hotels were found mainly in the larger conurbations and industrial areas. They catered largely for the business market. Group E hotels, on the other hand, show a definite weekend peak which becomes even more pronounced in the spring and autumn months. These hotels were found mainly in the rural and seaside areas and were catering for the holiday market with short-weekend breaks. Their annual peaks were derived from people taking short, second holidays outside of the main holiday period. Three other groupings of hotels were also identified. Each had a different combination of midweek, weekend or no occupancy peaks at different times of the year.

By identifying these patterns of variation in demand, the manager is better able to develop the market strengths of the hotel, and counteract the market weaknesses.

Other time cycles

It is tentatively proposed that the demand for accommodation may also be subject to other time cycles. A monthly cycle may be apparent in business hotels, due to that market segment being subject to expenses and budgets allocated on a monthly basis. A similar pattern may also arise from annual budgeting. For instance, the public sector appears to spend money at short notice where there are funds still available in a budget which must be used before the end of the financial year in March. Finally, a four-year cycle has also been proposed[10] brought about by such factors as the hotel's own pricing and marketing strategies, in combination with macroeconomic performance and customer attitudes.

Whilst such demand patterns do exist, understanding them is complicated by market segmentation. Since hotels do not cater exclusively for one type of customer, but deal with a mix of market segments, the hotel is faced with patterns derived from each type of segment. Segments can be categorised in a variety of ways. These include:

- purpose of visit, e.g. business, pleasure;

- party size, e.g. individual, group;

- nationality, e.g. national, EEC, international;

- travel stage, e.g. terminal, transit;

- price group, e.g. economy, middle, upper.

In the unlikely case of a hotel which attracted all of these market segments, the manager would need to aggregate 48 separate daily, weekly and annual cycles, or 144 different patterns. It is perhaps not surprising that there is little evidence at present of managers using forecasting techniques to aid their decision-making processes, although as technology becomes more readily accessible their potential contribution to effective planning may well become apparent.

The demand for accommodation is also susceptible to external forces that are not easily forecast. Such events may be local, national or international and the impact of them on a particular hotel is very difficult to judge. London hotels suffered low occupancy in 1974/75 due to terrorist bombings in London hotels. The United States' air-raid on Libya had a similar effect in 1986. Conversely, national events such as the royal weddings and the Queen's Jubilee had the opposite effect.

The hotel manager is faced with a very complex pattern of demand. By identifying these patterns and their relationships with different market segments, he or she is in a position to use various combinations of the marketing mix to maximise the utilisation of the hotel's capacity.

ESTABLISHING CAPACITY

The application of a particular marketing mix to the hotel business will depend largely on the relationship between the capacity of the unit and the identified patterns of demand for its services. Decisions taken initially to determine the capacity of the unit are therefore crucial to the operational management of that unit. The procedure for determining the capacity of a hotel is illustrated in figure 5.3.

Before considering the factors that will influence physical capacity, it is necessary for decisions to be made about the capacity strategy. There are two basic strategies.

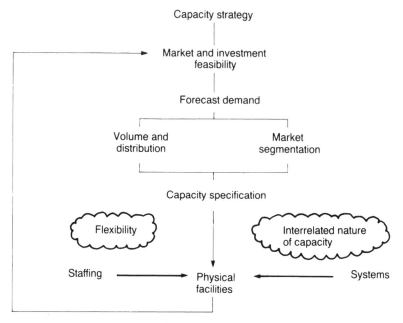

Figure 5.3   *The capacity planning process.*

The 'chase demand' strategy[11] requires a system which will allow for the efficient adjustment of capacity levels to cope with fluctuations in demand. This is difficult to achieve in hotel operations due to the fixed nature of plant, but minor adjustments can be made as will be discussed later in this chapter. The alternative strategy is to operate with fixed capacity, thereby eliminating the need or capability to adjust for changes in demand. This strategy therefore has two options. Either there can be considerable excess capacity to cope with peak demand leading to under-utilisation of resources off peak, or capacity can be fixed at a level to ensure high capacity utilisation all the time. This latter option results in customers being turned away during peak periods, but it may be possible to shift this excess demand to off-peak periods. This chapter is largely about how to resolve the issue of operating with fixed capacity.

Before building a new hotel or buying an existing property, it is usual to carry out a market and investment feasibility study. This makes a systematic assessment of the market for the proposed development, predicts the likely operating results for the next four or five years, and provides a realistic assessment of the viability of the total investment over that period. The study begins with the collection of basic data relating to the location of the property – the local area, the towns, population, transport links, and so on. The next step is to define the market area and identify potential sources of demand – institutional, recreational and staging. It should then be possible to quantify the total market area and, in the light of existing competitive facilities, predict the likely level of demand for the proposed hotel. It is then possible to prepare financial projections for the property at different capacities to arrive at the optimum profitability and return on investment.

As well as predicting the total volume of demand for the property and its pattern over time, the market feasibility study should also identify the market segments to be catered for and their likely needs. These too must be incorporated into the capacity planning decision. Such an assessment identifies the number of twin, double or single rooms, the number of suites or executive rooms, and the required ancillary services, such as bars, restaurants and so on. All sections of the hotel should have capacities appropriate to the forecast volume of business to ensure bottlenecks do not exist. For instance, the number of rooms has implications for the size of the reception area, car park and linen room.

At this stage it is also important to consider the flexibility of the facilities and the interrelated nature of the hotel's capacity. When designing the facilities due account should be taken of the operational problems of managing capacity by providing for maximum flexibility, to cope with periods of high or low demand or changes in the customer mix.

Another aspect that should be considered at the planning stage is that the ability of the hotel to satisfy demand is not solely determined by its physical size, but also by the ability of management to convert that capacity into usable capacity through the operational systems installed and the level of staffing provided. For instance, a hotel using a computerised hotel guest accounting system requires such a system to have enough memory to cope with the total capacity of the hotel. The speed of the system in accessing and printing data will determine the number of terminals required at peak demand and hence the number of staff required. The usable capacity of the system will depend not only on this staff's ability and skill, but also on the number of customer queries and their queueing behaviour. Other factors include the number of check outs that pay by cash or credit card. All other subsystems in the hotel must also be considered in terms of their compatibility with the hotel's physical capacity.

So, although the strategic investment decision is outside the scope of the unit manager, the decisions taken about capacity and systems will have a direct influence on the way in which the hotel's demand and supply is managed.

MANAGING CAPACITY IN DIFFERENT TYPES OF HOTEL

This book is primarily concerned with what managers are required to do on a day-to-day basis to improve the performance of existing operations. In general, unless they own the hotel themselves, they are not in a position to build new capacity. They operate in a context that is largely capacity constrained. This focuses attention on the need to optimise the volume of demand, although it is possible to modify supply too.

There are basically two circumstances in which a manager may need to take action: either demand exceeds supply or vice versa. There are three alternative strategies in response to both these scenarios:

Scenario	Strategy
Supply exceeds demand:	• Increase demand
	• Reduce supply
	• Redistribute supply
Demand exceeds supply:	• Reduce demand
	• Increase supply
	• Redistribute demand

A third scenario is theoretically possible, i.e. demand exactly matches supply. But even then a manager may need to consider one or other of the six strategies, since it may be possible to improve profitability by changing the mix of business, e.g. modifying demand from different segments of the market.

We shall consider each of these six strategies in turn, identify their relevance to the four main types of 'hotel', and select the key components of the marketing mix that are essential for the effective execution of each.

Increase demand

The first strategy is that of 'increasing demand'. The assumption underlying this strategy may be either that total demand is below total capacity, or that demand at certain times is low, or that demand from more profitable market segments is weak. For the independent hotel, demand can be increased by a number of different tactics, for example:

- product modification such as changing room use;
- altering distribution channels by identifying alternative sources of demand such as conferences or tours;
- pricing discounts;
- promotion, through advertising, sales drives, publicity and public relations.

The chain hotel will also use all of these same tactics.

Hospitals will rarely wish to increase demand, since by implication this suggests the need to make people ill. Private hospitals, however, may attempt to attract patients away from the National Health Service by using all the tactics outlined. If a situation did arise where an NHS hospital found itself in an excess supply situation, it may take part in an information campaign to make the public aware of the availability of hospital beds, if only to stave off a possible threat of closure.

In the hostel sector, we can distinguish between the commercial and non-commercial sectors. Hostels operating commercially have little or no opportunity to modify their product, distribution channels or promotion, and tend to rely on price adjustments alone. Non-commercial hostels, such as those run by the Salvation Army or a prison, would potentially be pleased to find that the demand for their services was less than their ability to supply. The reality of the situation in these sectors regrettably appears to be that the demand continues to outstrip supply significantly.

Reduce supply

The second strategy is that of 'reducing supply', on the basis of the same assumptions we made in the first case. Implicitly this strategy is selected instead of the former because it is believed that it is impossible or very difficult to create additional demand and that it is desirable or essential to reduce costs.

For the independent hotel, supply can be reduced by closing individual rooms, perhaps for redecoration, or a section of the building such as a floor or wing, or closing the whole hotel during the off-season. These tactics are essentially modifications to the product. Similar tactics can be employed by the chain hotel, although in extreme circumstances the chain has the expediency of selling off a particularly unprofitable unit, as indeed many chains have done.

The hospital may respond to low demand by closing wards or units. Commercial hostels also can close sections or complete premises by selling or conversion to alternative use, but it is unlikely that non-commercial institutions would take such a course of action.

It is clear that supply reduction strategies are concerned with only one component of the marketing mix, namely the product, whereas demand strategies involve all four components.

Redistribute supply

'Redistributing supply' is the third strategy. The hotel will have been designed for a specific capacity for a specific market segmentation mix. This mix of market segments may not materialise either because of poor forecasting or changes in the environment. It may therefore be necessary to change the supply of different accommodation types to meet the new pattern of demand.

For the independent hotelier this means changing the type of room available, e.g. converting twin-bedded rooms into executive singles, or combining rooms to make suites, or converting bedrooms into *en suite* bathrooms or meeting rooms. The chain hotel, in addition to the room conversion tactic, may also consider a complete move into a different market sector by upgrading to a different crown rating. It could also shift into a different division of the company and thereby acquire a new brand identity.

The hospital, however, has limited opportunity to redistribute supply but may find it beneficial to convert under-used facilities. Hostels will find great difficulty in making any change in their market segmentation as they tend to be locked into one specific area, for instance halls of residence.

Case study 5.1   Hotels in Singapore

The hotels in Singapore in the mid 1980s all faced a situation of over-supply. This was due to a significant increase in the number of bed spaces available following an investment boom in hotel properties. In 1983 there were 14,500 bed spaces; by 1986 there were 24,000. This coincided with a world-wide economic slump, negative growth in the Singapore economy for the first time in twenty years, and a general decline in tourism to the island state. So, occupancy rates for 1984 averaged 74.3 per cent and fell dramatically to 66.3 per cent in 1985.[12]

What makes the Singapore case interesting is that all the major hotels collectively responded to the over-supply situation. The Singapore Hotel Association is a very strong trade association and has significant influence within the government-sponsored Tourist Board. SHA's first response was to stimulate demand through sales and marketing promotions, trade shows and media advertising. Several joint efforts were made to stimulate business in conjunction with the Tourist Board and also Singapore Airlines. Specific market segments were identified, such as Japan and Taiwan; new concepts were developed, such as 'Christmas at the Equator' and 'Singapore Explorer'; and aggressive sales were made to major conference organisers, such as ASTA. The advantage of generating convention business is that convention visitors on average spend 7.6 days in the city and S$1,600, which is twice as long and twice as much as the typical tourist.

The other major strategy adopted was to reduce supply. This was done by shutting off some parts of the largest hotels. More importantly, many of the new hotels voluntarily agreed in conjunction with SHA to defer their opening dates by as much as 12 months.

Despite this, the hotels have found that price reductions have been necessary. Between 1978 and 1982 room rates had doubled, but by 1985 they had fallen to a point only 50 per cent higher than the 1978 rates. This has made Singapore highly price competitive in the Far Eastern tourist market, especially since the majority of its large hotels are less than ten years old.

Reduce demand

In response to the situation where demand exceeds supply, we identified three more alternative strategies. The fourth strategy is to 'reduce demand'. The reason for this seemingly irrational course of action is to take advantage of more profitable market segments – in simple terms to make more money out of fewer people.

The obvious way to discourage customers and at the same time increase revenue is to put the prices up. In reality the independent hotel may not need to increase its quoted 'rack rate' or full-price tariff, but merely reduce the amount of discounting to particular groups of clients. Chains can also reduce their level of discounting, although individual units may find this difficult to put into practice due to discounts agreed at corporate level between the chain and corporate clients. A further tactic available to the chain is to carry out a complete refurbishment and up grade its unit, thereby enabling it to charge substantially higher rates.

Hospitals approach this strategy in a completely different way. They are able to reduce the patients' length of stay, although this, like the hotels' tactics, is still a modification to the product component of the marketing mix. Commercial hostels' only tactic is to affect demand through increasing prices, whereas non-commercial hostels have little or no direct influence on the patterns of demand.

Increase supply

'Increasing supply' is the fifth strategy we have identified. For all four types of 'hotel', this response entails modifying the product by building additional capacity, expanding through acquisition, using external facilities on a temporary basis or increasing capacity within existing facilities. This can be done by adding beds, such as in the Little Chef Lodges which have sofa beds that convert a twin-bedded room into a family room. It can also be done by adding 'sales' opportunities. For instance, airport hotels and some non-commercial hostels may 'sell' the same space twice over in one twenty-four hour period.

Redistribute demand

Finally, there is the sixth strategy of 'redistributing demand', primarily from the periods of excess demand to those of low demand. Independent hotels may therefore attempt to move hotel bookings that they are unable to accept at one period in time to alternative dates. Chain hotels can in addition use the referral system to move demand from one hotel to another.

Hospitals can use rescheduling of known patients to alleviate peaks and troughs, although they cannot predict emergency cases. They may also attempt to move patients from in-patient care to out-patient care, or may even resort to suggesting private medical treatment, thereby redistributing the pressure on bed space to a different time or a different place.

Commercial hostels have little opportunity to redistribute demand as, particularly in halls of residence, demand is constrained by external factors. Non-commercial hostels may be able to make some redistribution through the use of the double-shift systems identified above.

Summary

From this analysis, several key features emerge:

1. Chain hotel operators can employ all the tactics available to independent hoteliers, but in addition they have some opportunities denied to the independents. This may be one reason for the recent expansion of hotel consortia.

2. Not surprisingly, approaches to modifying supply depend entirely on tactics relating to the product component of the marketing mix.

3. Hospitals tend to manage their capacity through the manipulation of their product, and only rarely utilise other components of the marketing mix.

4. There is a tendency for hotels to be largely market-oriented, with hospitals and hostels being product-oriented.

5. The strategy of redistributing demand depends largely on modifying the place component of the marketing mix in all types of 'hotel'.

In identifying the courses of action available to different types of hotel in a variety of capacity situations, it must be remembered that these courses of action are not discrete. That is to say, the hotel manager may be carrying out many of the alternatives suggested all at the same time. For instance, in an off-peak period the short-term focus may be on stimulating demand, whereas longer-term objectives for the high season may involve actions designed to shift demand or increase supply. There will also be a tendency for the manager to adopt strategies that are directly under his or her control and which are relatively easy to adopt. This is the main reason for using price as the principal strategy in capacity management.

Whilst we have identified the alternative courses of action, we have not described in any detail how to go about implementing any of these particular strategies. We shall therefore examine each element of the standard marketing mix – product, place, price, promotion – and identify specific approaches, procedures or techniques in dealing with them.

PRODUCT DEVELOPMENT

There are a number of ways in which product development can take place. In essence this is the concept of modifying the hotel product in order to improve either the level of occupancy or the contribution from customers or both. Where demand is weak or weakening, product development can also help to reduce costs, by closures during off-peak periods.

There are basically four main approaches to developing the product:

1. modify opening time of the unit;
2. change the usage of rooms;
3. alter the amenities of the unit;
4. increase or decrease the total unit capacity.

It is important to remember that any change to the product is likely to have implications for the other elements of the marketing mix. Product development must therefore be carried out in the context of the total marketing mix and consideration be given to the fit between all elements.

Modifying the opening time of the hotel is an apparently simple option to take, since unlike other product development options it appears to involve no capital investment. There are broadly three patterns of opening in the hotel business:

1. open all year, e.g. city centre hotels, hospitals;
2. open during one high season, e.g. seaside/tourist hotels;
3. open during periods of peak demand, e.g. college hostels.

Within these three broad patterns it is also possible to remain partly open, only reducing total capacity by closing down some part of the unit.

In theory most operators would prefer to remain open all year. This maximises the opportunity for revenue, maximises the possible usage of the capital plant and equipment, and enables staff to be retained on a permanent basis. The decision to close down for part of the year is made if the income from remaining open is less than the cost of staying open, that is to say some contribution is made to the unit's fixed costs. This does not mean that the hotel need operate at a profit during off-peak periods, only that it reduces the loss it may incur from being closed. This is illustrated in table 5.2.

Table 5.2 *Average monthly operating revenues and costs.*

| | Off peak | | High season |
| | Closed | Open | |
	£	£	£
Revenue:			
Rooms	nil	27,000	81,000
Food and beverage	nil	12,000	40,000
Other departments	nil	1,000	4,000
Total	nil	40,000	125,000
Expenses:			
Cost of sales	nil	16,000	37,000
Payroll costs	500	18,000	42,000
Administration	1,000	2,500	4,500
Energy	1,000	2,500	3,500
Property operation	2,000	2,000	2,000
Total	4,500	41,000	89,000
Profit/(Loss):	(4,500)	(1,000)	36,000

The second approach to product development is to modify the usage of rooms. This can be done at relatively low cost by increasing occupancy through the addition of Z-beds or sofa beds. This usually is accompanied by a change in price. For instance, three-star chain hotels in London take parties of students off-peak in January at a substantial discount per student. But they accommodate these customers in triples, so that the income per room is reduced proportionately less than the discount offered, as illustrated here:

	Rack rate	50% discount rate
Per person	£30	£15
Income/double room	£60	£45

Room modification may also involve some greater expenditure through refurbishment, redecoration or upgrading of bedrooms by the addition of *en suite* bathrooms and so on. Such changes may shift the hotel out of one product range into another, i.e. from a three-star to a four-star category, with major consequences for the total marketing mix.

This may also be the case with the third approach, namely modifying the amenities of the hotel. There are a wide variety of ways in which this may be done. They include the introduction of direct dial telephones in each bedroom, improved restaurant and bar facilities, in-house conference and meeting rooms, and the addition of 'club' facilities. A major trend in UK hotels in the 1980s has been the development of health/sports clubs. For instance, Crest Hotels have built such facilities at their hotels in Maidenhead, Oxford and Bristol, whilst the Grand Hotel, Eastbourne, has spent £1.5 million on a complex that includes an indoor swimming pool, a fully equipped gymnasium, a solarium, a sauna, a beautician and hairdressing salon and the original open-air pool.

Finally, the fourth approach to the product is to develop additional capacity in the form of an extension to the existing premises. Such extensions are often carried out using funding from the Tourist Boards.

The success of product development in helping to manage capacity is supported by research. A survey into the occupancy of hotels in the Yorkshire and Humberside area found that improved occupancy was helped by 'more rooms with private bathrooms, investment in rooms and facilities, a better range of services, and a successful restaurant'.[13]

DEVELOPING THE HOTEL'S DISTRIBUTION CHANNELS

Of the four Ps, place is often the most difficult to comprehend and apply to the hotel industry (largely thanks to McCarthy's wish to find four words all beginning with 'p' to describe the elements of the marketing mix). Place actually refers to the distribution process required to get the product to the customer. This concept appears difficult to apply to the hotel business because, unlike a consumer product, a hotel cannot be physically channelled through warehouses, wholesalers and retail shops. However, consideration of the physical distribution of the hotel product and the differing distribution channels that could be used can provide opportunities for making adjustments to the overall marketing mix.

In marketing terms the physical distribution of a product involves order processing, materials handling and inventory management, as well as packing, warehousing, transportation, installation and customer service. When dealing with an intangible immovable product such as a hotel the aspects of packing, warehousing, transportation and installation have limited significance, although it is well worth paying attention to such details as the packaging of the product in relation to its image using brochures, letter headings, key cards, etc., to making sure that guests find it easy to get to your hotel by good signing, by providing maps or by providing courtesy transport to and from airports and stations, and to making sure that guests are able to operate all the facilities in their rooms by providing clear instructions or staff guidance. As in any service industry, customer service is of paramount importance and will be considered in detail in chapter 7. The materials handling aspects of distribution in hotels are dealt with in the food and beverage, housekeeping and maintenance departments and have already been mentioned in chapter 3. The prime focus of this section therefore lies with order processing and inventory management, both of which are the primary concern of the reservations department of the hotel. The reservations department handles the incoming enquiries for accommodation, checks the availability of room stock for the period of the enquiry and makes the decision to accept or reject the booking based on previously determined criteria. This department therefore has effective control over the success of the unit's demand management policies.

The principles of operation of a hotel reservation system are the same whether they are being handled by a simple manual bookings diary of a sophisticated computer system. The first stage in handling an enquiry is to collect all necessary guest information quickly and accurately. This can either be done manually, writing information onto a printed form or by computer using direct data entry onto an on-screen form. In either case the form should be laid out in a logical sequence which can be followed when taking a reservation either by telephone or in person at the front desk. A computer system can be programmed to carry out checks on the data as it is entered, for instance to check that the departure date entered is after the arrival date entered, so making the operator aware of possible errors. Another feature which is available on some computer systems is an on-line guest history, which looks back over past records to try to identify if an enquirer has stayed in the hotel before. This data can then be used to speed up the reservation process and provide an impressive service to the guest but, unfortunately, the technical difficulties involved in identifying one particular guest from large numbers of previous guests with the same name or initials make its benefits difficult to achieve.

Table 5.3 *Examples of room codes used for reservations.*

Code	Explanation
S	Single
T	Twin
D	Double
TRP	Triple (three single beds)
FAM	Family (one double and one single)
–ST	Studio (a single- or double-bedded room with a couch converting to an additional single bed)
–SUIT	Suite (a single-, double- or twin-bedded room with a separate sitting room)
–MINI	Mini-suite (a single-, double- or twin-bedded room with a lounge area but not in a separate room)
–B	Room with bath (this would only be a necessary suffix if some rooms did not have a private bathroom)
–S	Room with shower
–W	Room with WC only
L–	Prefix used to denote a room of superior/luxury standard for which a higher room rate could be charged
X–	Denotes an executive room offering higher standards of accommodation and additional facilities such as bathrobes, trouser press, special check-in, etc. Higher room rates are charged

The second stage of the process is to check the availability of the accommodation type that the guest is requesting. In any reservation system some form of shorthand is required to refer to different types of accommodation. Table 5.3 gives a typical system used for hotel reservations.

Once the room type has been specified the system should be able to give details of availability as quickly as possible and in a way which is easy to understand. If accommodation of the type requested is not available on that date then alternatives should be provided, giving other types of accommodation available on that date or alternative dates when that accommodation type is free.

The last stage of the process is to make the decision as to whether to accept or reject a particular booking. These accept/reject decisions are based on three areas of concern:

- Do we want to accept a booking from this particular guest?

- Does the booking fit into the present pattern of business?

- Is it within hotel policy to accept this booking?

There may be certain VIP (or CIP – commercially important person) guests who we would wish to accommodate even if the hotel is full and there may be certain guests who because of previous behaviour in the hotel or poor credit rating we would not wish to accommodate even if the hotel is empty!

The second set of factors to consider is the pattern of business at that time. What is the current occupancy level on that date and what from previous experience is likely to be the conversion rate of provisional reservations to confirmed bookings? What is the level of enquiries for accommodation at that time as an indication of the pressure of business for that period? How do advance reservations for the period this year compare with reservations for the same period at this time last year?

The third area to consider is how well this booking fits into hotel policy. Most hotel companies will set target average room rates (ARR) to be achieved for a particular period. Accepting a large party booking at a substantial discounted rate may adversely affect the ARR and so should not be accepted at that time. Marketing objectives may dictate that rooms should be sold only to particular market segments at particular times of the year. For instance, a hotel may keep a certain number of rooms for private clients who come all year round, even though there may be short periods when they could fill those rooms completely with conference or tour business. A further policy requirement may be to block off a number of rooms for a provisional group reservation, for maintenance or redecoration, or when rooms have been allocated to travel agencies or airlines to sell.

These accept/refuse decisions are obviously very difficult to make and although research is being conducted to develop an expert system based on a microcomputer to assist in making them,[14] most hotels rely on the expertise of their front-office managers, reservations supervisors or head receptionists. If the only person dealing with advance reservations was also the person with the expertise to make effective accept/reject decisions then the quality of those decisions could be guaranteed. However, most hotels will employ a number of reservation clerks and reservations may also be taken by receptionists, managers and sales office staff. There is therefore a need to use a series of codes on the availability chart used for reservations to allow the booking to be accepted without constant referral to the 'expert'. These codes would be updated by the reservations supervisor or front-office manager on a regular basis so that all decisions taken are up to date. Some examples of availability control codes used by a major international hotel company are shown in table 5.4. These codes give control over accepting bookings but there needs to be a careful balance between having a sophisticated range of codes allowing detailed control and a system which is easy to understand and use.

Table 5.4 *Availability control codes.*

Code	Explanation
C	Closed to all tariffs. This code can be applied to one or more room types.
D	Open to major tariffs only. Limits bookings to those specified as major tariffs, e.g. full rack rate, corporate rate, weekend breaks, etc.
G	Closed to selected tariffs. Allowing only particular tariffs to be booked, e.g. only weekend breaks or only conference tariff or only full rack rate.
R	Request only. Have to ask the 'expert' about this one.
S	Sell through. Bookings cannot be taken to start on this date but bookings prior to this date can be taken to sell through it.
M	Minimum stay. Only bookings for a specified number of nights can be taken, e.g. four nights over Christmas or Bank Holidays, etc.
N	No one-night stays.

The reservations function represents a hotel making a direct sale to a customer with no intermediaries in the distribution channel. A high percentage of hotel reservations are made directly by the customer. On the other hand, factors such as distance and language barriers separating buyers from sellers in an international context may make it advisable to involve an intermediary. The number of intermediaries may be up to three or four, the main types in hotel distribution being:

- corporate sales offices and central reservations of the hotel organisation itself, as well as referral sales from other hotels in the chain;

- organisations whose main business is the promotion and sale of travel and accommodation, such as travel agents, hotel representatives, computerised reservations services, tour operators and incentive travel planners;

- organisations who offer travel and accommodation as a complementary service to their main business activity, such as American Express, car rental companies and motoring organisations;

- organisations with a general interest in the promotion and organisation of tourism such as tourist boards, tourist information centres and convention and conference bureaux.

Most hotel companies employ some form of specialist sales team within the organisation. This can be organised on a centralised basis with one office handling the sales effort for one geographical area or for one market segment. Increasingly, however, companies are devolving responsibility for sales from a centralised office to regional offices and in some cases to the appointment of sales managers at unit level. These sales offices form an additional link in the reservations chain and the free flow of information is a prime requirement for their effective operation.

Perhaps the most common form of indirect sales for a chain hotel comes from referral business from other hotels in the group or from a central reservations office.

Similar benefits are achieved by the independent hotel joining a consortium such as Best Western, Pride of Britain or Consort, or by being part of a franchise such as Holiday Inns, Holidex.

Case example 5.2   Trusthouse Forte Fortres III

Recognising that historically it had not paid enough attention to the rooms management aspect of its hotel operations, in the mid 1980s Trusthouse Forte embarked on a campaign to improve its rooms management effectiveness through a management development programme. Before this development could take place it was necessary to ensure that the operating system was capable of meeting the demands that were likely to be placed upon it. Over £5 million was spent on developing a computerised reservations system called FORTRES. This system was evolved over a number of years, initially in a small number of units and using different hardware. In its Phase III form it comprised a central reservations computer linked to IBM hardware and modified Carahost software. The configuration of the system is illustrated in figure 5.4.

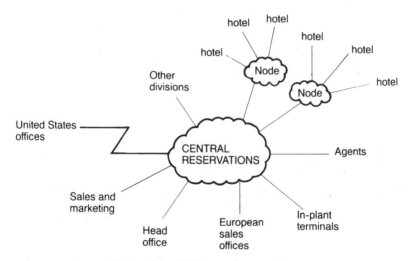

Figure 5.4   *THF central reservations.*

The system is based on 'distributed data processing' (DDP). Each hotel has its own microcomputer-based reservations system. This operates completely independently of the central computer but it can communicate with it through a series of regional nodes. A call to THF central reservations is routed to the office in Aylesbury where it is dealt with by an 'agent'. These agents have access to the central computer which stores comprehensive details of every THF hotel world-wide, as well as current availability on-line from the hotel itself. If the booking is completed, the agent takes all the customer's details and these are sent to and stored in the hotel's system.

The system gives each hotel control over its own reservations. It can still operate normally in the event of a central computer or transmission line fault but it also gives immediate access to hotel reservations from any of its agents. In addition to the agents working in the Aylesbury office, there are links to head office, UK sales and marketing departments, European sales offices and other divisions of the company, such as

Gardner Merchant. Another feature of this distribution channel is that it allows certain customers direct access to the system through 'in-plant' terminals. In this way regular or prestige customers such as American Express, Thomas Cook, Hogg Robinson, Esso, GEC and Boots are able, from their own offices, to book directly into any THF hotel in the UK. The transatlantic link also allows direct booking to the THF associated properties in the USA.

The major problems of any centralised system are those already identified in relation to keeping availability up to date and the operation of the system itself, such as the speed of response to calls, frequency of call termination and coping with peaks. Sophisticated call logging devices can be used to monitor all calls coming into the office and give information for different time periods. It is then possible to set targets, such as average delay in answering, to be no more than 6 seconds, and for it to be accurately monitored.

The problem for the hotel manager is to select from the variety of possible distribution channels the most suitable one for a particular market and particular product offering. The more convenient and accessible that channel is, the more likely it is to be successful. The trend in the tourist industry in general is for the concentration of firms across all aspects of tourism provision, that is to say airlines, car hire, hotels and credit companies. It is estimated that in the USA by the 1990s there will be six major travel service organisations offering a totally integrated service package and a one-stop distribution channel for that package.

PRICING

We have already seen that product development may also entail modification to the pricing policy of the hotel. We shall not deal here with alternative pricing techniques and their implications as we shall examine these in some detail in the next chapter when we look at improving contribution. We are concerned here with the issue of how consumers perceive price and hence how it affects their purchase decision.

In order to do this we must consider the elasticity of demand for accommodation. This can be expressed as :

$$\text{Elasticity of demand for accommodation} = \frac{\% \text{ change in number of rooms sold}}{\% \text{ change in price of room}}$$

Thus the elasticity measures the sensitivity of room sales to price change. Where a change in price brings about a greater percentage change in the quantity sold, the demand is elastic. When a change in price causes a smaller percentage change in the quantity sold, demand is inelastic. It has generally been believed that demand for accommodation from business travellers was relatively inelastic, whereas pleasure travellers were sensitive to price and hence demand from them was elastic.[15]

Whilst this concept is relatively easy to understand, it is extremely difficult to apply, especially in the hotel industry with the distinctive features we have identified (see pages 71 to 73). This is due to the fact that elasticity may vary from one location to another, from one market segment to another, and from one time of the year to another. Thus, for instance, it can be speculated that top-class London hotels have inelastic demand all year, whereas tourist hotels in London may have inelastic demand only in the summer months. However, the top-class hotel would always have a relatively higher level of inelasticity than a tourist hotel, since up-market customers are less price sensitive than down-market ones.

HOTEL PROMOTIONS

The final element of the marketing mix that can be modified and managed in order to improve occupancy is that of promotion. This can broadly be subdivided into advertising, sales promotion, merchandising and publicity/public relations. Although merchandising is largely concerned with the in-house promotion of facilities and services to customers already resident in the hotel, we shall deal with this here. We shall not deal with each approach to promotion separately, but identify key elements in putting together any promotion in a service industry context, specifically for hotel operations.

The first key point is that this process is part of the *overall marketing strategy* of the hotel. The promotional campaign developed must be congruent with the nature of the product, the distribution channels used, and the pricing policy of the unit.

The second key point is to identify the *purpose* of promotional activity. Lovelock and Quelch[16] have identified three categories of people at whom promotion may be aimed, and for whom there is a range of reasons for carrying out the promotion:

1. Customers:
   - individuals or groups
   - increase awareness
   - encourage trial by non-users
   - increase purchase frequency of users
   - commit to purchasing over a long time period
   - reinforce other aspects of the marketing mix
   - obtain market research information.

2. Intermediaries:
   - persuade them to deliver a new product
   - persuade them to provide an additional push to an existing product.
   - insulate trade from a price increase.

3. Competitors:
   - move offensively or defensively against competitors (see page 101).

The third key point is the *process* by which such promotion is put together. A shortcoming of hoteliers is the tendency for them to start with the advertisement or promotional concept and then work backwards towards who it should be aimed at and why it should be done. In fact, the actual advertisement/promotional concept should be nearly the last stage in the process.

Stage 1: Identify hotel's strengths and weaknesses

Clearly this analysis is designed to enable management to work on improving any weaknesses in the product, and to enable the promotional activity to emphasise its strengths. There are three main sources of information from which this analysis can be made. First, the perceptions of management provide a low-cost, first-hand analysis, although this perspective is likely to be highly subjective. However, it can be reviewed and supported by analysis of data generated by the day-to-day operation of the unit, such as reservation cards, enquiry letters, the pattern of commission payments to travel agents, the type and frequency of use of credit cards, and so on.

The second source of information is the market itself. This is largely customers of the unit, or perhaps would-be customers. The general approach to investigating this viewpoint is market research, such as telephone surveys, mail shots, guest question-naires, and so on.

Alternative sources of market information are other hoteliers' views of the unit, which may be obtained informally over a drink or at a professional association dinner, and the views of consultants, such as marketing or media personnel, who may experi-ence the hotel as a guest to get first-hand knowledge of its style and ambience.

The final source of information concerning the unit's strengths and weaknesses is derived from a review of the external environment, locally, regionally and perhaps nationally. Such a review would encompass an analysis of what competitors are doing, what hotel construction is taking place, forthcoming events of importance (such as a royal wedding), modifications to transportation links (new motorways, by-passes), and so on.

Stage 2: Devise a position statement

Lewis writes:[17]

> Although the concept of positioning has been widely accepted in a range of industries, by most appearances it has largely escaped the attention of hotel marketers. Whereas position-ing relates to a property's subjective attributes (and how they differ from competitors' subjective attributes), hotel advertising has traditionally emphasized such objective product characteristics as number of rooms, prices, facilities, and amenities – characteristics in which competing facilities are generally quite similar.

He goes on to suggest that a position statement should do three things:

1. *create an image* by keeping the concept simple, clear and tangible;

2. *identify benefits* by clarifying the utility or value of the hotel to the consumer in terms of location, facilities, price, ambience or availability (or what Lovelock has called the utility of 'place', 'form', 'monetary', 'psychic' and 'time');

3. *differentiate the product* from competitive products by demonstrating the uni-que attributes of the hotel to its potential customer.

Stage 3: Select target audience

Once the hotel has a clear position statement, a decision can be made as to whom the promotion will be aimed at. The target audience may not necessarily be identical to the market segments at which the hotel is aimed. This is because it is unnecessary to promote to those market segments or parts of a market segment that will purchase a room or some other aspect of the operation in any case. For instance, a hotel res-taurant well patronised by the local community may not need to be advertised locally, but it may need to be promoted in-house to hotel residents.

There are four categories of target audience, each of which needs a slightly different approach in terms of what the promotional tool says and does:

1. *hotel guests* – this audience will be reached mainly by merchandising material and techniques, as well as some sales promotional tools such as prize promo-tions;

2. *individual potential customers* – these must receive an evocative, memorable image, usually through the medium of advertising;

3. *group customers* – these want information and value for money, so advertising must provide the information they require and sales promotional tools must stimulate interest. However, much of the sales effort to groups is carried out by the hotel company's sales force through personal contact with such clients;

4. *intermediaries* – these also require information rather than image.

Stage 4: Devise the promotion package

The promotional tool can be just one of the four types we have identified – advertising, sales promotion, merchandising or PR – or any combination of these four. In designing and planning the promotion package, six points should be considered:

1. *Product scope* – what aspect of the hotel is being promoted? Room sales and function business are largely made as planned purchases, whilst hotel food and drink sales are more likely to be impulse purchases. This has implications for which promotional tool to use.

2. *Market scope* – keep in mind the target audience for the promotion in selecting components of the package, such as the media through which the promotion will be communicated.

3. *Timing* – consider when, for how long and how frequently the promotional effort should be undertaken.

4. *Identify beneficiary* – particularly with regard to promotions aimed at intermediaries; keep clear who will receive the benefit of any such promotion.

5. *Competition* – if at all possible, design the promotion such that it cannot be copied by competitors or turned to their advantage.

6. *Return on investment* – promotion costs money. Attempts must be made to identify the return expected in terms of additional sales against the cost of the effort. Discounting, coupons and prize promotions must be carefully evaluated to identify the likely take-up rate.

Stage 5: Measure effectiveness

The final stage in the process of devising a hotel promotion is to evaluate the effectiveness or success rate of the campaign. Some forms of promotion are difficult to evaluate, particularly PR and advertising, whereas a sales promotion is relatively easy to evaluate since its take-up rate can be measured. It is for this reason that many hotel advertisements include an enquiry coupon or sales promotional offer in order to measure the type and scale of the advertisement's readership.

The final key point emphasises the way in which the advertising or promotion must reflect the *nature of the hotel experience*, which is fairly typical of most service experiences. George and Berry[18] suggest five factors to keep in mind with regard to promoting the sale of a service. First, the employees of a service business are a key feature of the provision of the service and should be regarded as a second audience of the hotel's advertising effort. The image created by advertising must therefore be congruent with the culture and work climate of the hotel. For instance, an advertisement that identifies as a distinctive benefit of the hotel its quiet, secluded location must operate such that the workforce are calm and unhurried. Likewise employees are another category of people at whom sales promotional ideas can be aimed. In-house staff competitions, bonuses related to sales and so on are all sales promotional ideas designed to encourage sales through personal selling.

Secondly, the intangible nature of services and the level of personal customisation of a service that can take place make word of mouth a powerful promotional tool. In other words contented customers carry out promotion on behalf of the hotel at no cost! Positive use can be made of this medium by encouraging customers to tell their friends, by giving out small mementoes with the name, address and telephone number of the hotel on them to act as a constant reminder (for instance, book-matches, key rings), by making the target audience of promotional activity so-called opinion leaders, and by using the comments of satisfied customers in promotional material.

Thirdly, we have already identified the idea of providing tangible clues to consumers in order to reduce the risk of purchasing a 'product' that they cannot see, taste, touch or hear until after consumption.

Fourthly, since a service has no physical appearance, promotional continuity must be maintained in all advertising, sales promotional material and merchandising, in order to focus customer attention on some readily identifiable symbol of the organisation, such as the company logo.

Finally, ensure that promotions promise what is possible. Do not make claims that cannot be met.

SUMMARY

This chapter began by identifying that the immediate consumption of a service by the consumer in contact with the service provider required a different approach to the marketing planning process than was the case with consumer products. In particular, the hotel manager became responsible for remixing components of the marketing mix in response to individual consumer needs. We briefly reviewed a range of proposals concerning the nature of the marketing mix for service business and concluded that the four Ps, proposed by McCarthy, were still relevant. The advantage of considering or adopting one of the other proposals lay in the insight they could provide about the nature of service provision.

We then went on to consider the nature of demand for the hotel 'product' and what customers sought when purchasing one or other of the different facilities on offer. The key element in managing customer demand is the effective utilisation of space or capacity. Hotels, typically, have a fixed capacity largely determined by the feasibility study that takes place at the time of construction. This fixed capacity is not aimed indiscriminately at the total market place, but is usually targeted at some specific market segments. Such segmentation arises logically out of the location of the hotel and deliberately out of the design and facilities incorporated into the hotel at the time of construction. This is further emphasised by the categorisation of hotels by star ratings or whatever, instituted by outside organisations.

Once the market segment has been established, the hotel manager faces two scenarios: either demand exceeds supply or supply exceeds demand. For each of these scenarios there are three alternative strategies available in order to improve the unit's occupancy. These strategies will vary according to whether the unit is an independent hotel, a chain hotel, a hostel or a hospital. In each case, however, the strategy involves the modification of at least one of the elements of the marketing mix – product, price, place or promotion.

Since effective capacity management depends upon modifying elements of the marketing mix, we then went on to identify in the hotel context the alternative approaches and techniques available to the manager for modifying each element. Product development focused on the opening times of the hotel, usage of rooms, amenities of the unit and total unit capacity. The development of distribution channels ('place') identified the key role that advanced reservation systems play in the sale of hotel accommodation. In considering price, we confined our analysis to an understanding of the concept of elasticity of demand, since chapter 6 deals with price in depth. And, finally, we looked at promotion: the purpose of hotel promotion, the tools available, the process of planning such promotion and key features of the promotion of services to consumers.

REFERENCES

1. Bell, M. L., 'Tactical service marketing and the process of remixing', in Donnelly, G., and George, W. R. (eds), *Marketing of Services*, American Marketing Association, Chicago, 1981.

2. McCarthy, E. J., *Basic Marketing: A Managerial Approach*, Irwin, 1964.

3. Levitt, T., 'Marketing intangible products and product intangibles', *Harvard Business Review*, May/June 1981.

4. Shostack, G. L. 'Breaking free from product marketing', *Journal of Marketing*, vol. 41, pp. 73–80, April 1970.

5. Booms, B. H., and Bitner, M. J., 'Marketing services by managing the environment', *Cornell HRA Quarterly*, pp. 35–39, May 1982.

6. Gronroos, C., 'A service-oriented approach to marketing of services', *European Journal of Marketing* vol. 12, no. 8, pp. 588–601, 1978.

7. Renaghan, L. M., 'A new marketing mix for the hospitality industry', *Cornell HRA Quarterly*, pp. 31–35, August 1981.

8. Buttle, F., *Hotel and Food Service*, Holt, Rinehart and Winston (Cassell), 1986.

9. Jeffrey, D., and Hubard, N. J., 'Weekly occupancy fluctuations in Yorkshire and Humberside hotels 1982–1984: patterns and prescriptions', *International Journal of Hospitality Management* vol. 5, no. 4, pp. 177–187, 1986.

10. Gamble, P. R. G., and Smith, G., 'Expert front office management', *International Journal of Hospitality Management* vol. 5, no. 3, pp. 109–114, 1986.

11. Sasser, W. E., Olsen, M. D., and Wyckoff, D. D., *Management of Service Operations*, Allyn & Bacon, 1978.

12. *The Arthur Young Survey of Singapore's Hotel Industry*, Arthur Young Management Consultants Pte Ltd, 1985.

13. Stacey, C., 'Boosting occupancy', *Caterer and Hotelkeeper*, pp. 53 and 56, 15 May 1986.

14. Gamble, P. R. G. and Smith, G., *op. cit*.

15. Abbey, J., 'Is discounting the answer to declining occupancies?' *International Journal of Hospitality Management* vol. 2, no. 2, pp. 77–82, 1983.

16. Lovelock, C. H., and Quelch, J. A., 'Consumer promotions in service marketing', *Business Horizons*, pp. 66–75, May–June 1983.

17. Lewis, R. C., 'The positioning statement for hotels', *Cornell HRA Quarterly*, pp. 51–61, May 1981.

18. George, W. R., and Berry, L. L., 'Guidelines for the advertising of services', *Business Horizons*, pp. 52–56, August 1981.

6 Increasing Income

Figure 6.1 *Secondary key result area: income.*

INTRODUCTION

With regard to improving financial performance, it is usual to focus on contribution as the means of increasing profitability. Contribution is the difference between variable costs and sales. Clearly, then, the two major factors with regard to improving contribution are the effective management of variable costs and the management of sales volume. We shall examine the management of costs in chapter 7 when we look in detail at the issue of productivity. In this chapter we concentrate on the concept of sales value. Sales value is made up of two components: the number of sales transactions, and the price charged. In the previous chapter we examined how the hotel manager might go about influencing and improving the volume of sales transactions, so this chapter is largely about price, and therefore about the key result area of increasing income (see figure 6.1).

The rate of inflation between 1970 and the mid 1980s has been in the region of 416 per cent. Whilst the investment and construction cost of new hotels has more or less kept pace with inflation, the pricing of hotel rooms has significantly exceeded this. For instance, in 1971 the Reading Post House was built at a cost of £2 million and its rack rate was £5 per night. In 1987, the University Post House at Guildford was built at a cost of £7 million whilst its rack rate is £63 per night. The current breakdown of investment cost in a new hotel of around 100 rooms with an average bedroom size of 2.6 square metres, excluding land costs, is as follows:

- *Building* – including site search, market survey, refinement on sites, viability study, outline brief, draft option agreements, outline planning permission, purchase negotiation, architect, engineer, quantity surveyor, detailed plans, tenders and board approval – as well as costs of construction.   36%

- *External* – landscaping, car parks, signing   6%

- *Services* – connection of mains utilities   20%

- *Pre-opening expenses* – interest charges, marketing, staffing   7%

- *Furniture, fittings and equipment* (this area of cost is rising very rapidly)   25%

- *Fees*   6%

HOTEL COST STRUCTURE

Focusing on price as the principal means of improving income is particularly appropriate for the hotel business, due to the high level of fixed or semi-fixed costs. Over 90 per cent of hotel capital is invested in fixed assets such as buildings, plant, fixtures and fittings. This gives rise to high fixed costs of depreciation, insurance and rates, and high semi-fixed costs of heating, lighting, maintenance, repairs and labour. Businesses with a high proportion of fixed costs are particularly vulnerable to a fall in sales volume. This has been well illustrated by Kotas,[1] as shown in table 6.1.

Table 6.1   *Effect of cost structure on profitability.*

| | Business A | | Business B | |
	Normal results £	Decreased sales £	Normal results £	Decreased sales £
Sales	10,000	9,000	10,000	9,000
Fixed costs	6,000	6,000	2,000	2,000
Variable costs	2,000	1,800	6,000	5,400
Total costs	8,000	7,800	8,000	7,400
Contribution	2,000	1,200	2,000	1,600

Reproduced with permission.

Although both business A and business B suffer a 10 per cent fall in turnover, business A, because of its high fixed costs structure, experiences a 40 per cent fall in contribution. Business B, however, has only a 20 per cent fall in contribution, since its fixed costs are relatively low. This clearly makes managing sales volume important in the hotel business. Furthermore, the implication of price as a means of improving income is emphasised due to the existence of a high differential between price and variable cost. As we have seen in chapter 5, the decision to remain open or to close during the off-season is based largely on the extent to which income generated is greater than the variable cost incurred. Since variable costs are proportionately only a small part of the cost (and hence the price charged), this provides a great deal of discretion for the hotel manager in terms of setting a price. For instance, the variable cost of providing a three-star hotel room for one night may be £5, but the standard tariff for such a room might be £35. Thus there is a £30 differential that can be exploited commercially to improve contribution.

The effective management of income is therefore in two stages. First, there is the setting of the tariff for each type of room in the hotel. This is largely a strategic decision, focused over the long term, and often based on the expected *average* costs of operating. Secondly, there is price modification, such as discounting, over the short term, based largely on the *marginal* cost principle we have previously discussed.

For each type of hotel – independent, chain, hostel and hospital – the unit manager requires different skills and techniques. The independent hotelier needs to know both how to establish a tariff structure and how to modify it. The chain hotel manager needs to understand not only how the tariff structure of his or her hotel was established, but also more importantly how to modify the established prices. The manager in the non-commercial sector will not focus his or her attention on the sales volume aspect of contribution, but will largely be concerned with cost management.

PRICING POLICY

Price is set originally in the context of corporate objectives. It is often assumed that profit maximisation is the only objective of commercial firms. In fact there is a wide range of possible objectives. Buttle[2] suggests four categories:

1. Profit-oriented:
    *   maximisation of profit
    *   satisfactory profit (satisficing)
    *   maximum positive cash flow
    *   target return on investment
    *   rapid payback
    *   harvesting.

2. Sales-oriented:
    *   maximisation of sales volume
    *   satisfactory sales volume
    *   market share gain or maintenance
    *   market penetration.

3. Competition-oriented:
    *   maintenance of price differentials
    *   matching competitors.

4. Cost-oriented:
    *   break even
    *   meet costs.

The selection of suitable pricing objectives is made as a response to factors over which the firm has little or no control, such as the level of demand, the type of industry, the structure of the industry, nature of competition, and the phase of market development.

Whilst the function of marketing is to influence *demand* for a particular product, most firms have little or no control over total demand, demand fluctuations or elasticity of demand. Likewise, the *structure of the industry* is complex. As we saw in chapter 1, there is greater concentration in the hotel industry, i.e. fewer but larger firms in the market, but relative to many industries, the hotel industry is extremely unconcentrated. This is the main reason for the *highly competitive nature* of the business. Whilst there may be local, geographical monopolies, such as only one hotel in a town or new resort, these only exist for the non-discretionary traveller. Such hotels do face competition from hotels in alternative locations. Finally, the phase of market development affects the pricing objectives and hence the policy selected. For instance, launching a new hotel in a new market, a firm may decide to match the quality of the competition but at a lower price in order to create competitive advantage. However, in mature markets, pricing policy is often based on the idea of price discrimination, with the product priced according to the elasticity of demand of the segment at which it is aimed.

Other factors that will affect the selection of policy are not external to the organisation. These are factors over which the firm can exert some control. These include *product considerations* such as the prestige of the hotel, the level of differentiation, age of the unit and its position in the market. There are also the *resources of the firm* in terms of its ability to absorb loss-making periods or units and so on.

Once a clear pricing policy objective has been established, an appropriate tariff structure can be determined and suitable pricing techniques can be used to calculate prices.

TARIFF STRUCTURES

There are a wide range of alternative tariff structures in the hotel business, ranging from the all-in tariff to a complex price for each of the hotel's services. The selection of a particular structure is dependent largely on the market at which the hotel is aimed. Indeed, a hotel can have several tariff structures, with one for each of its market segments. In broad terms, business customers tend to accept room-only tariffs with ancillary services prices individually, whereas pleasure travellers prefer all-inclusive rates.

Each type of structure has implications for how the hotel is managed. A hotel that prices only its accommodation has to be far more aggressive in its internal marketing and merchandising than a hotel offering an all-inclusive rate. The focus of management in hotels with all-in rates is much less on marketing and much more on cost analysis and reduction. All-in rates also reduce the complexity of administration and customer accounting, although control of sales must still be maintained.

PRICING TECHNIQUES

These techniques are used to establish prices and tariffs over the long term. For each category of pricing objective there are different techniques available. These are:

1. Profit-oriented:
    *   target rate of return
    *   marginal pricing
    *   IMPS (Integrated Menu Pricing System)
    *   base pricing.

2. Sales-oriented:
    *   marketing oriented pricing (MOP)
    *   prestige pricing
    *   loss leader
    *   psychological.

3. Competitor-oriented:
    *   follow the leader.

4. Cost-oriented:
    *   cost plus
    *   factor pricing
    *   actual cost approach
    *   break even.

Not all of these approaches are suitable for setting room tariffs. However, they may be used in a hotel for the setting of prices in bars, restaurants and ancillary areas. Since we are largely concerned with the contribution derived from room sales we shall concentrate on the pricing techniques used to establish room rates.

Profit-oriented techniques

Profit-oriented pricing techniques are used extensively in the commercial hotel sector. This is largely because the main alternative, cost-oriented techniques, takes no account of the level of capital invested, which typically is high for hotels.

Target rate of return

The target rate of return method starts with the level of return required from the investment. The particular approach adopted for hotels is known as the Hubbart formula, and was developed for the American Hotel and Motel Association. By taking an estimate of the total investment cost, both fixed and working capital, stating the target rate of return and estimating the fixed and semi-fixed operating costs, it is possible to calculate the required gross operating income. If the profit from non-rooms is estimated, the required rooms profit can be calculated by taking non-rooms profit away from the gross operating income. By adding estimated rooms operating costs to required rooms profit, the required rooms revenue per annum is established. By dividing this by the estimated number of room nights, the average room rate is determined. This is illustrated in table 6.2.

The advantage of this method is that it focuses on profit, it takes into account and integrates costs, revenues and prices, and it is relatively simple to calculate. Its major weaknesses are that it ignores price elasticity of demand and the impact of local competition, it requires forecasts of future costs and occupancy rates which are difficult to establish with any accuracy, and it regards pricing as independent of the rest of the marketing mix. As we have seen, price is only one of the four Ps.

Table 6.2   *Example of tariff setting using the Hubbart formula.*

A.	Total investment cost	£900,000
B.	Target rate of return	10%
C.	General operating costs	£200,000
D.	Required gross operating income	£290,000 (B% of A + C)
E.	Non-rooms profit	£20,000
F.	Required rooms profit	£270,000 (D − E)
G.	Rooms operating costs	£230,000
H.	Required rooms revenue	£500,000 (F + G)
I.	Number of room nights	42,000
J.	Average room rate	£11.90 (H : I)

Marginal pricing

The major alternative profit-oriented technique is marginal pricing. This method is more sophisticated and requires an understanding of the relationship between demand and price as well as of the cost structure of the business. This sophistication also means that this method can be used by firms with sales-oriented pricing objectives. Buttle[3] provides examples of how this approach is employed in hotels.

The approach requires a demand function and a cost schedule. A simple demand function might be:

$$Q = 7,500 - 50P$$

where Q = quantity
          P = price.

So the function above means that maximum sales volume is 7,500 (room nights), and that for every £1 charged we expect to lose 50 rooms. This can be shown as a graph as in figure 6.2.

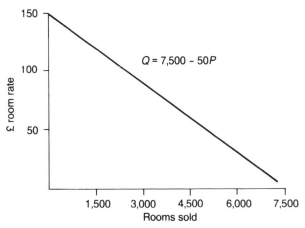

Figure 6.2   *Demand schedule ($Q = 7,500 - 50P$). Reproduced with permission.*

The cost schedule is based on the formula:

$$TC = FC + VC$$

where TC = total cost
          FC = fixed cost
          VC = variable cost.

In this example, let fixed costs be £100,000 and variable cost £5 per room night, so that:

$$TC = 100,000 + 5Q$$

This too can be shown graphically, as in figure 6.3.

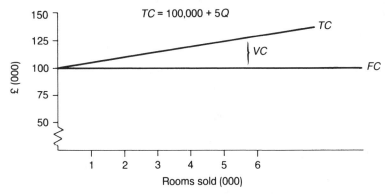

Figure 6.3 *Cost schedule* ($TC = 100,000 + 5Q$). Reproduced with permission.

The two schedules can be combined to show the level of profit achieved at any given level of volume and price, based on the following formula:

$$Z = TR - TC$$

where
Z = profit
TR = total revenue
TC = total cost.

Since total revenue is price multiplied by quantity, and total cost has been established as £100,000 + 5Q, the profit formula can be expressed as:

$$Z = P \times Q - (100,000 + 5Q)$$

so that:

$$
\begin{aligned}
Z &= P(7,500 - 50P) - 100,000 - 5(7,500 - 50P) \\
&= 7,750P - 50P^2 - 137,500
\end{aligned}
$$

Thus by subsituting different prices (P) in the above formula, it is possible to establish levels of profit achieved. This is illustrated in table 6.3.

Table 6.3 *Marginal pricing example.*

Room rate (P)	7750P	50P^2	137,500	Profit
10	77,500	5,000	137,500	−65,000
20	155,000	20,000	137,500	−2,500
50	387,500	125,000	137,500	125,000
75	581,250	281,250	137,500	162,500
77.50	600,625	300,312.50	137,500	162,812.50
80	620,000	320,000	137,500	162,500
100	775,000	500,000	137,500	137,500

Reproduced with permission.

If the data from table 6.3 were graphed, the profit would be shown as an inverted 'U' shape. This is because at the point of maximum profit, i.e. £162,812.50, the sale of a room at £77.50 exactly balances the contradictory influences of the demand and cost schedules.

Although more sophisticated, this technique also has some weaknesses. Like the target rate of return method it requires estimates of costs data. In addition, demand schedules are costly to derive, and will change with changes in market conditions, such as price competition. It makes no allowance for non-price variables that may affect demand, and it ignores cost and demand complexities. To facilitate the derivation of a formula that expresses demand as a function of price, the manager needs to call upon his or her own judgement, comparisons with similar products, market surveys, test marketing and market simulation. It must be remembered that the demand formula used above is highly simplified. There are likely to be more than just two variables, and the function is unlikely to be a straight line over the whole range.

IMPS and base pricing

The base pricing method and IMPS are examples of profit-oriented pricing techniques which are used in menu pricing rather than rooms.

Sales-oriented techniques

Market-oriented pricing

This technique is particularly appropriate for establishing room tariffs for a new hotel development. First, the target market is established and hence the nature of competition for this market segment. This enables the organisation to establish a product position appropriate for the competitive state of the target market and set a room tariff complementary to this product positioning.

The alternative sales outlets are then analysed to establish what proportion of sales will be made direct to guests, through travel agents, through conference organisers, and so on, and hence what discounts are conventionally offered to these different channels. The room tariff is then adjusted for each channel to ensure that margins are maintained at the level expected. For instance, travel agents may expect a 10 per cent discount whilst tour operators may expect a 25 per cent margin. On a tariff of £40, then, for direct guest sales the hotel will receive the full £40, on sales through travel agents it will receive £36, and on sales to tour operators it will receive £30.

Once the proportion of sales through each channel has been estimated, it is then possible to calculate total annual revenue. This is illustrated in table 6.4, assuming 40 per cent of sales of a 100 bedroom hotel are to guests, 40 per cent are through travel agents, and 20 per cent are to tour operators.

Once the total revenue is established, the desired level of profit can be deducted to establish the total annual running costs. For instance, if the target profit was to be £350,000, annual operating costs in the example in table 6.4 must not exceed £978,600. From this the impact of sales less than forecast, or costs higher than estimated, can be calculated to establish the impact on profitability.

The advantages of this approach are that price is formulated in the context of the total marketing mix, notably product and place. It combines demand, cost and competitive considerations, and it can be combined with breakeven analysis to establish the payback period on capital investment. It, too, requires market research and fore-

Table 6.4 *Total revenue using MOPS for a 100 bedroom hotel.*

Channel	Room nights no.	%	Achieved room rate £	Revenue £
Direct	14,600	40	40	584,000
Travel agents	14,600	40	36	525,600
Tour operators	7,300	20	30	219,000
Total	36,500	100	27.30 (av.)	1,328,600

casting techniques to be effective, and the value of the technique depends largely on the accuracy of these.

Other sales-oriented techniques

The other three approaches to sales-oriented pricing are not based on formulae. *Prestige pricing* is based on the concept that, contrary to the accepted laws of economics, there are some products for which demand increases as the price increases. *Leader pricing* is the concept of pricing one element of the product mix low so as to attract sales, whilst *psychological pricing* utilises a range of approaches for setting price according to what it is perceived the customer is prepared to pay. None of these approaches is really suitable for setting prices in the first place, but we shall consider them again later when we look at how the manager may adjust prices in the short term in order to meet pricing objectives.

Competitor-oriented techniques

The approach of *follow-the-leader* pricing is quite common in the hotel industry. That is to say a hotel establishes its price based on what a competitor is charging. It is particularly likely where independent operators are in competition with a chain hotel. For instance, if a three-star chain hotel has a tariff of £32.50 for a single room, an independent hotelier would set his prices 10 per cent lower – £29.25. For the hotelier the approach has the advantage that it is inherently competitive and very easy to calculate. But it is a very dangerous approach as it takes no account of the specific capital structure, operating costs or profit objectives of the business.

Cost-oriented techniques

Cost-oriented techniques are largely used in the setting of prices in catering operations. The *cost-plus method* is widespread. Either a percentage mark-up is added to the cost, or a set amount added. *Factor pricing* is setting price by multiplying the cost by a standard factor, such as 2 or 10. *Actual cost pricing* is a variation of the Hubbart formula, in that sales targets and profits are established, and all costs except food are taken away from the sales less profit target to establish a food cost ceiling. Menu items are then selected on the basis that their cost stays under this ceiling. These techniques are not applied to room pricing largely because they are unsuited to products with a high fixed cost element, requiring indirect cost allocations across a range of products.

Breakeven method

The final technique is the breakeven method. This has relevance to the not-for-profit sector of the hotel industry. In this sector, income can be derived from sales revenue to individual customers such as with college students in a hostel, or income can be a lump-sum budgeted amount from external sources of funding such as in the NHS. In both cases, it is necessary to establish what level of volume will result in total costs being met by the income available.

Breakeven pricing also uses the formula:

$$[TC = FC + VC]$$

It is usual to assume that the variable costs are the same for each unit of output so that there is a linear relationship between variable cost and sales volume. In practice, this relationship may not be linear due to economies of scale (i.e. as volume increases, variable unit costs fall) or improved performance based on past experience. Once again, sales revenue is seen as derived from the volume of sales and price:

$$[TR = Q \times P]$$

Breakeven occurs when $TC = TR$. this is shown on figure 6.4. In this example, $TC = TR$ at 20,000 bed nights. Breakeven occurs when income of £600,000 pays for the fixed costs of £500,000 and the variable costs of £5 per bed night. Any further sales would create a profit.

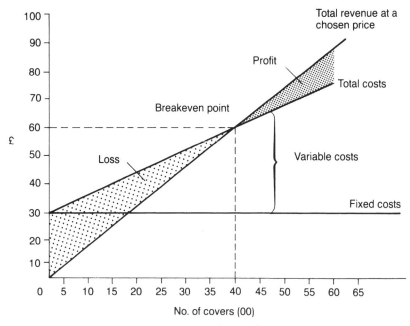

Figure 6.4 *Breakeven chart.*

Normally the unit contribution formula is used to establish the breakeven point. The unit contribution is the price less the variable unit cost, so the number of sales to be made to cover fixed cost is the fixed cost divided by the unit contribution. From the example above:

$$Q = \frac{FC}{P - VC}$$

$$20,000 = \frac{500,000}{(30 - 5)}$$

This formula can be reworked to establish price, so, for instance, the not-for-profit hostel manager would calculate the price knowing exactly the volume of sales, i.e.

$$P = \frac{FC}{Q} + VC$$

MODIFYING PRICE

Once price has been established in the context of corporate objectives using the appropriate pricing technique, it is common for the unit manager to modify this price. As we have seen, the demand for the hotel product is extremely complex, with different market segments having different elasticities of demand that are likely to vary over the course of a year. In addition, the different channels through which sales are made may also lead to price modification. And finally, changes in the external environment such as the opening or closing of a locally competitive hotel also affect the pricing decision.

The decision to modify the price, usually in the form of some sort of discount on the rack rate, must be made on the basis of improving performance, or at least minimising the effect of a fall in demand. Current practice in the industry is that major hotel chains expect and budget for 20–25 per cent of their potential sales revenue to be at a discounted rate. This means that a very large proportion of actual customers are receiving some sort of discount. However, there is growing evidence[4] to suggest that many operators are discounting to improve sales volume with a detrimental effect on profitability. This is due to the misconception that a 10 per cent reduction in rates will result in at least a 10 per cent increase in occupancy. This would only be the case if demand was neither elastic nor inelastic. However, even business travellers are becoming more price conscious, so that demand for hotel accommodation in the UK is likely to be elastic rather than inelastic. The implications of this are that a 10 per cent reduction in rates should always result in an increase of sales volume of more than 10 per cent. Even then, however, price cutting may not be more profitable, since this ignores the variable cost of providing the room. Therefore a 10 per cent rate reduction requires a 15 per cent increase in occupancy if the variable cost element is 25 per cent of the room rate.

For example, take a 100 bedroom hotel with an average room rate of £40 and an average occupancy of 70 per cent. If the variable cost is 25 per cent of average room rate, the contribution towards fixed cost is £30 per room. If this £40 rate is discounted by 10 per cent to £36, the contribution is reduced to £26. The level of total contribution before the rate cut was 100 rooms at 70 per cent occupancy times £30, i.e. £2,100 per day. If the contribution is now only £26, the occupancy rate needed to maintain the same level of daily contribution is found by dividing £2,100 by £26, i.e. 80.8 per cent. The percentage increase in occupancy from 70 to 80.8 is:

$$\% \text{ increase} = \frac{80.8 - 70}{70} \times 100 = 15\%$$

In addition to the misconceptions about the effect of discounting prices, there is the long-term impact of instituting a price-cutting policy. First, there will almost certainly be competitive reaction. Therefore the short-term competitive advantage gained will almost immediately be eroded. Thus whilst the specific demand for the product may be elastic, the aggregate demand for accommodation is unlikely to be so. If all hoteliers discount, there is not likely to be a significant increase in the number of people using hotels. Secondly, if rates are cut in order to generate business, it is extremely difficult to restore prices to their previous level when the environment is healthier. There is a great deal of consumer resistance. In 1982, Robert Hazard, the President of Quality Inns International, is quoted as saying:[5] 'When fall (autumn) comes and the discount programme ends, Holiday Inn may find that its guests resent paying the higher prices. It's hard to start a discount programme, but harder still to stop it.'

Therefore the key element in any discounting policy is to identify if one or more of the following is being achieved:

- new business is being generated, i.e. customers who would not otherwise be buying hotel rooms;

- business is being maintained during a seasonal trough;

- discounts are aimed at specific market segments whose price sensitivity is clearly different to the market segment for which the rack rate is set, e.g. tour operators, travel agents, etc.

There is little or no point in generating sales by discounting which only draws business from competitors, since the inevitable retaliation by competitors will only result in an overall lowering of rates across the board.

Given that the rationale for lowering price has been clearly established, there is still the question of how to decide on what basis rates should be reduced. At what levels should the discounts be set? In some cases, the discount price is established by trade practice, for instance the level of discount expected by travel agents or tour operators. Travel agents command discounts by virtue of the number of bed spaces they are prepared to purchase in advance. This large-scale guaranteed advance booking results in a 15 to 20 per cent discount, which the travel firm can pass on to its clients.

As well as travel agents, other bulk purchasers of accommodation are so-called 'room-brokers'. In the UK the two largest are Room Centre and Expotel, both of whom provide a centralised reservations service and pass on their bulk discounts to clients. Between them they make nearly 2 million reservations a year.

Another approach is for individual firms to negotiate a discount price. This is often done when an organisation requires a large number of bed nights over a period of time, either for a specific conference or to accommodate personnel regularly visiting one specific location. Some hotel companies automatically offer corporate discount schemes to regular users. Trusthouse Forte, for example, instituted in 1985 their gold and silver cardholder schemes, so that companies who spend more than £50,000 each year receive a 5 per cent discount and those who spend more than £150,000 receive 8 per cent discount. This discount includes food and drink as well as accommodation.

Finally, discounts for maintaining seasonal business are likely to be based on a psychological approach, by taking into account the consumer's perception of price. This is particularly true of weekend break pricing. For instance, Westin in the USA offers a flat rate of 50 per cent discount on all rooms and suites on Fridays, Saturdays and Sundays.

ACHIEVING FULL POTENTIAL

In recognising that price will vary at different times of the year and for different market segments, it is important to ensure that the yardstick for measuring good performance is both fair and accurate. The standard yardstick used throughout the hotel industry is occupancy rate. However, as we have seen, it is possible to increase occupancy at the same time as profitability decreases. Lovelock[6] has suggested that an appropriate measure should establish the extent to which an organisation's assets are achieving their full revenue generating potential. He proposes the idea of an *asset revenue generating efficiency index* (ARGE). This is based on the assumption that it is unreasonable to expect a hotel to operate at 100 per cent occupancy at the standard rack rate. Since occupancy is likely to be less than 100 per cent and discounts will be offered, we need to be able to establish what is a reasonable level of expected revenue from this combination of different levels of occupancy at different rates.

For example, in a 200 bedroom hotel with a rack rate of £50, the theoretical total revenue generating potential is £10,000 per night. If 60 rooms are occupied at the rack rate of £50, and another 60 rooms are occupied at 40 per cent discount, i.e. £30, then the occupancy rate is 60 per cent and the average room rate is £40. This gives the average unit price efficiency rate of 80 per cent (£40 as a percentage of £50). The ARGE is therefore this average unit efficiency rate multiplied by the occupancy rate ($0.8 \times 0.6 = 0.48$) = 48 per cent. That is to say the hotel is operating at 48 per cent of its full potential.

Not only is this a more effective measure of actual performance than the occupancy rate on its own, but the concept can be applied to setting operating targets in terms of maximising revenue from sales. This can be illustrated by considering a new hotel, with 100 twin-bedded rooms. To keep the illustrative example relatively simple we shall assume the hotel has only three room rates:

- £40 per night for two persons;
- £30 per night for single occupancy;
- £20 per night for single or double occupancy off-season.

We shall also assume that the hotel has three distinct periods of demand during a typical year:

- off-season – October to December;
- peak season (business travellers) – January to April;
- peak season (tourists) – May to September.

It is assumed that business travellers will be largely single occupancy, whilst tourists will be double occupancy.

For each operating period it is therefore possible to calculate a target ARGE by determining what proportion of total occupancy it is reasonable to expect to be generated by the different market segments. This is illustrated in figure 6.5.

Figure 6.5 has nine different cells, with each cell representing the proportion of rooms to be occupied at a given rate for each distinct period. This enables the ARGE for each period to be calculated, so that for the off-season 60 per cent of the occupancy will be at the off-season rate, 20 per cent at the single rate and 20 per cent at the double rate. Thus the ARGE target for this period is 65 per cent. This example assumes that the discounting creates 100 per cent occupancy throughout the year, but

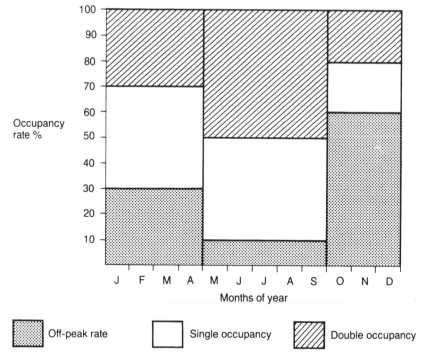

Figure 6.5 *Matrix of revenue expectations for different periods and different client groups.*

it is also possible to build into this model the idea that some rooms will not be sold by showing cells with zero revenue.

The illustration also suggests that for each distinct period, the relative proportion of sales to each market segment is continuously the same proportion. That is to say, for instance, irrespective of the day of the week in the off-season the proportion of double occupancy sales will always be 20 per cent. This is not the case. The percentage sales volume for each period is an average performance over that period. Thus during the off-season it may be that during the week, double occupancies are quite high, but almost non-existent at weekends. However, the overall effect is that double occupancies do not represent more than 20 per cent of a week's business.

Similarly, the illustration suggests a marked change from one period to another in terms of the type of bookings accepted. This too is not true. There will be a transition period, during which the proportion of one type of booking will change. So long as *overall* for the period, the type of sales reflect the target, it does not matter that there are fluctuations on a daily or weekly basis within the same period. If this is problematic, the model can be made considerably more sophisticated and targets can be set for each month or even each week. But the value of the concept is partly in its simplicity, and the effort required to plan a highly complex ARGE matrix is unlikely to be offset by the benefits gained.

The advantages of this approach are:

• prices are set to reflect the demand curves of different market segments;

• there is recognition of the impact of seasonality;

- clear targets can be set to sales and marketing personnel, including receptionists, in terms of the type of client they should approach and the price to be charged;

- correct decisions to *refuse* business of the wrong type can be made. It is common for receptionists and front-office management to be faced with the issue of whether to accept an advance booking from a tour group some months ahead, or risk waiting to fill the same space with travellers at the full rate at short notice. With the use of the matrix, the number of discounted bookings that can be taken is clearly established.

ADDITIONAL REVENUE FROM OTHER DEPARTMENTS

So far we have concentrated on income derived solely from the sale of accommodation. Of course in a hotel, income is also derived from sales in other departments of the hotel, assuming that the unit does not operate a fully inclusive tariff, such as at Club Mediterranée. The other operating departments can be subdivided into two main areas: food and beverage, which includes bars, restaurants, banqueting and floor service, and other operating departments, which includes telephone, laundry, florist and so on.

Whilst the concept of the ARGE index is an effective tool for understanding and maximising revenue derived from room sales, we must also consider revenue derived from these other departments. The hotel manager therefore seeks to maximise *income per guest night*:

$$\text{Income/guest night} = \frac{\text{Room sales} + \text{Ancillary sales}}{\text{Number of residents}}$$

So far we have only concentrated on the room sales part of this objective and identified approaches to maximising the average room rate. We also need to consider approaches to maximising the revenue generated as 'ancillary sales' from the other operating departments. For instance in 1983, only 44.3 per cent of total sales revenue in hotels was generated by accommodation; meals and refreshments generated 29 per cent, alcoholic drink 21 per cent, and other goods and services made up the rest.[7]

Ancillary sales are derived from two distinct market segments: hotel residents and non-residents. The effective management of these two quite separate groups of customers is fundamental to profitability. For instance, it is quite common for a hotel to develop a reputation for its restaurant that attracts clientele from the locality, to the extent that the unwary first-time resident who decides to eat in the restaurant on his first night in the hotel finds that he is unable to do so because it is already fully booked. Such is his frustration, the hotel is likely to lose repeat sales of accommodation which are far more profitable than restaurant sales.

The extent to which residents will spend additional money in the hotel will depend on the range of additional services available, as well as the occupancy rate. But the key factor is the market segment served by the unit. Thus a hotel may operate at the same occupancy midweek and at weekends, but find that its additional revenue generated is different for the two periods, because one type of customer uses the hotel during the week, and another type stays at weekends.

Just as it is possible to discount the rack rate for corporate customers or tour operators, it is possible to discount ancillary services. In effect this is what usually happens when offering an all-inclusive tariff. The allocation of income across departments usually results in them all operating at lower levels of profitability.

SUMMARY

The manager of a hotel is made responsible for maximising the full potential of the operating unit. One of the major ways in which this can be done is by managing the price at which his product is 'sold'. There are two stages to price setting. First, there is the setting of the standard rack rate by using a technique appropriate to the objectives of the organisation. In the commercial sector, the three main methods are the Hubbart formula, marginal pricing and market-oriented pricing. In not-for-profit organisations, the breakeven approach is mostly used. Once price has been established, the manager may have to alter this price tactically in order to attract new business, maintain demand in slack periods, or meet the demands of different market segments, particularly corporate customers. In order to measure fully the effectiveness of this action, we advocate the concept of an index based on the asset revenue generating efficiency of the unit.

The ARGE concept draws together the idea of capacity management and income generation. This can be summarised in the following formula:

$$\text{Income performance} = \frac{\text{Rooms sold} \times \text{Achieved room rate}}{\text{No. of rooms} \times \text{Room rate} \times \text{Available nights}}$$

The number of rooms is determined by the original feasibility study of the hotel (see page 74), and the available room nights by the policy concerning when to keep the hotel open (see page 80). In this chapter we also identified how room rates might be set. This provides the maximum level of sales achievable in a given period. Income has to be measured against this possible maximum. It is derived from the level of rooms sold, which was discussed in chapter 5, and the actual room rates charged, which was discussed in this chapter on page 103.

In addition to rooms income there is also the additional revenue generated by ancillary departments. The opportunities for such additional sales will depend upon the tariff structure, but assuming there are additional sales opportunities, these can be viewed as a 'multiplier' derived from the volume of room sales and the market segments that use the hotel.

REFERENCES

1. Kotas, R., *Market Orientation in the Hotel and Catering Industry*, Surrey University Press, 1975.

2. Buttle, F., *Hotel and Food Service Marketing*, Holt, Rinehart and Winston (Cassell), 1986.

3. Buttle, F., *op. cit.*

4. Abbey, J., 'Is discounting the answer to declining occupancies?' *International Journal of Hospitality Management* vol. 2, no. 2, pp. 77–82, 1983.

5. Hazard, R., 'Discounting hotel rooms: counterproductive effort', *Canadian Hotel and Restaurant*, p. 16, August 1982.

6. Lovelock, C. H., 'Strategies for managing demand in capacity constrained service organisations', *Service Industries Journal* vol. 4, no. 3, pp. 12–30, November 1984.

7. Business Statistics Office, *Results of 1983 Catering Enquiry*, HMSO.

7 Managing Customer Service

Figure 7.1 *Secondary key result area: service.*

INTRODUCTION

This chapter is concerned with the secondary key result area derived from the inter-face between employees and customers (see figure 7.1). In any service industry this encounter is of prime importance in determining the customer's overall satisfaction with the experience. It is essentially an encounter between two individuals. However, the context within which this interaction takes place distinguishes it from other in-teractions. It is only by recognising the key features of this service encounter that the manager can hope to influence its outcomes and therefore the satisfaction which the customer derives from it.

The management of service is not made easier by the hotel context due to the potential stress under which service contact employees operate. Such stress has been identified as being associated with the 'boundary role' that services workers, i.e. any employee who comes into contact with customers, play in their organisations. Unlike many organisations, in many service firms – including hotels – practically all levels of the workforce from the most senior to the most menial can and do come into contact with the customer. For senior personnel this contact may be considerably less stressful due to the perceived status and experience of their position than for a junior member of staff.

In order to provide a satisfactory service encounter, service firms have adopted a number of strategies for managing the interaction, such as the provision of 'scripts', changes in the design of the service delivery system and influencing the organisational climate. The contribution that such approaches make to the successful running of the business are less financially apparent than those designed to generate income or improve productivity, but they are just as necessary to the long-term performance of the hotel. Without good service and satisfied customers the hotel will ultimately fail. In the short term, well managed service encounters also make the hotel a pleasant place to work for everyone concerned and will contribute marginally to the income derived from ancillary services as described in the previous chapter.

SERVICE AS A KEY RESULT AREA

Due to the intangible nature of the social contact involved in the service encounter, it is difficult to define in concrete terms the results that would be expected in this area. By looking in more detail, however, at the parties involved in the encounter it is possible to identify their own particular requirements which should lead to a stricter definition of a successful service experience.

- *The customer.* A customer taking part in a service encounter has two major expectations. First, the activities involved in satisfying the need for the interaction must be accomplished successfully. If a guest wants to exchange foreign currency at a reception desk, achieving a successful exchange of pesetas into pounds sterling in terms of accuracy and speed will be of paramount importance. Secondly, the guest wants to be treated in an appropriate manner.

- *The service provider.* The employee of the service firm engages in service encounters for a large part of the working day and these interactions are central to the employee's self-perception. Most front-of-house employees want to feel that they do their jobs successfully and have selected their career fully aware of, or indeed because of the fact, that their work will bring them into contact with people. They want to provide the right service for the guest. This in turn will involve two elements: the successful completion of the task and satisfying these interpersonal needs through interactions.

- *The organisation.* The organisation has three requirements: first, that all customers should be satisfied with the service they receive; secondly, that the employees are satisfied with the work that they do; and thirdly, that the service has been successful to the organisation in terms of increasing sales, increasing profitability or maintaining competitive advantage.

This analysis stresses the complex nature of the service encounter and the variety of expectations that are attached to providing a successful service. In simple terms this complexity can be reduced to two major dimensions:[1] the procedural dimension involved in the technical aspects of delivering the service to the customer, and the convivial dimension involved in how well the server relates to the customer as a person, establishes rapport with him or her and meets their interpersonal needs. The procedural dimension is therefore concerned with such aspects as the flow of service, its timing, how well the customer's individual requirements can be met, anticipation, communication, customer feedback and effective supervision and monitoring. The convivial dimension is concerned with the server's attitude and approach, body language, tone of voice, tact, attentiveness, guidance, the use of names and the server's ability to sort out customers' problems or complaints.

MANAGING THE SERVICE ENCOUNTER

As the results of the service encounter are of fundamental importance to the success of the hotel operation as a whole, the manager needs to take a proactive approach to controlling the encounter. It is not feasible or desirable for the manager to be present at every single such interaction, but that does not mean to say that the same sort of influence over behaviour cannot be attempted as achieved by training staff in technical skills such as bedmaking or serving drinks.

The influence that the manager has on service interaction is illustrated in figure 7.2. This figure provides the framework for analysing and discussing the effective manage-

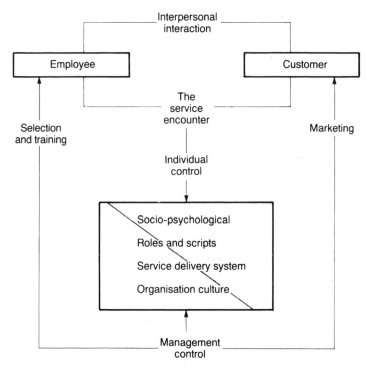

Figure 7.2 *A model of management influence on service.*

ment of service followed in this chapter. It illustrates that management's *direct* control on the interaction is small, i.e. largely through the selection and training of employees and through marketing to customers, relative to the level of control the participants themselves have over the interaction. The manager does have influence over the role employees play, the scripts they use, the design of the service delivery system, and the organisational culture, which *indirectly* affect control over each interaction the employee is engaged in. The model suggests that the level of influence by the manager is greater over culture and system design than over those relating to interpersonal and socio-psychological factors.

THE MEETING OF INDIVIDUALS

At a basic level of analysis the service encounter is an interaction between two individuals, a dyadic interaction, and will therefore follow the normal pattern for such occasions. This pattern will normally consist of a number of stimulus response exchanges. This interaction process involves the reception and interpretation of perceptual clues, the making of appropriate responses both verbally and non-verbally and the opportunity to give feedback and take remedial or responsive action. Each individual will have his or her own personal characteristics and perceptions of the other individual, his or her own motivations and level of social competence. The circumstances will have an effect in terms of the time the interaction occurs, its location, method of conduct, the nature of the participants and the reason for the encounter.

There has been a tendency in the hotel industry to consider only the service provider's side of the encounter and to stress the importance of developing employees' social skills through training, role play exercises and so on. The service encounter must, however, involve the customer as well. It is the interaction of two persons which depends in the first instance upon the social, economic and personal characteristics of them both. In any interpersonal situation, the personal characteristics of the individuals will make a significant impact on the exchange. The individual personality or temperament – both of the employee and the customer – will be relevant as will their general level of intelligence. It has been found,[2] however, that people can behave socially in quite different ways depending on the situation they find themselves in. In one situation a person may be shy and retiring but in another they may be dominant and outgoing. People on holiday staying in a hotel may well display different behaviour patterns than if they were staying in the same hotel on business. In fact some hotels have encountered problems of this kind when encouraging their business clients to return with their wives for weekend breaks. The customer has been dissatisfied with the weekend package primarily because their own requirements have changed but the service offered by the hotel has not. When registering on business the customer may want fast, efficient service with the minimum of fuss and interference – the customer as the dominant element. When staying on pleasure, however, the customer may want a lot more attention, to be looked after – a much more submissive approach.

There are, however, certain characteristics which do seem to persist from one interaction to another. These include a person's need for dominance or dependence, their need for warmth or aggression in encounters, their extroversion or introversion, stability or neuroticism, their overall way of looking at the world, their social and cultural background and their self-image or self-esteem. The conclusion to be drawn here would be to suggest that, although a person's behaviour may not be as predictable from one situation to another as we might expect, there is a stable core from which we could expect a range of similar behaviour patterns to be drawn. Similarly, although we can through training encourage an individual to display certain behaviours in a service encounter, they will not be sustained consistently in the long term if they do not fit into the individual's psychological make-up. This has obvious implications for the recruitment and selection process.

A second feature which will affect the interaction of the customer and the employee is their perception of the other's status, personality, age and so on. Just as the customer's perception of the employee will be influenced by their personal appearance, their uniform, the customer's expectations and the surroundings they are in, so the employee will form rapid, largely automatic, judgements about the customer. The placing of customers into clearly defined types – known as stereotyping – can mean that an employee will adopt an approach to a customer who they have placed in a particular group that is not wholly appropriate. One feature which British Airways discovered when they were researching the performance of their ground crew in providing guest service was a strong tendency to stereotype all customers within seconds of the encounter starting. Once established this stereotype was very hard to break and resulted in many poor service encounters. Part of British Airways' very successful 'Putting People First' campaign has been to reduce the level of stereotyping so that customers are seen more as individuals and are given a service more directly suited to their needs.

Just as some people are more skilled in manipulative motor skills such as driving a car or chopping vegetables, so different levels of competence in social skills can be identified. The interaction between two socially skilled people will be very different from that between two socially less competent people. Although it is difficult for us to affect the social competence of our customers, it is possible to develop the social competence of our staff through training and experience. It is also possible to develop their awareness of customer's social skills and so adapt their approach accordingly.

A further characteristic worth considering is the individual's objectives and needs which are likely to change from situation to situation. A person may be looking for support, protection and guidance, as is the case with new employees during induction or a tired guest arriving at reception. A person may be looking for warmth and friendship and may behave in such a way as to encourage a friendly response. A third identifiable need is for power to control others' behaviour. The need for business customers to have control over the service they receive in a hotel has been identified[3] as an important factor in determining their overall satisfaction with the hotel experience. A fourth need is that for approval, confirming a person's self-image. Other needs such as the sex drive and aggression will be restricted by social taboos but some customers may still attempt to fulfil these needs on hotel employees whom they regard as subordinate.

Most encounters in a hotel will occur in order to carry out a particular task and this task will provide the initial motivation. Once the encounter has started, however, the other motivating forces can be brought into play.

FEATURES OF THE SERVICE ENCOUNTER

The service encounter, however, has a number of special features that characterise this specific form of social interaction,[4] and which modify the four issues relating to dyadic interactions discussed above, i.e. personal characteristics, interpersonal perceptions, social competence, and objectives and needs. Personal characteristics in service encounters are modified by the work environment and the specific roles assigned to participants. Interpersonal perceptions are also modified by these, as well as the suspension of status and the fact that the interaction is usually between strangers. Objectives and needs are modified by the task-based nature of the interaction which means that specific goals have to be achieved through specific functions (as we identified in chapter 4). This emphasises the duality of the service encounter where interpersonal success is combined with getting things done.

What emerges from this analysis of how the service context modifies typical interpersonal encounters (see figure 7.3) is that the social competence of the participants

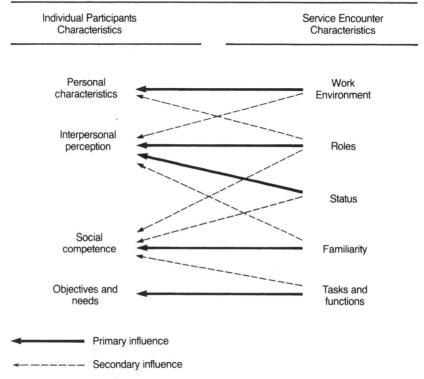

Figure 7.3   *The potential effect of the service encounter on participants.*

remains unaffected by the fact that they are engaged in providing and receiving service. However, due to the often transient nature of the service encounter there is no time for the interpersonal relationship to develop – participants have to 'get it right' first time. This emphasises the importance of social competence.

Before going on to examine the manager's role and options in managing these circumstances, we shall discuss each of the modifiers identified above in the context of hotel service provision. First, these encounters take place as part of a work environment. This fact is acknowledged by both parties. Although when the hall porter offers to assist a guest with his luggage he is providing a 'helping hand', the customer recognises that this is part of the job he is paid to do and will distinguish it from being assisted with his luggage by a stranger on a train. The second modifier is that the roles adopted by the participants are well recognised and understood. Hotel receptionists are expected to welcome customers with a friendly smile and to carry out their specific administrative duties efficiently.

As well as modifying personal characteristics, the work environment and roles will affect interpersonal perceptions. In addition, in any service encounter there may be a temporary suspension of the status enjoyed by the parties concerned. In a hotel situation every guest must be treated as the more important of the two participants in the service encounter. Deference is part of the service provider's role. Fourthly, the nature of these encounters is usually the meeting of two strangers but a customer is more likely to disclose information of a personal nature to a service employee than to any other stranger. For instance, the barman in a hotel is regularly the person that customers will confide in.

With regard to objectives and needs, service encounters have specific goals which need to be achieved and of which both parties are aware. In a hotel, for example, upon arrival both the customer and the receptionist are aware that a registration form of some sort must be completed, a room allocated and the key handed over. The activities undertaken during the exchange between the two parties is focused on a specific function and is restricted by the nature and content of the service to be delivered. The content of the interaction is likely to remain closely related to the task in hand. The type of information exchanged during the encounter will also be predominantly concerned with the task in hand.

In a hotel this can present a somewhat confused picture since a hotel guest will exchange task-specific information with service providers, such as asking for a drink, but they will also chat with hotel staff about apparently non-task related topics. This apparently social chat is in fact more task-related than at first appears as it is the function of the hotel to make the customer feel secure and comfortable.This type of interaction is therefore in this sense fulfilling a task-related role.

SOCIO-PSYCHOLOGICAL FRAMEWORK

So far in this chapter we have considered the service encounter from the perspective of the meeting of individuals, and have stressed the factors involved in the differences between individuals which make interaction so difficult to predict and therefore to manage. We shall now consider the first of the four indirect controls managers have over the service provision as identified in figure 7.1. The perspective of social psychology is not so much on the differences between individuals but rather on the nature of the interaction itself, between people and their environments and the sharing of this behaviour and experience.

The focus of attention from this standpoint is that social interaction involves a form of exchange and that it is from the interdependence of the parties that satisfaction with the encounter is derived. Exchange theory as proposed by Homans[5] suggests that all social action involves both cost and benefit for the individual, who will, in any social situation, look to maximising the benefits and minimising the costs. In a service encounter the benefits may include receiving the required products and services, financial gain or attention or status, but may involve the costs of effort, financial expenditure, stress, inconvenience, discomfort or embarrassment. The achievement of maximum benefit and minimum cost is dependent on the response of the other party – the behaviour of one party will have an immediate effect on the behaviour of the other party. The overall character of the interaction is governed by the mutual responses of the individuals.

In an ideal situation the behaviour of one individual would result in the mutual satisfaction of both parties – the desired outcomes of both parties would correspond. The opposite situation is where the interests of one party are totally at odds with the interests of the other. Friends meeting for a social evening out would be an example of the first situation, and a negotiation between unions and management over an industrial dispute an example of the second. Between these two extremes, there is a range of situations where some interests correspond and others are in conflict. This is typical of the service encounter where, for instance, the service provider is trying to get the customer to spend as much money as possible by offering additional services or products but the customer, although interested in having the 'extras', is also concerned to stay within budget. The interaction can be seen therefore as a delicate balance between conflict and co-operation which will proceed smoothly as long as the behaviour of one party is recognised as 'acceptable' – within the range of behaviours the other would normally expect in this situation. If for some reason one party behaves in an 'unacceptable' fashion then the other will become defensive and resort to safer but potentially less satisfying behaviour.

This interdependence approach to looking at interpersonal interaction starts from the premise that both parties are equal and have the same degree of control over the encounter. In the service situation, however, there are a number of ways in which one party has more influence on or control over the encounter than the other.

Status

The balance of status in the service encounter is almost always in favour of the guest. Service providers are always expected to smile at guests and treat them courteously. They are expected to pay particular attention to their appearance. And the guest is in control not only of the right to begin and end the interaction but also the direction and nature of the interaction. It is a 'natural' part of taking a job in the hotel and catering industry that you occupy a low status position where the customer is always right.

The effects of this status differential are a little more difficult to determine. The obvious situation would be that this relative deprivation of the service provider would result in a feeling of hostility to the guest and the greater the status difference the greater the hostility. Shamir,[6] however, argues that the conflict is due to the natural ignominy of the service position being at odds with an individual's self-esteem and therefore that there will be less conflict if the guest can be seen to be of a much higher status than the service provider. In fact some service personnel get very positive feelings from serving customers they see as being high status.

Culture

Hotels are places where people from a wide variety of cultural backgrounds meet. They are places where guests are having to cope with unfamiliar surroundings, unfamiliar customs and procedures and perhaps an unfamiliar language. These guests are subject to considerable stress and anxiety as they struggle to make sense of the environment around them. The service provider has to cope with a stressed and anxious guest, and may indeed be having to cope with similar cultural difficulties himself.

Territory

It is quite common for employees to become attached to their place of work and regard it as part of their 'territory', feeling stress when other people enter that space.

Chambermaids often complain about guests who enter *their* rooms and get them dirty. It is also quite natural for a customer who has paid for a room for the night to regard that room as part of their territory and feel upset if others, such as the chambermaid, try to invade it. The guest is even provided with 'Do Not Disturb' notices to stop this invasion!

Role ambiguity

Using a theatrical metaphor, both the customer and the service provider are playing roles; just as actors who do not know their lines can upset a theatrical performance, so customers or staff who do not know the script can upset the service performance. This is particularly true of players who are new to the scene. The new employee who has not worked at this establishment before or may not have done this sort of work before and to whom the task has not been properly explained will suffer from this type of role ambiguity.

Similarly, a guest who has not stayed at your establishment before will be unaware of how they are expected to behave. For example, a guest arriving to check in at the Inn on the Park for the first time may be unaware that registration is carried out at the tables in the lounge area of the foyer and spend a considerable period of time wandering around looking for the reception desk. This ambiguity can result in considerable stress and embarrassment.

ROLES AND SCRIPTS

The second area of potential management influence is the application of role and script theory to the service encounter. A role can be defined as the pattern of behaviour typical of or expected of people in a particular position. The effective and productive operation of most business activities, including hotels, depends on the breakdown of the total activity of the business into specialised and discrete tasks assigned to individuals or groups of employees. This specialisation enables workers to become skilled and proficient through training and practice, and thereby improve the economic operation of the business. Following on from the creation of specialised jobs, specific employees are expected to perform specific tasks in specific ways. These expectations arise not only from management who originally defined the jobs, but also from colleagues and from customers.

All these expectations come together to define the specific role of the employee, which will in turn determine that person's behaviour. Part of this behaviour will relate to the interpersonal interaction of the service encounter. For some hotel jobs, customer contact and interaction is limited, as in the kitchen or housekeeping. For other hotel employees, it is a major part of the job to interact with customers, such as in the hotel's front office or restaurant. These high customer contact positions are known as boundary roles and are subject to particular stresses. Before attempting to manage interpersonal interactions, management must ensure these boundary role stresses are minimised.

Boundary role positions suffer from five types of role stress, in addition to the role ambiguity previously mentioned. First, they are subject to *role conflict*. This conflict arises because the role occupant or employee has expectations imposed on him or her from both inside the organisation and outside it. These may be contradictory. For instance, a chance hotel customer may resent having to pay in advance, but this is almost certainly likely to be company policy. Conflict arises from the receptionist's dual role of 'welcomer' and 'cashier'. Often, such conflict is derived from the failure of management to match policy with customer needs and expectations or the failure to communicate these expectations to the employee. The customer's dissatisfaction with the policy is directed at the employee, who has little room for manoeuvre.

Secondly, boundary role stress can be derived from *inter-client conflict*. In this situation, an employee is faced with two or more customers requesting or demanding different things. This may be due to customers' different time dimensions, some requiring speedier service than others, or social dimensions, some requiring more personal attention than others.

A third problem is *role overload*. This is caused by employees having too many things to do at once. A frequent cause of this type of stress in hotel reception is from the dilemma posed by the telephone ringing at the same time as a guest comes to the counter. More and more hotels are separating the administrative, non-contact roles of the receptionist from the interactive contact roles, to ensure that guest contact staff can concentrate just on this role without interruption.

Role incompatibility refers to the stress that may be caused by placing a person in a role for which they are unsuited. This may arise where the role of the person has changed and hence modified the extent to which the employee is brought into contact with customers. For instance, the introduction of carvery and buffet services in restaurants has increased the frequency of contact between kitchen personnel and customers. Such staff, unused and untrained in this type of activity, may be stressed by the situation.

Finally, there is *multiple-role conflict* which is caused by staff having to switch between roles, as behaviours which are suitable for one role may become unsuitable for another. Stress is caused by confusion and uncertainty about which role to adopt. In a study conducted by Voss in 1984,[7] he identified that receptionists in general performed eight major roles. Of these he identified six which he thought were applicable to the hotel receptionist:

1. *the contact role* – coming into direct and frequent contact with customers either on the telephone or face to face;

2. *the filter role* – providing a filter during the initial contact with the customer to establish the exact nature of the encounter and therefore the best person to deal with it;

3. *the scheduling role* – scheduling the customers to match the hotel capacity available;

4. *the selling role* – the promotion of other hotel services and amenities;

5. *the control information role* – the collection and preparation of information in a central point to facilitate management control;

6. *the invoicing role* – preparing final bills and invoices for the customer.

It was suggested that hotel receptionists are not involved in the other two roles:

7. *of diagnosis* – making an initial diagnosis of the customer's problem or requirements;

8. *of despatch* – the allocation of the required resources to deal with the customers request.

It is easy to see, however, that hotel receptionists *are* involved in diagnosing the customers' problems whether that is following a request for information or dealing with an advance reservation, and also in the despatch of resources such as the allocation of rooms during check-in. It is possible, then, that hotel receptionists need to play all eight roles at various times during a normal working day.

The responses of employees to role stress can take several forms.[8] These include avoidance of contact, psychological withdrawal and automatic behaviour, overacting, educating the customer, and controlling the interaction. The manager must be aware of these symptoms in order to be able to identify the possible cause of the stress that is causing this undesirable behaviour.

Contact avoidance can range from lack of eye contact whilst talking to a customer to ignoring a customer completely. Withdrawal and overacting are two opposite extremes of behaviour, the former involving the employee 'switching off' and responding to the situation with the minimum automatic behaviour acceptable, and the latter being exemplified by employees behaving over expressively in an effort to conceal their true feelings. Withdrawal tends to occur when contact staff wish to distance themselves from customers, whereas overacting tends to occur when staff wish to reduce the disparity of status between themselves and their customers.

Educating the customer is usually evidenced by staff informing customers of rules and regulations about the interaction imposed on the staff member by the organisation. The customer does not need to know of such 'rules' but the employee hopes to ensure compliance and reduce conflict from the customer. Finally, there are a wide variety of options staff may adopt in an effort to control the interaction and remove the initiative from the customer. For instance, cabin personnel on airlines may leave the seat belt sign switched on longer than necessary in order to confine customers to their seats in order to make trolley service easier.

Since these behaviours are not desirable, the manager can adopt the standard responses to staff performance failure. These are:

- to define more carefully the job staff are expected to do;
- to design the job to make compliance more likely;
- to train existing staff more effectively in their jobs;
- to take care in selecting the right sort of staff for their intended positions.

In some situations it may be easier to change the customer's expectations of the service they will receive than it is to change the employee's.

Such responses may be required in the context of service provision, but there is an additional strategy that builds on the recognition of the participation in the encounter by the customer as well as the employee. This extra strategy is based around the idea of 'script theory'. Most if not all interactions between customers and employees will involve verbal communication, such communication naturally emerging from the context in which the exchange takes place. These exchanges tend to result in the natural emergence of key words and phrases recognised and used by both participants. These words and phrases form patterns that are repeated and hence provide a framework for the development of a specified script for both participants to follow. For instance, it is quite usual for telephonists to be trained to respond to callers in a quite specific way. The Holiday Inn standard response is 'Thank you for calling the Holiday Inn, Place name. How may I help you?'

The hotel manager is faced with a choice between two broad alternatives. The first is to be prescriptive and define exactly what the script should be and how staff should present it to the customer. A well written script will be designed in such a way as to elicit precise and appropriate responses from the customer. In the hospitality industry, the best example of this is in the fast-food sector where counter personnel are trained to make specific statements and ask specific questions throughout the entire service encounter.

The second alternative is to allow service provision staff to use their own words and phrases within the context of the particular situation. To overcome possible communication problems and role stress, staff may be trained in communication and interpersonal skills. One particular technique which was tried out by British Transport Hotels in the 1970s was transactional analysis.[9] This technique attempts to explain to service employees why people behave in the way they do and enables them to interact more effectively. Another technique used by the Carlton Tower Hotel in the late 1960s was T groups, where staff are sensitised to customers' attitudes and feelings through the discussion and analysis of their own behaviours.

Between these two extreme options it is possible to specify a script which incorporates a choice of alternative statements from which the employee can choose. For instance in the Disney organisation, employees are selected for the *roles* they are to play at *auditions*, not at interviews, and they are provided with their scripts with a small number of possible deviations. Once they are *on stage* they are always expected to respond in role and follow their selected variation of the script.

The basis for choosing between these two broad alternatives will depend on a range of factors, notably the social competence of the personnel and the nature and context of the interaction. Prescribed and detailed scripts are most appropriate when staff have low social competence, speed is an important part of the customers' expectations, the exchange needs to be accurate, and customers seek a secure and reliable interaction. In the hotel context possible interactions of this kind could take place when making a room reservation, when checking in to the hotel and when checking out of it.

The increasing sophistication of information technology and the increasing acceptance by customers of such technology does potentially enable the removal of the service provider from this interaction altogether. The automatic bank teller machines are an excellent illustration of this. Already in large American hotels it is possible for a customer to check out of his room by using a keyboard linking the hotel computer to the bedroom's television set. By keying in the appropriate number the customer's bill is displayed, and by keying a second number this can be charged to the customer's account or credit card.

Personalised scripts are most appropriate in situations where there is a complex exchange between the provider and the customer, where customers seek individuality, and where staff are socially competent. Such an approach is particularly appropriate in circumstances where the customer is seeking information or is unaware of or unable to articulate his specific needs. For instance, a customer asking a porter to recommend a theatre that he would enjoy visiting.

Both approaches have potential pitfalls. The prescriptive approach may increase the likelihood of staff switching off and adopting an automatic mode of behaviour. This may give the customer the impression of an uncaring and insincere level of service, exacerbated by the fact that the non-verbal signals transmitted by the employee, showing this uncaring attitude, are likely to swamp out the warm and caring scripted verbal message which is being transmitted. The employee is also ill-equipped to cope with service encounters where the customer deviates from the expected responses. This leads to the usual response from the service employee of 'I'm not sure I'll have to ask the manager.' The personalised approach, on the other hand, has the danger that the staff's lack of competence or experience can lead to poorer levels of service than the hotel would like to provide, as well as lead to higher levels of role stress.

SERVICE DELIVERY SYSTEMS

Given the nature of the hotel service with a large number of intangible components to the product and the reasonably high element of customer/server interaction, it is natural that the customer's perception of the hotel product will be strongly influenced by the nature of the service encounters experienced. Indeed the process of the service encounter is a major part of the total product. It follows therefore that it should be possible to influence the nature of the service interaction by affecting the design of the process – the service delivery system.

Attempts have been made to analyse service processes using adapted manufacturing process techniques.[10] This technique of service 'blueprinting' breaks the process down into a series of interconnected steps and identifies the points at which it is possible to offer options in the system. A guest making a reservation, for instance, reaches a point at which a number of different room types or tariff types representing different options in the service may be offered. From this sort of analysis it is possible to identify two major dimensions of service processes: their complexity, and their variability or 'executional latitude'. Complexity refers to the number and intricacy of the steps required to perform the service process, whereas variability is the amount of freedom allowed or the range of service options available at each step in the process.

It is possible then to design a service delivery system which is either more or less complex or allows more or less variability. Increasing the complexity of the hotel service would involve offering additional services or enhancing existing facilities, so increasing the number of steps the customer passes through. The addition of leisure complexes to hotels provides a good example of an attempt to increase the complexity of the operation. Reducing the complexity of the operation would involve a narrowing of the service offered, stripping the service down to a minimum. It could be argued that apartment hotels and all-suite hotels are examples of reducing the complexity. Increasing the variability of the service involves giving the guest wider ranges or service options, providing greater customisation and flexibility. An example here would be the provision of executive floors with separate registration and check-out points offering a wider range of guest services. Reducing the variability is concerned with offering a uniform standardised product of reliable service quality but with very few, if any, options. The development of budget hotels such as Little Chef Lodges provides evidence of this sort of process.

The implications of this analysis are that the service interaction should be designed to fit the complexity and variability of the service process, and that managers should be aware that if they are attracting different markets requiring different service processes then the service interactions will also need to be altered. A service process with low guest server contact offering a largely standardised product can be managed in a largely mechanistic way using standard operating procedures, rules and regulations. This technique could not work, however, in a system offering high guest contact and a large range of options, where employee self-management and peer referencing techniques are more appropriate.

In addition to the nature of the process, service encounters do not take place in a vacuum. The design of the unit, the nature of the physical environment, the availabiltiy of plant and equipment and the procedural requirements of the operation will all affect the quality of the service provision. Service encounters have three main elements relating to communication, social interaction and task achievement.

Communication can be either verbal or non-verbal. Verbal communication can be facilitated or enhanced by the service delivery system ensuring that the environment is conducive to information exchange. Attention should therefore be paid to the prevention of extraneous noise, the efficacy of equipment such as telephones and public address systems, and to the comfort of the environment within which the communication takes place. Often, this type of communication will involve the exchange of information. Service providers can be supported in this exchange by adequate resources such as good signing in the unit, supporting documentation such as maps and plans, speedy information retrieval systems, and the display of information such as those on electronic cash registers in bars or coffee shops.

Non-verbal communication is particularly important in aiding effective social interaction. This too can be supported by physical design such as ensuring staff address customers at the same height to encourage eye contact, locating equipment such as VDUs so that staff do not need to turn their backs on customers, and so on. Social interaction in the hotel reception area was improved by Trusthouse Forte by the replacing of the typical reception counter with a low pedestal desk at which both the receptionist and the customer could sit. Ironically, this innovation was discontinued because the introduction of computerised front-office systems demanded too much space for the component items of equipment than such a desk could provide.

Social interaction can also be supported by providing for the physiological and psychological comfort of the employee. Aspects of this would include the provision of clean and comfortable facilities for staff to change in so that they can present themselves in the best possible way, and the provision of practical and flattering uniforms. There is also the ubiquitous practice of expecting staff to wear name badges in the belief that social interaction between staff and customers is enhanced. Little or no reliable research has investigated the extent to which this is true. It can be argued that some staff feel threatened by this disclosure and resent being addressed by customers on a personal basis, especially when they cannot respond in a similar way. This practice increases the status differential between the two parties.

Finally, service encounters predominantly involve getting something done and this is made easier and more efficient if the correct tools, equipment and layout are available.

ORGANISATIONAL CULTURE

The final influence on the service encounter, which of all four, management has the most control, is organisational culture. The culture of an organisation refers to the underlying attitudes and beliefs held by managers and employees. Culture has been analysed in a variety of ways and is also referred to as climate or social architecture. Whilst there are subtle differences of interpretation between these terms,[11] for our purposes it is sufficient to use the term culture in discussing the impact informal attitudes and beliefs have on effective service provision. These attitudes and beliefs are shaped by the rationale for the existence of the organisation, its history, the influence of key organisational members, notably the founders and senior executives, the size of the organisation, and the degree of stability in the organisation's environment. For instance, the Marriott Corporation has undoubtedly been affected by the fact that the Marriott family are Mormons.

Definitions of the culture of an organisation range from the formal dictionary definition (i.e. 'the integrated pattern of human behaviour that includes thought, speech, action and artifacts and depends on man's capacity for learning and transmitting knowledge to succeeding generations') to the informal description of 'the way we do things round here'. Every organisation has some form of culture and this may be more or less strongly expressed. In some organisations it is very difficult to identify a coherent culture, whereas in others there is a very strong sense of culture with all employees knowing the goals of the organisation and working toward them. Whether weak or strong, culture has tangible effects through a strong influence on who gets promoted, what clothes people wear, what decisions are made and ultimately the success of the business.

The main elements of any corporate culture are its values, its heroes, its rites and rituals and its cultural network. *Values* are the basis of the corporate culture; they provide a sense of common direction for all employees and guide their day-to-day behaviour. Values define the character of the organisation and create a sense of identity for people throughout the company. They are closely linked to the way the company aims to achieve success in response to the business environment it operates in and are frequently expressed in slogan-like phrases. For instance, McDonald's has a very strong culture based on the idea of QSCV – Quality, Service, Convenience and Value – developed through intensive induction and training programmes for franchisees and supported by inspections and competitions to find out who best reaches the McDonald's standard.

This identification of people who best fit corporate values leads to the development of corporate *heroes* – people who have been successful by sticking to corporate values. They provide a role model for other members of the organisation and at the same time illustrate that success lies within the grasp of all employees. They can become symbols of the company to the outside world and can come to represent what makes this company special, setting the ideal standard of performance and motivating employees.

The motivational force of corporate culture is reinforced through *rites and rituals* which seek to communicate to employees what they are expected to do and the way they are expected to do it. They set out standards of behaviour, they call attention to the way in which procedures are to be carried out and they provide opportunities for the organisation to let off steam through organised events.

The *cultural network* is the informal organisation through which much of the communication of the culture takes place. It is the hidden hierarchy which ties together all parts of the company irrespective of titles or level. One aspect that all studies of organisational culture stress is the central importance to the success of the company of the people of the organisation and the need to build a culture which takes these people into account.

Not all organisations can or indeed should develop the same type of culture. They should develop the culture which is appropriate to the business environment within which the company operates and which matches to its overall values. It is possible to break organisational cultures down into four main types: power, task, role and person.[12] In some industries, and for some organisations, there is a clear fit between the 'model' culture and the actual organisation.

A *power culture* is based around the founder/chief executive of the organisation holding a highly significant and influential position. A *task culture* focuses the attention of the organisational members on the purpose and activities inherent in the organisation. A *role culture* is based around the roles that individuals play in the organisation. Such a culture has the structure of a typical bureaucracy. Finally, the *person culture* is typically found in academic circles and the professions as it is based around the needs and wants of the participants.

In the hotel industry, there is no clear relationship between hotel organisations and any one of these culture types, National Health Service hospitals, because they operate within the public sector, tend towards role-type cultures. Organisations with strong chief executives, such as the Forte family in THF and Cyril Stein in Ladbrokes, it might be argued, have power-type cultures. However, in general terms, it would seem that, traditionally, task-type cultures would be the most appropriate for hotel operations to have, but this may not be the most suitable for the development of an appropriate level of service.

Harrison[13] has proposed that within each of these four cultures there is a distinctive service style, which is a separate issue from whether the organisation provides good service or bad. One organisation may provide a highly efficient but impersonal service, which is not necessarily any worse than the organisation that provides a relaxed and friendly service.

In a *power culture* the style of service emphasises status and prestige. This leads to differentiation in grades of service to different types of customer. This sort of approach can be found in many independent hotels and restaurants, particularly serving a high-class or wealthy clientele. If there is a strong focus of power in the organisation who takes a direct interest in the standard of service then this will become an important and central issue. For instance, the late J. W. Marriott is said to have read every customer complaint letter personally and frequently made surprise tours of inspection at 4 o'clock in the morning. If these chief executives within power cultures act in a strong and benevolent manner then the quality of service is likely to reflect that benevolence. This is most likely to be the case in small, owner-managed operations and will be good for business. However, as many power cultures rely on fear as a motivational force this can lead to a very servile approach to service, where service personnel dare not step outside the expected laid-down standards.

The typical *task culture* has a service style associated with getting the job done and a sense of achievement. It concentrates on the 'doing', where the customer becomes the 'target' of the service. Thus customers rely on the service provider's expertise and desire to do the job 'correctly'. This orientation is dedicated to excellence, innovation and professional standards, which may well be above those expected by the customer. If this type of organisation sees service as central to its mission, it will make every effort to achieve the highest possible standards.

The style of service typically found in a *role culture* revolves around the organisation's preoccupation with systems, efficiency and profitability. Service style will therefore provide an efficient service for the typical customer, with a high degree of standardisation. Customers see these organisations as offering predictable standards at a reasonable cost, but little warmth. As customer needs have over recent years become increasingly complex, more differentiated and less predicatable systems have had to be designed which can cope with providing a range of options. But this increased complexity of operation has reduced the reliability of the service provision. Employees in a role culture therefore tend to respond in seemingly rigid and uncaring ways because they are controlled by organisational policies. This can cause dissatisfaction for the employee who joins the organisation in order to provide customer care, but finds the ability to do so constrained by rules and regulations. Attempts to improve service standards in this culture will concentrate on training and close supervision, on the assumption that the employees need changing not the system.

The *person culture* exists to provide support for and to satisfy the individual needs of its members. This type of organisation has no superordinate goals – it has no organisational objectives, only the collective objectives of its members. It has little structure and control mechanisms are only possible by the mutual consent of all the members. It is therefore difficult to find examples of this type of culture in the purely commercial field, although there are examples of hotels working as co-operatives and Israel has a number of kibbutz hotels run as part of the normal kibbutz operations. If a person culture were to be centred around the concept of providing service it would be expected to emphasise values of co-operation, caring, belonging and responding. The service style would be to listen to customer needs, understand them and respond to customer concerns, with a feeling of teamwork and mutual support. In this situation the emphasis is not on designing efficient systems, and consequently service delivery can go wrong. But if it docs, there will always be a sympathetic person who will listen to the customer's problems and concerns and will attempt to put things right.

Case example 7.1   British Airways

A recent example of the management of culture to effect a major change in the level of service provided has been carried out by British Airways. In 1978 British Airways were suffering from overmanning, fierce competition and rocketing fuel prices. Staff throughout the company seemed to be generally detached from this reality, although a major cost cutting exercise reduced staffing levels dramatically – from 60,000 to 35,000 in five years – and brought home the serious nature of the problem.

In 1983 Colin Marshall was appointed Chief Executive. With his experience of service industries, he identified the meeting of customer needs as the key area requiring radical change and instigated a programme to improve awareness and implement an effective strategy.

The first phase of this programme was a market research survey amongst air travellers with BA and other airlines to identify BA's image. BA emerged as aloof, detached, not caring, not friendly, but technically competent, showing British cool and having an ability to cope with crises.

The second phase was an internal research project with customer contact staff to find out their views of customers. The major result of this survey was to identify a strong tendency to jump very quickly to stereotypes and deal with the stereotype and not the individual.

This research resulted in the development of a three-phase programme – the 'Putting the People First Campaign' designed to bring about a new orientation for customer contact staff.

1. *PPFI: The Putting the People First Event.* This was a two-day event organised by an outside consultant – Time Manager International – run for approximately 170 people at a time from a range of customer contact positions. This event, with lots of AVA and theatrical effects, attempted to cover basic personal development relating to handling feelings, handling the first four minutes of an encounter, coping with stress, self-preservation techniques, and so on. This programme ran day in, day out for two years covering some 23,000 employees.

2. *The initiation and support of 'Customer First Teams'.* A sort of quality circle,

these teams comprised volunteers looking for ways to improve the customer service experience in their particular work area. This has produced not only some significant suggestions for improvements which have since been implemented company-wide but also a feeling that staff have some measure of control over the service experience they deliver.

3. *The 'Customer First' training review.* Having attempted to develop customer contact staff awareness of customer service it was then necessary to review all other training programmes and incorporate this new approach. In some instances this involved rewriting small sections; in the case of cabin crew it involved the complete redesign of the *ab initio* training programme.

This original initiative has been supported by further programmes. PPF2 was a one-day event similar to PPF1 but for support staff, e.g. in engineering and finance. This attempted to show support staff the importance of customer contact even though they may not have direct contact other than through colleagues who they may deal with during their working day. *All* BA staff have now been through this programme. PPF3, which completed its run in December 1986, was an internal exhibition put on by the various departments within the company to show the rest of the company what that particular section does all day – the title of the session was indeed 'A day in the life'. This followed a desire expressed in PPF1 and 2 to find out more about what everybody else did.

The programme was also supported by a number of management initiatives. Perhaps the most significant of these was the establishment of a 'Customer Service Department', comprising a small team whose job it was to monitor market research reports, talk to customers and staff, etc. This department has grown in significance and has helped to produce Customer Service Standards and a Service Quality Audit. It has now become one of the seven major departments in the marketing sector of the company with *line management* responsibility for all customer contact staff (excluding cabin crew).

It was realised during the implementation of the PPF programme that a somewhat larger change in management style and overall organisational culture was essential if the aims of the PPFC were to be achieved over the long term. No amount of training and exhortation of customer contact staff would bring long-term results if the management style of the company did not reflect the PPF approach. This resulted in the 'Managing People First' programme – again with a three-phase approach:

1. Research was carried out amongst BA's top managers to elicit their views as to how a BA manager should manage, what they considered to be important and where they saw the gaps. This resulted in the identification of five areas: Trust, Teamwork, Taking responsibility, Clarity of vision and Motivation. These five elements were built into a five-day residential programme which concentrated on the approach, the 'right things to do' not the 'how to do it's.

2. A series of training courses on adopting the appropriate management style already identified.

3. The tying in of rewards to management performance related to the identified ideals set by BA. This procedure, which is in an early stage of implementation but is gradually spreading through the organisation, is based on regular (three monthly) appraisals against pre-identified criteria. These are then computer processed to obtain an annual report on the individual, which also gives in-

formation as to performance in relation to other managers, and information about the performance of the appraiser in relation to other appraisers. This report then provides the basis for the calculation of a financial bonus.

There are one or two key issues which seem to be raised by this experience. First, a company in the service industry field has realised the importance of the customer service experience to their continued success to the extent that it has become a key corporate value. Secondly, having accepted customer service as a key value it is not simply a matter of training customer service personnel in customer contact skills, but it also involves support staff and management, and, indeed, a fundamental change in corporate culture. Improving customer service has repercussions not just for those in direct customer contact but for the whole organisation.

SELECTION, TRAINING AND MARKETING

The two areas over which the manager has direct control that can be used to influence the service encounter are those concerning the selection and training of staff, and the 'selection and training' of customers, otherwise known as marketing.

As mentioned in chapter 4, managers can attempt to influence employee performance in general from a number of approaches – job design, the skills and abilities of individuals, and their motivation to do the job. Attempts to affect the service performance can follow similar lines, concentrating on the aspects of recruitment and training. Recruitment practices should be aimed at attracting and selecting the right person for service positions; the difficulty is in deciding what the 'right' person is like in more detail than simply being willing and cheerful.

Management must make a conscious effort to find out what sort of service customers want and to develop standards of performance which reflect those expectations. These standards of performance can then be used as the basis for developing personnel specifications and training programmes. The 'right' person for one establishment where customers expect minimum but reliable service may be someone who sticks closely to their given script, but an establishment offering a customised service may be looking for individuals with a strong need for scope in their jobs, who do not wish to be tied down and have a desire to express themselves.

This service-oriented approach to personnel management should be continued through to the induction programme where it may be more appropriate to concentrate first on service skills rather than start straightaway on developing technical knowledge and skills. It should be carried further through into training programmes and into the criteria for appraisal and promotion. The overall organisation of the workplace should aim to produce a satisfying work climate and this can be enhanced by staff giving other departments – internal customers – the same service they would give the guest – the external customer.

Training staff in giving service can follow four basic models. The traditional approach uses the behaviour modelling technique where staff are shown the correct way of dealing with a customer based on previously identified standards. Staff are then encouraged to adopt this way through the use of role play exercises, video replay, and so on. This can be a very effective way of training staff but it does engender a rather rigid approach which may not be suitable to all situations.

The second style is to use a high profile event based on transactional analysis (TA) techniques, as used by British Airways, SAS and Thistle Hotels. This consists of a one- or two-day multi-media event addressed to audiences often involving 100–200 people, which in a very professionsl package introduces participants to 'strokes', 'discounts', assertiveness and stress management. Done well this style generates an enthusiastic response, but because of the short time involved it cannot hope to cover all the complexity of TA and there is doubt as to how long this type of 'hype' will last in the day-to-day reality of the workplace.

A third approach is based on staff involvement and uses the basic idea of a quality circle (see page 161) where staff are encouraged, probably through management guidance or direction, to consider how they can improve the service given to the customer.This approach needs the commitment of both managers and supervisors and the provision of resources by which the ideas generated can be tried out in a practical way. Commonwealth Holiday Inns of Canada in the UK have introduced the idea of 'service chains' of this nature and have identified specialist customer service trainers in various departments through their hotels.

A final style may be to encourage staff to develop their customer service skills by the use of incentive schemes or competitions where they are judged against the previously identified performance standards. This style has been used by a number of the high street banks.

None of the above techniques could be expected to work in isolation. They should be part of an integrated approach to customer service awareness and development.

The concepts of selection and training can be extended to the customer where the marketing strategy of the organisation is used to attract – or select – a certain type of customer to the establishment and advertising and promotional material can be used to give the customer awareness of – or training in – the sort of service to be expected. It is important that the marketing strategy gives the correct impression of the organisation and that advertisements do not make false promises about service standards. A famous example was the case of British Rail which started a series of very well designed national TV adverts stressing the friendliness and helpfulness of British Rail staff. Unfortunately, the training programme which was tied in to the advertising campaign was only one third completed and the advertisements only succeeded in raising customer expectations to a standard that BR could not deliver. Any changes in service standards to systems must be communicated to the customers so that they too understand their role and respond accordingly.

Advertising can be used as an effective means of teaching customers their part of scripts. As discussed earlier, a script includes not just spoken communication, but also actions and behaviour patterns. For instance, many hotels have tried to solve the problem of long queues at morning check-out time by using express check-outs based on pre-completed credit card vouchers. One reason for the poor response to this innovation may be the lack of information provided about the service. Likewise, customers can 'learn scripts' they are not meant to learn through poorly designed advertising. One hotel chain which ran an advertising campaign stressing the individuality of its units, illustrated this with a picture from one of their hotels of a room with a four-poster bed. This generated new custom, but only for that specific room, as well as many requests from regular customers for that specific room. The demand was so great many customers were disappointed and staff became increasingly frustrated at having to deal with enquiries about just this one room.

Just as it is possible to think of marketing as having a personnel-type function with regard to customers, it is also possible to think of personnel managers having a marketing role within the organisation. Berry[14] argues that, as employees are so crucial to the provision of services, the 'philosophy and practices of marketing' should be applied to them as well as customers. It has also been suggested that this concept of *internal marketing* can be thought of as the in-house mirror image of the organisation's external marketing effort. There should be an internally consistent set of the four Ps – Product, Place, Price and Promotion – that match the external set.[15]

A significant example of this is the role of advertising and promotion within the organisation. Employees of an organisation are often just as much an audience for media campaigns and public relations activities as customers. Their perception of their workplace and their role within it will be affected by such exposure. More important-ly, any potential conflict between the image portrayed with actual performance must be avoided. It should be quite usual for staff to be informed and instructed about any procedural dimensions resulting from a marketing initiative. For instance, front-office staff would be told about the level of discount to offer people taking a weekend break offer, as well as any conditions applying to such reservations. But the internal-marketing-oriented organisation will go further than this and develop with staff an understanding of the convivial dimension too (see page 162). The staff will be told about the purpose of the campaign and the expected impact this will have on sales and occupancy. In addition, the implications of the promotion with regards to the type of customer likely to be attracted will be identified, so that staff recognise that they may be required to act differently to bargain-break customers, whose needs may be diffe-rent to those of other customers.

SUMMARY

This chapter has described the nature of customer service from a number of different perspectives to provide an insight into the complexity of the problem facing the manager attempting to manage the service encounter. This chapter began the analysis by looking at the service encounter as the meeting of two individuals and looked at the differences between these individuals and the way this affected the interaction. This, it was seen, was also affected by the specific nature of the service encounter itself. It was then suggested that the encounter should be looked at as one where the actions of one party affected, and were in turn affected by, the actions of the other party – that a successful interaction was based on the interdependence of the customer and the service provider.

The customer and the service provider can be seen as playing out a series of roles which have identifiable scripts, but which are also subject to stress which in turn will affect the success of the interaction. The manager has an increasing role to play in determining the scripts people use. The manager is also able to influence the interac-tion through the design of the service system itself which can reduce or enhance the amount of service the customer is allowed.

It was also shown that the style of service that is provided will reflect the style of the organisation itself – the organisational culture. Managers can attempt to change the service style through changing that organisational culture – or perhaps more likely, that a change in culture will also involve a change in service style.

The topics of selection and training were also discussed as ways in which the mana-ger can not only seek to have a direct influence on the service encounter from the employee side, but also through marketing have some influence on the customer side.

Assuming that the people who are appointed to service positions in the organisation applied for those posts because they like giving service (they would not have been appointed otherwise, surely) and that customers want the 'good' service the employees want to give, then, the only person who can get in the way is the manager. If the manager requires certain (unnecessary) forms to be filled in, certain procedures and rules to be adhered to that may interfere with the natural progress of the service interaction, then they will be creating considerable stress for the employee[16] and for the customer. It does seem that if we want our staff to be enthusiastic about giving service then the manager must also share and take part in that enthusiasm.

REFERENCES

1. Martin, W. B., 'Defining what quality service is for you', *Cornell HRA Quarterly*, pp. 32–38, February 1986.

2. Gergen, K. J., and Marlowe, D. *Personality and Social Behaviour*, Addison Wesley, London, 1970.

3. Nightingale, M. *Determination and control of quality in hospitality services*, MPhil thesis, University of Surrey, 1983.

4. Czepiel, J. A, Solomon, M. R., Surprenant, C. F., and Gutman, E. G., 'Service encounters: an overview', in Czepiel, J. A. *et al.* (eds), *The Service Encounter*, Lexington Books, Massachusetts, 1985.

5. Homans, G., *Sentiments and Activities*, Routledge and Kegan Paul, 1962.

6. Shamir, B., 'Between service and servility: role conflict in subordinate service roles', *Human Relations* vol. 33, no. 10, pp. 741–756, 1980.

7. Voss, C., Armistead, C., Johnston, B., and Morris, B., *Operations Management in Service Industries and the Public Sector*, Wiley, 1985.

8. Shamir, B., *op. cit.*

9. Lockwood, A. J., and Jones, P., *People and the Hotel and Catering Industry*, Holt, Rinehart and Winston (Cassell), 1984.

10. Shostack, G. L., 'Designing services that deliver', *Harvard Business Review* vol. 62, pp. 133–139, January/February 1984.

11. Mill, R. C., *Improving Productivity in the Hospitality Industry*, Van Nostrand Reinhold, 1986.

12. Handy, C. B., *Understanding Organizations*, Penguin, 1981.

13. Harrison, R., *Organisational Culture and Quality of Service*, Association for Management Education and Development, 1987.

14. Berry, L. L., 'Strategic management and marketing in the service sector', in Gronroos, C. (ed.), *Swedish School of Economics and Business Administration Research Reports*, 1982.

15. Jones, P. L. M., 'Internal marketing', *International Journal of Hospitality Management* vol. 5, no. 4, pp. 201–204, 1986.

16. Parkington, J., and Schneider, B., 'Some correlates of experienced job stress: a boundary role study', *Academy of Management Journal* vol. 22, no. 2, pp. 270–281, 1979.

8 Improving Productivity

Figure 8.1 *Secondary key result area: productivity.*

INTRODUCTION

Productivity is becoming a major issue in service industries. In the UK service organisations now employ over 50 per cent of the workforce. Since this sector of industry
has traditionally had relatively low levels of productivity, this has major impllcations
for the national economy. Indeed it has been argued that this is a contributory factor
in causing inflation.[1] Blois[2] argues that this inflationary push and lack of productivity are largely due to labour costs increasing more steeply than prices. Baumol[3] argues
that not all service industries are the same. Some services have been subject to

technological innovations, such as telecommunications, and hence their productivity
has significantly improved. Others, like the hotel business, he describes as 'stagnant
personal services' (stagnant in the sense of no real improvements in productivity)
which are typified by direct contact with consumers and in which quality is closely
related to labour-time expended.

This emphasis on labour and labour costs is typical of most approaches to productivity in service industries. Labour is a large proportion of the total costs of providing a
service and it is perceived as being a variable cost over which management can exert
some control. However, labour is not the only element in the cost structure of the
business.

PRODUCTIVITY – INPUTS AND OUTPUTS

Productivity is usually defined as:

$$\text{Productivity} = \frac{\text{Outputs}}{\text{Inputs}}$$

Input refers to the resources used in making a product or providing a service, whilst
output is the product or service itself. These may be measured in financial terms, i.e.
as costs and revenues, but not necessarily as we shall see.

Early approaches to productivity identified two broad strategies. Firms, particularly
those with high fixed costs, should concentrate on increasing output whilst holding
inputs steady – the so-called 'market-oriented' approach. Alternatively, for those
firms with a high proportion of variable costs, the strategy of 'cost reduction' should

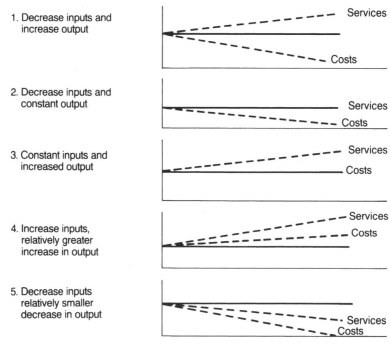

Figure 8.2 *Models of improving productivity.* Reproduced with permission.

be adopted, i.e. hold output steady but reduce costs. But this model of market orientation or cost reduction is too simplistic. There are in fact five ways in which the ratio of inputs to output can be improved, as illustrated in figure 8.2.

Let us consider each of the five possibilities shown in figure 8.2 in turn.

1. *Decrease inputs and increase output.* This option is theoretically possible, but is unlikely to occur very frequently. For the manager it is difficult to forecast how a reduction in input can increase output and difficult to monitor effectively.

2. *Decrease inputs and constant output.* This option identifies circumstances where existing provision is inefficient – that is to say corrective action should be taken by changing the inputs to achieve the same level of output but at lower cost.

3. *Constant inputs and increased output.* This option also implies inefficiency, in that the same inputs could produce more output. Unlike option 2 which looks at the operation's costs, this option suggests a marketing approach.

4. *Increase inputs, relatively greater increase in output.* This too is a market-oriented approach, but one that recognises that the change in output can only be achieved at some extra cost.

5. *Decrease inputs, relatively smaller decrease in output.* This option assumes that a cost reduction exercise will have some impact on output, but that the fall in output will be more than offset by the savings made.

For a hotel manager wishing to improve productivity, the value of these five options is that they provide a clear framework for considering any particular action aimed at affecting productivity. These options help to forecast or predict the likely effect of a change and set criteria for measuring the impact of that change. But putting these ideas into practice in the hotel industry presents some special problems.

PRODUCTIVITY IN THE CONTEXT OF HOTEL OPERATIONS

The definition of productivity as the ratio of inputs to outputs is simple to state but complex to apply in the context of service industries in general, and the hotel industry in particular. There are three main issues.

First, there are a very large number and variety of inputs/outputs that occur in the daily operation of a hotel. It must be remembered that most productivity measurement and productivity improvement programmes have originated in manufacturing industry. In the manufacturing sector, the inputs needed to make a specific item of output, such as the parts needed to make a radio, are relatively easy to identify, measure and account for. This is largely because the product is standardised, so that many hundreds or thousands of identical goods are manufactured. In services and hotels, however, each service transaction with each individual consumer is unique. The transaction may differ only slightly or drastically from one customer to the next. And this difference may be deliberately customised by the service provider in response to customers' needs, or it may occur due to the breakdown of the service transaction (see chapter 7). So the first major issue can be stated as:

Issue 1 **Neither inputs nor outputs are easily standardised**.

The second issue follows on from the first. Many service providers, including hoteliers, attempt to standardise their provision, or at least some parts of it, despite the difficulties. For instance, the decor in hotel rooms may be identical. They do so largely as a response to provide comfort and security by ensuring that there are no surprises for their customers. But whilst customers may find such standardisation non-threatening, this does not mean to say that they all react in exactly the same way to identical inputs. So that in our example, some customers will like the bedroom decor, others will be indifferent, and others will dislike it. This second major issue can be stated as:

Issue 2   **Relationships between inputs and outputs are not constant**.

Finally, in service businesses, both inputs and outputs are made up of tangibles and intangibles. We discussed this in chapter 1 and exemplified it by considering Shostack's model of service provision (see page 9). One of the reasons why it is so difficult to standardise *all* inputs and to guarantee their impact on output is that the intangible components are complex and difficult to control. This intangibility has a further implication, however – it is almost impossible to measure them directly. Indeed an underlying theme of this book has been that hotel management is difficult to provide well largely because so much of the manager's role is concerned with managing intangibles. Thus attempts to measure inputs and outputs for productivity improvement reasons will almost always be difficult and the results are likely to be imprecise. This third issue can be stated as:

Issue 3   **Not all inputs/outputs can be measured accurately**.

Any approach to productivity improvement in the hotel industry must therefore tackle these issues. Flynn[4] has proposed an approach to performance measurement in the public sector that can fruitfully be applied to services in general and hotels in particular. He identifies four components of service provision, and defines them as follows:

1. *Inputs*: physical assets, such as plant and machinery, and labour which are combined in some way to create a series of intermediate output.

2. *Intermediate output*: the capacity to provide the service.

3. *Outputs*: the actual output achieved.

4. *Outcomes*: the impact which the service may have on the consumer.

This model is shown in figure 8.3.

Let us illustrate this with an example. The housekeeping staff service rooms with new linen and so on (inputs). In this way, each day a number of rooms become available for sale (intermediate output). But not all of these rooms are necessarily sold, only a proportion of them (actual output). The hotel's customers that have purchased the room have a wide range of experiences, such as a peaceful night's sleep, comfort, security, and so on (outcomes).

From these four components it is possible to identify where productivity fits in, along with its relationship to capacity management and quality. Productivity is concerned with the *efficient* use of resources. In this approach there are two types of efficiency:

- Efficiency 1 = the ratio of inputs to intermediate output, e.g. the unit cost of providing a room per night.

- Efficiency 2 = the ratio of inputs to output, e.g. the cost of providing rooms in relation to sales generated.

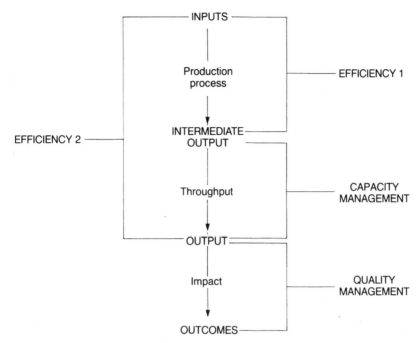

Figure 8.3 *Model of efficiency improvement for the service industry.*

Capacity management is in effect the ratio of intermediate output to actual output. We have considered approaches to making sure that optimum use of the hotel's available space is made in chapter 5. Finally, *quality* is the issue of *effectiveness* in ensuring the output is translated into desirable outcomes.

This chapter is therefore only concerned with *efficiency* and as such concentrates on inputs and intermediate output. This resolves to a great extent the three issues we have previously identified. By eliminating the qualitative, intangible elements and concentrating on inputs defined as assets or labour, we can reasonably standardise both inputs and outputs, expect some sort of constant relationship, and relatively simply measure them. We must not forget *effectiveness*, but we shall deal with this highly complex matter when we consider how the hotel manager should manage quality in the next chapter.

This approach to productivity improvement also fits with our original model of hotel management. In this model, productivity was seen as the management of assets and labour (see figure 8.1). It has been regarded as the making of choices between these two alternative resources to produce the desired output. The customer does not enter into the issue since we are largely concerned with producing intermediate output, which may or may not actually be taken up by customers. So the combination of assets and employees is to do with efficiency. The combination of assets with customers is to do with capacity utilisation, turning intermediate output into actual output. And the combination of employees with customers is to do with effectiveness, helping to turn output into successful outcomes.

So both employees and assets have two roles to play. They must be efficient, by producing output at the lowest possible cost, and they must be effective, in terms of providing customers with the type of experience each one desires.

MEASURES OF PRODUCTIVITY

In the last section we identified two types of efficiency. The value of these two alternative ways of measuring efficiency is that much of the confusion about performance is removed. For instance, a hotel could have a highly efficient housekeeping staff, with high levels of productivity. Using the standard approaches to productivity measurement this might not be very clear because the cost of the housekeeping department would be compared with sales revenue, i.e.

$$\text{Productivity of housekeeping dept.} = \frac{\text{Rooms revenue}}{\text{Housekeeping staffing costs}}$$

But, whilst the rooms division manager may have some control over labour cost, the income generated by the sale of the rooms will depend on the rate at which each room is sold. For instance, the housekeeping department of a 100 room hotel with 100 per cent occupancy at full rack rate will be seen as more productive than the housekeeping department of an identical hotel selling all its rooms at discounted rates.

The above example uses financial measures to identify efficiency 2. But to identify correctly the performance of the two housekeeping departments we need to compare efficiency 1. This also could be done by using financial measures, for instance by comparing staffing costs with rooms available for sale at full rack rate. Whilst this makes comparison for productivity reasons possible, it confuses the picture with regard to actual performance. It is therefore probably desirable to use non-financial measures with regard to efficiency 1. Using the same example we could compare the number of man-hours and the number of rooms serviced, i.e.

$$\text{Productivity of housekeeping dept.} = \frac{\text{Number of rooms serviced}}{\text{Number of man-hours}}$$

So productivity can be measured financially and in physical terms. It is also possible to combine both a financial measure and a physical measure in one ratio. This is illustrated in table 8.1.

Table 8.1 *Example ratios of Productivity*

	Physical measures	Physical and financial measures	Financial measures
Raw materials	No. of portions served	No. of bar customers	Food revenue
	Weight of commodity used	Cost of liquor sold	Food costs
Labour	Housecount	Total room sales	Total added value
	Total employee hours	Chambermaid days	Hotel payroll
Energy	Total guestrooms	No. of cooked meals	Hotel revenue
	Total kilowatt hours	Total cooking costs	Total energy costs

Adapted from Ball, Johnson and Slattery.[5]

In the hotel there are two performance measures that are almost sacrosanct. One is occupancy rate (in hotels) and the other is gross profit (in catering). Both of these are measures of productivity, expressed as a percentage simply by multiplying the ratio by 100. Occupancy is a physical measure:

$$\text{Occupancy rate} = \frac{\text{Number of rooms occupied}}{\text{Total number of rooms}}$$

Gross profit is a financial measure:

$$\text{Gross profit} = \frac{\text{Food cost}}{\text{Net food sales}}$$

Comparisons, using these two measures, are often made in two ways. Within each unit performance is measured over time, i.e. from one week to the next or the comparable week this year with last year, and between operating units, usually within the same chain but sometimes against the performance of other hotels. The use of these measures is ubiquitous, and performance targets are frequently set in these terms. For instance, in the past, some hotel chains have had a target gross profit percentage for all their hotels irrespective of their size, type of catering facility, level of function business and so on, although modern trends are towards a more flexible approach based on the specific characteristics of each operation.

Both of these measures suffer from the same weakness as in the example we cited above. Occupancy rate measures throughput and is concerned with capacity management. Gross profit measures efficiency 2 in a highly aggregated way. Neither of them measures efficiency 1. The hotel chains would argue that at the end of the day they are only interested in profitability, and both occupancy rate and GP per cent enable them to monitor this closely. But hotel managers should be aware that these measures do *not identify the inefficient hotels*. Ball, Johnson and Slattery, in conjunction with Holiday Inn, identified that some better measure of productivity performance was required, particularly focusing on labour productivity.

With regards to inputs, their study developed the useful concept of 'full-time equivalent employee' (FTEE). This overcomes the problem of measuring staffing inputs when coping with full-time, part-time and casual staff that are typical of hotel operations. So for any particular time period, such as a month, the labour input can be standardised and expressed as FTEEs. For example,

$$\text{FTEE for May} = \frac{\text{Total hours worked in May by all staff}}{\begin{array}{c}\text{Number of hours}\\\text{in working day}\end{array}} \times \begin{array}{c}\text{Total working}\\\text{days in May}\end{array}$$

So that, assuming the working day was eight hours and staff work a five-day week excluding weekends, there are 22 working days in May. If there were 1,720 total hours worked in the entire month, this is the equivalent of 10 FTEEs (1,720 divided by 8 × 22). By standardising in this way it is possible to compare more accurately performance over time and between units.

Ball, Johnson and Slattery compared this input measurement with two output measures: the number of customers served and the amount of revenue generated. Both of these suffer from the problem we have previously identified, namely they measure efficiency 2. Comparing FTEEs with number of customers is slightly better than comparing it with revenue, since this eliminates any variance in performance caused by customers changing their average spend. It is only appropriate to measure it against revenue if it can be argued that employees had to some extent control over the spending habits of the customers. In housekeeping this would not be so; in the bars and restaurant it could be. This difference in context also has other implications for the way in which productivity should be measured.

There is nothing wrong with measuring efficiency 2, if this desired intermediate output matches the actual level of demand. Thus in the banqueting department, the two measures FTEE:customers and FTEE:revenue are appropriate. Due to the predictability of the banqueting department's activities, efficiency 1 and efficiency 2 should be identical. The same is true to a certain extent in the housekeeping department with regard to servicing rooms. Since the number of rooms to be serviced is known in advance, admittedly only the night before, it should be possible to match the labour input to the actual output. In this case, housekeeping staff have a shorter time frame in which to do so than banqueting, and they may employ a proportionately greater number of full-time staff which also creates some inflexibility.

But in the hotel's bars and restaurants there is a much greater chance element in the actual level of output, despite past trends and table reservations. The labour input is therefore determined on the basis of some level of intermediate output that subsequently may be in error. By measuring FTEE:customers in this context, it is not clear whether poor productivity arises because there were too many employees or too few customers.

APPROACHES TO PRODUCTIVITY IMPROVEMENT

So far we have discussed what is meant by productivity, the problem of applying the concept in the hotel and other service industries, and ways in which it can be measured. But we have not discussed how to go about actually *improving* the ratio of inputs to outputs. Whatever the particular approaches or techniques adopted, the manager must always understand these issues we have identified. In this sense productivity improvement is carried out at three different levels. At the organisational level there are broad goals to be achieved concerning outcomes. This requires more than just the application of productivity concepts, but also an understanding of quality issues too. For each major department within the operating unit, there will be actual output targets, which may involve capacity management and productivity ideas. And finally within each department, there will be specific objectives with regard to intermediate output that will require the application of productivity techniques to efficiency 1 type problems.

All the evidence from other industries, especially manufacturing, suggests that productivity improvement can be achieved in a wide variety of ways. It is insightful to differentiate between the overall approach that can be adopted and the specific techniques applied within the particular approach. We argue that the approach adopted should be appropriate for the type of unit. Thus the approach adopted in the hotel industry will be broadly similar across hotel, hostels and hospitals, but will be different to the approach adopted in engineering or mass production. Within the hotel industry, this broad approach will vary according to the size of the organisation, the size of the operating units, the management style, level of unionisation and so on. There may also be external factors such as regional differences in wage rates that affect decisions about productivity improvement ideas.

The way in which the approach to productivity will vary will be on the basis of both formal and informal criteria. These should not be taken as separate from each other, but as two ends of a continuum. Under the formal criteria are included the structure of the organisation, delegation and authority, cost allocation, remuneration policy and other aspects of the organisation over which planning and control can be exercised. At the other end of the continuum are informal criteria that support productivity improvement, such as organisational climate and culture, involvement strategies, decision-making processes and people development. Rather than change the organisation to make productivity happen, these informal ideas change the attitudes and behaviour of people within the organisation. We argue that, in the hotel industry, particular emphasis should be placed on informal ideas for developing an approach due to the high labour cost and high contact nature of the activity.

The ideas associated with the formal approaches are largely to do with structure and accountability. Productivity gains are derived from making changes to the production process. It is therefore essential to know:

- What are the inputs to the activity?
- Who manages these inputs?
- What do the inputs cost?
- What is the behaviour of cost with variation in output?
- What elements of cost are controllable?
- What is the desired level of output?

So for productivity to be improved, managers and supervisors must be provided with this sort of information, delegated authority over their activities and be allowed to modify the inputs and costs over which they have control. There are a variety of ways in which this can be made possible or be facilitated.

First, the organisation can delegate to staff at all levels the setting of productivity goals and objectives. This will almost certainly need to be supported structurally by appointing a productivity co-ordinator or by setting up a productivity committee. The role and scope of the co-ordinator or committee will vary according to the size and style of the organisation.

Secondly, the organisation must analyse all its operating costs and identify the level of management at which authority for costs is appropriate. For instance, the laundry room supervisor might be accountable for expenditure on soap powder, the executive housekeeper might be responsible for labour costs in that department and the rooms division manager may have overall responsibility for the total costs of servicing rooms. For those costs that are clearly and directly associated with a revenue-generating department (or profit centre), it is relatively easy to assign responsibility. But in a hotel there are a large number of costs not directly attributable to operating departments – typically energy costs, personnel and administration, and other overheads. These elements of cost contribute to the total output of the hotel, but cannot easily be included in the operating costs of any one specific department. Such costs have to be allocated in some way.

General overhead costs can be assigned to profit centres according to benefits received, responsibilities or some other logical measure of use. There are a number of methods for allocating costs, but all depend on the selection of an allocation base, i.e. the factor used to determine how much is allocated. The 'Uniform System of Accounts for Hotels' suggests some typical allocation bases.

Allocated costs:
- Rent

Allocation bases:
   – % according to revenue source
   – square feet of area occupied

- Insurance (contents) – square feet of area occupied – square feet plus investment in fixtures/furniture
- Telephone   – number of extensions
- Energy costs   – cubic feet of area occupied
- Marketing   – ratio to sales
- Wage administration – number of employees

The three main methods for allocating costs are the direct method, the step method and the formula method, in ascending order of complexity. The direct method takes all overhead costs and allocates them to profit centres according to the appropriate bases. This ignores the fact that some of the overhead costs will be derived from running non-revenue generating departments (or 'service centres'). For instance the personnel office will use up energy as will all the other offices, but this is allocated on the basis of the relative proportion of space occupied only by profit centres. To overcome this, the step method assigns all costs to every department irrespective of whether they are profit or service centres. Then the costs of the service centres are allocated to the profit centres in turn. For example, table 8.2 illustrates how energy costs might be allocated in a simple hotel with two profit centres (rooms and F & B) and two service centres (energy and payroll).

Table 8.2   *The Model Hotel: allocation of energy costs.*

Revenue & costs:

	Revenue	Cost of sales	Labour	Other	Profit (loss)
Rooms	24,000	0	4,500	1,800	17,700
F & B	12,000	4,600	4,400	1,500	1,500
Energy			1,000	2,200	(3,200)
Payroll			1,300		(1,300)

Allocation bases:

	Square feet	No. of employees
Rooms	15,000	6
F & B	3,000	6
Energy	1,000	1
Payroll	1,000	1

1. Direct method:

Expense	Amount	Base	Proportion to:		Amounts to:	
			Rooms	F & B	Rooms	F & B
Energy	3,200	sq. ft.	83.3%	16.6%	2,667	533
Payroll	1,300	empl.	50%	50%	650	650
					3,317	1,183

2. Step method:

Expense	Amount	Base	Proportion to:			Amounts to:		
			Rooms	F & B	Energy	Rooms	F & B	Energy
Payroll	1,300	empl.	46.1%	46.1%	7.7% 600	600	600	100
Energy	3,200 +100	sq. ft.	83.3%	16.6%		2,749	551	
	3,300					3,349	1,151	

In the future, technological innovation may remove some of the need to allocate costs using these methods. One analysis[6] argues strongly that at least with regard to energy costs submetering is a feasible alternative. That is to say, submeters are installed that identify the precise usage of energy in each specific department of the hotel. Coupled with thermostats and controls that enable the staff in the department to control this usage, it is argued that this will result in reduced costs and better accountability. It is possible that this concept could also be applied to other activities, such as usage of centralised computer time and so on.

Indeed the introduction and adoption of technology, and changes to the service delivery system itself, is a third formal approach that can be used to improve productivity. One particular example of this is the impact that computers and information technology will have on efficiency in the industry. At the beginning of the chapter we saw that Baumol has coined the phrase 'stagnant personal services' and we suggested that the hotel industry might be typical of this category. Research [7] suggests that this might not be an entirely true picture of hotels.

Information technology is having three major impacts. First, the use of computerised point-of-sale hardware enables closer monitoring of labour productivity, measured as covers per man-hour for instance, and hence managers are able to arrange staff rotas to reflect more accurately peaks and troughs in customer traffic. Secondly, many of the administrative and clerical roles have become highly efficient, producing more accurate information and a greater throughput of paperwork with considerably fewer staff. Thirdly, and perhaps most importantly, the introduction of computer technology into the front-of-house activities has reduced the clerical and often tedious aspects of the work, so that receptionists, cashiers and enquiry clerks are left free to concentrate on the more qualitative, service aspects of their role.

Finally, another formal aspect of approaches to productivity is the way in which remuneration and reward systems are designed to facilitate and encourage productivity. With labour cost such an important element it is clear that the potential for improvement may stem largely from the workforce's ability and willingness to increase their input, i.e. produce more per man-hour. Clearly employees have to be given some incentive to do this. Such incentives can take the form of bonus payments, wage rate increases and so on. One specific approach is the Scanlon plan.

As well as these formal, organisational approaches, hotel managers must also implement informal strategies aimed at encouraging and supporting productivity improvements. A climate must be created so that employees of the organisation are made aware that productivity is important. This can be achieved through the communication channels of the organisation, such as in-house journals, posters, notices and memoranda. It can also be made part of the induction process for new employees and of on-the-job training programmes. The aim of this communication is not simply to provide information, but to create an environment conducive to productivity that is based on trust and co-operation. It is not simply a question of asking employees to work harder, but to work more intelligently and creatively. Such trust will be difficult to create if the workforce has a sense of threat about their jobs. Stable employees, who have worked for the organisation over a period of time, are much more likely to generate good ideas and adopt new working practices, so long as they feel safe about their future employment. The hotel industry tends to have a large proportion of seasonal, casual and part-time members of staff, but nonetheless there should be a core of full-time staff around whom such initiatives could be based.

As well as awareness and the right sort of climate, employees must share in the benefits of productivity. Whilst these can often be formalised, as with regard to reward systems, other elements such as a sense of job security may be equally important. Managers and supervisors must pay attention to employees who work well and give them due praise. Recognition and a sense of achievement will greatly enhance the motivation to work productively. Where productivity has been placed high on the agenda, feedback on the levels of productivity achieved on a weekly basis may also contribute to maintaining interest and generating enthusiasm for improved performance. The 'publication' of such information can also be accompanied by a workplace meeting to discuss the issue. This can also be helped by the adoption of a 'no harm' policy. That is to say, if an employee comes up with an idea that may not be particularly productive, but which can do no harm, then it should be implemented. Whilst little or no benefit may be derived from doing so, it clearly identifies that ideas and suggestions are acted upon and does much to create the right sort of productivity-oriented atmosphere. Such approaches may be rare in hotels and service industries, but many companies in the manufacturing sector have found these effective means of stimulating interest.

Werther[8] argues that managers too must adapt and modify their own beliefs and attitudes if they are successfully to manage productivity. Effective decision-making requires five steps:

1. identify the problem or opportunity;
2. generate alternatives;
3. select the optimum solution;
4. implement;
5. control/feedback.

In the UK, managers tend to act fast and only involve their employees at the implementation stage. There is a feeling that managers are paid to put problems right. But there is the danger that resistance to change by employees may slow down or prevent successful implementation. In Japan, managers take much more time over the identification of problems and generating alternatives, and they involve their staff in that process. In this way, the remaining three stages are carried out well, due to the early commitment and support of all involved. This latter approach is particularly useful in the area of productivity (and quality) management. Involvement by employees in the decision-making process taps the hands-on experience of the people actually doing the work. The idea of a suggestion box for staff to put their ideas and comments anonymously to management has long been superseded. In some organisations there is a suggestion 'system'. An employee discusses an idea with his or her supervisor, this is written up and recorded, reviewed and evaluated. If it is implemented and savings are made, the employee receives a financial reward commensurate with the level of savings made.

Whether formal or informal approaches are adopted, the intention is to make productivity improvement possible. This does not guarantee that it will happen, although we would hope that it might. Usually specific techniques are applied, both to enact and to measure effectively improved productivity. But without the support of the approaches we have outlined, it is extremely unlikely that the techniques applied on their own will be successful. For instance, time and motion study might show how portering staff could work more efficiently, but employee resistance both to the study and to subsequent implementation could prevent the productivity gains from occurring. But backed up with the right organisational climate, employee involvement, management encouragement, incentive payments and so on, then there is a real chance to make progress.

TECHNIQUES FOR IMPROVING PRODUCTIVITY

The techniques that can be used in the productivity field are very wide ranging. Some are simply measurement techniques, others generate solutions to problems, and some do both. They include:

- work simplification
- short-interval scheduling
- task-unit scheduling
- ergonomic analysis
- value analysis
- zero-based budgeting
- methods analysis
- time and motion study
- simulation modelling
- work sampling
- job enrichment programming
- quality circles.

What the manager needs to know is which of these fits with the particular problem he or she is facing. Many of the techniques originate from manufacturing and hence concentrate on the evaluation of highly repetitive tasks. In the hotel situation such work situations are rare and almost certainly are only to be found back-of-house, as front-of-house staff attempt to customise the service they provide.

Techniques that enable the analysis and evaluation of work processes are estimating, time study, activity sampling and method study. Such techniques can measure not only what employees are doing, but also the frequency of use of plant and equipment. Such techniques may be of value in identifying opportunities for productivity improvement in a hotel if they can cut down on 'travel time'. That is to say, the length of time employees spend in moving from one part of the unit to another.

A second group of techniques is aimed at the more effective use of the workforce by better scheduling of their time. Such scheduling may be based on the data generated by the previous range of techniques, from forecasts of demand, or from carrying out a detailed task element analysis. From this it is possible to schedule the activities of staff over their shift period and also to roster on duty the most appropriate level of staff for a given period.

Case example 8.1   The Excelsior Hotel

The Excelsior Hotel carried out a study of its house porters, responsible for cleaning public areas and offices. Whilst the standard of cleanliness was high, the monthly cost was averaging nearly £2,240 in labour cost alone. Although a mixture of full-time and part-time staff were employed, at slightly different hourly wage rates, this was the equivalent of 6.5 FTEEs. A typical week's rota is shown below:

	Sun.	Mon.	Tues.	Wed.	Thur.	Fri.	Sat.
J. Carruthers	off	7–3	7–3	7–3	7–3	7–3	off
W. Arbuthnot	off	9–5	9–5	9–5	9–5	9–5	off
J. Finchley	off	7–1	7–1	7–1	7–1	7–1	off
T. Harrison	8–1	off	off	off	off	off	8–1
P. Briggs	off	3–7	3–7	3–7	3–7	3–7	off
A. Hammond	7–3	off	off	off	off	off	7–3

In addition to the rota hours, all staff on the rota worked some overtime, amounting to 20 hours per week at time-and-a-half.

In an effort to reduce the cost, the hotel initiated a study similar to task-unit scheduling. First, they identified all the tasks the cleaning staff were required to do. These were grouped according to location, and some additional tasks were added. For instance, a corridor was identified as being best cleaned by a particular team of staff. The frequency with which the area required attention was established, and the length of time to carry out each task was estimated. Precise work measurement was not carried out as there were too many tasks to measure, and the experience of the housekeeping staff provided an accurate enough estimate. This produced a list of daily tasks, along with the frequency and time for each. Part of this list is shown in table 8.3.

Table 8.3 *List of daily tasks, their frequency and time required.*

Task	Type of location	Number of locations	Frequency	Time estimate	Required minutes
F. hall – spot clean	Room	1	2	16.00	32.00
– sweep	Floor	1	3	3.30	9.90
– mop	Floor	1	1	6.30	6.30
– polish	Floor	1	1	8.00	8.00
Main doors	Door	2	2	5.00	20.00
Baggage room – clean	Room	1	1	5.00	5.00
Lounge – dust	Room	2	2	6.30	26.00
– vacuum	Floor	2	1	7.15	14.30
– windows	Room	2	1	3.00	6.00
Corridor – spot clean	Corridor	4	2	4.15	34.00
– vacuum	Floor	4	1	3.30	14.00
Lifts – sweep	Lift	3	2	1.45	10.30
– dust	Lift	3	2	1.30	9.00
Brass & chrome etc. . . .	Item	12	1	2.00	24.00

Once this was established it was possible to calculate the total monthly hours, by taking the daily tasks and multiplying them by 30, the weekly tasks and multiplying by 4, and adding these totals to the time to be spend on monthly tasks. This theoretical analysis of how long these tasks required showed a total of 900 hours, which at the average hourly rate meant a potential saving of £110 per week and a reduction in FTEEs to 5.2.

Since the study showed savings could be made, the analysis had to be translated into work schedules for each cleaner that would enable a reduction in part-time staff and overtime. This was done by assuming three full-time staff would each work a seven-and-a-half hour day, with a half-hour for lunch. These three shifts were marked out on paper as three parallel lines subdivided into quarter hour periods. From the lists of tasks, those tasks that had to be completed during a certain time of the day, such as vacuuming the front hall, were identified and marked on the shift schedules. Other tasks were then allocated to the three workers taking into account their location, travel time, equipment availability, break times, and so on. Once most of the tasks had been allocated, those remaining were either covered by part-time staff or allocated as overtime. For each cleaner a clear work schedule was produced, part of which is shown below:

7.00 – 7.35	Spot clean front hall, sweep, mop and polish floor.
7.35 – 7.45	Main doors.
7.45 – 7.55	Sweep and dust lifts.
7.55 – 8.05	Clean and vacuum corridor A.
8.05 – 8.20	Dust and vacuum lounge.
8.20 – 8.30	Clean and vacuum corridor B.
etc. . . .	

Thirdly, there are the techniques aimed at questioning all inputs and re-examining their role and importance. Value 'engineering' breaks down any activity into its component parts and attempts to identify any parts that are not needed or redundant, or any parts that could be substituted by a cheaper alternative. For instance, the substitution of personnel-based floor service by in-room bars and beverage making facilities is a typical example of a value analysis of service provision. A value judgement was made that most customers would accept the lack of personal service for the benefit of having almost immediate provision whenever they wanted it. The substitution contributed to productivity by lowering the inputs, i.e. it was more cost-effective to replace labour with capital equipment, and by raising outputs, i.e. the presence of in-room facilities substantially increased the take-up of beverage sales in most cases.

Another technique in this category is zero-based budgeting. Each item of expenditure, particularly overhead costs, is analysed in terms of its cost, purpose, possible alternatives, performance measures and potential benefits. Underlying this is the assumption that the need for any item of cost may at least be queried and that the current activity is not necessarily the most appropriate way of achieving objectives. Working from a zero-base, the manager is required to justify expenditure in each area. For example, rather than relying on increasing the advertising budget each year in line with inflation, the marketing manager is asked to justify the budget based on the anticipated advertising plan for the coming year. The budget is therefore set in line with need and not historical precedent.

Finally, there is another group of techniques aimed less at reducing cost and more at improving output. Such techniques are associated with team building, job enrichment and quality circles. Since these also play a significant role in the management of quality, we shall discuss these in the next chapter.

A STRATEGY FOR PERFORMANCE IMPROVEMENT IN HOTELS

So far we have identified a wide range of approaches and techniques, illustrating some of them in some detail. We suggested that in considering these, particular approaches and techniques should be combined in a coherent strategy specifically designed to improve productivity in hotel operations. But we have not identified what this strategy should be like. Indeed, there is very little evidence to substantiate any particular combination of features. Venison[9] approaches this issue, but his evidence is personal and anecdotal.

Staw[10] has proposed three possible configurations, one of which might be appropriate for hotels. The strategies are based on the individual, the group and the organisation.

The *individually-oriented system* would include such features as:

- rewarding good performance through individual remuneration schemes, such as bonuses;

- individual performance targets;

- on-the-job training and staff development;

- task unit scheduling;

- promotion policy based on skills of personnel;

- job enrichment;

- work and method study.

Both formal and informal approaches support the individual's contribution to the operation's performance. This strategy is typical in the UK and USA and reflects the socio-cultural norms of business and society.

The second strategy is a *group-oriented system*, which in the context of hotels could be regarded as the different departments of the unit. The productivity approaches and techniques included in this system would be:

- organising work and rotas around groups;

- quality circles;

- group bonus payments;

- intra-group selection and training of new personnel;

- allocation of separate social space for each group;

- departmental cost allocation;

- productivity co-ordinator.

In this system, groups become very strong and begin to set performance norms for themselves. A strong sense of group loyalty can create an ethos of hard work and intra-group co-operation.

Finally, the *organisation-oriented system* selects from the range of options those features that develop productivity for the total organisation, or in this case the whole hotel:

- strong organisational climate, with clear culture based on 'myths', 'rituals', and so on;

- job rotation around the unit;

- guarantee of long-term employment;

- few status distinctions between employees;

- widespread dissemination of information about the organisation's performance.

- remuneration includes profit-sharing;
- consultative style of management;
- productivity co-ordinating committee.

This approach builds up a strong 'corporate' loyalty that is seen in some hotel groups, particularly amongst management personnel. The American hotel chains are particularly good at achieving this, not just to improve productivity, but also for the beneficial effects it can have on service, income and quality.

What evidence there is suggests that the organisation-oriented system is the best approach to adopt in the context of hotel operations. But this area needs a great deal more analysis and research before a clear picture emerges.

SUMMARY

Productivity is one of the three secondary key result areas in our model of hotel management. In this model it is the interface between assets and employees and is concerned with decisions concerning the resources of the hotel. The standard definition of productivity is the ratio of inputs to outputs. There are five variations on the way in which this ratio can be improved. In the hotel industry the measurement and performance of this improvement is made difficult by the complexity and intangibility of both inputs and outputs. These difficulties are resolved by the model of productivity, which differentiates between efficiency 1, efficiency 2, and effectiveness.

Using this model, we went on to make a critique of the ways in which productivity is typically measured in the industry and offered some alternative measures. Before attempting to initiate any specific improvements, the manager must develop a particular approach to productivity that draws on a wide range of formal and informal criteria. Once this has been done, techniques can be applied to measure and initiate improvements. We concluded that potentially the most coherent and appropriate strategy for productivity improvement in hotels was an organisation-based system, that puts together a package of approaches and techniques which mutually support each other to make a significant impact on performance.

REFERENCES

1. Whiteman, J., *The Service Sector – A Poor Relation?*, Discussion Paper No. 8, National Economic Development Office, 1981.

2. Blois, K., 'Productivity and effectiveness in service firms', *Service Industries Journal*, pp. 49–59, November 1984.

3. Baumol, W. J., 'Productivity policy and the service sector', in Inman, R. P. (ed.), *Managing the Service Economy, Prospects and Problems*, Cambridge Univerisity Press, pp. 301–318, 1985.

4. Flynn, N., 'Performance measurement in public sector services', *Policy and Politics* vol. 14, no. 3, pp. 389–404, 1986.

5. Ball, S. D., Johnson, K., and Slattery, P., 'Labour productivity in hotels: an empirical study', *International Journal of Hospitality Management* vol. 5, no. 3, pp. 141–147, 1986.

5. Redling, M. H., and Goland, L. M., 'Submetering of hotel utilities', *Cornell, HRA Quarterly*, pp. 45–50, February 1984.

7.   Whittaker, M., 'Technology and employment in hotels and catering', unpublished paper, Brighton Polytechnic, 1986.

8.   Werther, W. B., 'Out of the productivity box', *Business Horizons*, pp. 51–59, September – October 1982.

9.   Venison, P., *Managing Hotels*, Heinemann, 1984.

10. Staw, B. M., 'Organisational psychology and the pursuit of the happy/productive worker', *California Management Review* vol. 28, no. 4, Summer, 1986.

9 Managing Quality

Figure 9.1 *Central key result area: quality.*

INTRODUCTION

There is no doubt that quality in the hotel industry is an important issue. Many organisations overtly use this word in their advertising and promotion directed at their customers and in their standards of performance manuals directed at their staff. For instance, the Ladbroke hotel chain instituted a quality programme called 'Quality '85' during the summer of 1985. Other companies have directed the focus of their advertising campaigns towards aspects of their product that are quality related. Thistle Hotels included this statement in a 1986 advertisement: 'So while every Thistle Hotel guarantees a standard of accommodation and business facilities equal to and in many cases better than that offered by international hotel chains, then that is where regimentation ends and individuality begins.' More succinctly, Holiday Inns have used the slogan: 'A better place to be.'

In the hospital sector, too, there is an increasing awareness of the role of hotel services in providing quality patient care. This has been brought about by the introduction of general management into the NHS, the impact that the hospital enquiry had on standards, the removal of crown immunity from prosecution, and the threat of privatisation. Many health authorities have responded to these external factors by developing the role of the hotel services manager, many of whom are being appointed to health authority boards.

It is therefore no accident that quality is central to our conceptual model of hotel management (see figure 9.1). In this model quality is the interface of all three primary areas: employees, assets and customers. By its very nature, therefore, we regard quality as both *central* to the role of hotel management and the most *complex* of all the key result areas.

WHAT DO WE MEAN BY QUALITY?

Quality has sometimes been confused with 'the best'. Dictionary definitions talk about quality as 'the degree or standard of excellence of something', and naturally enough hoteliers do not wish to think of providing a product that is substandard. This is particularly true if hoteliers tended to have a product-oriented view of their business. The provision of quality is therefore a technical problem. The room itself is seen as the product, and the problems of quality management are therefore associated with ensuring high and consistent standards.

Today, many more hoteliers are consumer-oriented and therefore take a much less narrow view of quality. The modern concept of quality is 'fitness for purpose'. This shifts the evaluation of quality away from the provider, i.e. the hotelier, onto the consumer. Hoteliers no longer need to provide the best, but the best that the consumer's money can buy. Thus quality is no longer just a technical problem, but a behavioural one too. The hotelier has to be aware of the consumers' attitudes and perspectives in order to be able to provide quality.

The definition of quality that we shall adopt is that of the British Standards Institute:[1] 'The totality of features and characteristics of a product or service that bear on its ability to satisfy a given need.' There are many other different approaches to quality, each of which is supported by its own jargon. It is now becoming accepted that for quality to be effectively introduced into an organisation, it has to be totally integrated into *all* activities of the firm. This belief originated with the Japanese who took up this idea of 'total quality control' in the 1950s. At the end of the 1960s, Juran, a leading expert in this field, recommended that a more apt description of the approach is 'company-wide quality control'.

Finally, there is the school of thought that believes 'control' is too narrow, and that 'quality management' is more appropriate. In 1985, Hart and Casserly[2] advocated that 'total quality management' combines all the elements needed to 'imply that quality is a discipline to be implemented throughout an organisation, and it suggests the complete dedication essential to making a quality programme work'.

CUSTOMER PERCEPTIONS OF QUALITY IN HOTELS

Quality is important in the hotel industry because of a number of factors, some of which have always existed and some of which are more recent trends. Any industry that markets a product in a highly competitive market, competing for the consumer's disposable income, needs to be aware of quality issues. Since quality relates to consumer's needs and expectations, the standards adopted by the industry are mostly established by its customers, and these standards have been changing. There has been a growth in 'consumerism' in general, which has resulted in customers expecting to receive products and services that are acceptable. Companies have also been able to produce higher quality products because technology has developed that assists them to do so. In the hotel industry much of this is derived from advances in computer technology that has resulted in much higher quality of provision through increased speed and accuracy of reservations and billing procedures. British consumers have also travelled more widely than ever before, due to package holidays and cheaper transportation. They have returned from foreign countries with new ideas and standards about hotel provision, now reflected in the range of services and facilities becoming available in British hotels. Hotel organisations themselves have fuelled higher quality expectations amongst customers by using the concept of quality as a marketing tool, as identified above.

However, the hotel industry's response to changes in quality perception are less marked than in other service industries, where the pace of change has been much swifter. This is due to several factors:

- Modification to the hotel 'product' requires a fairly substantial capital investment. For instance, Crest Hotels' implementation of their 'leisure' club into their Maidenhead unit has cost them £750,000.

- The time scale involved in renovating and improving premises and provision is lengthy and may be inhibited by restrictions as to the time of year that the work may take place, i.e. the off-season.

- A large proportion of the hotel market is made up of 'mediated demand', that is the reservation of accommodation is made on behalf of the end-user by a third party, either a tour operator, travel agent or corporate business.

- The frequency of purchase of hotel accommodation is relatively low compared with other services, such as eating out. It therefore takes some time for consumers to influence the quality of provision.

- The responsiveness of hoteliers is physically constrained by the structure of the hotel itself. It is extremely difficult to bring up to modern standards hotels that were built in an earlier age, and which have rooms that are typically much larger than modern hotel bedrooms, and may have bathrooms not adjacent to each room.

- Hotels may not find it easy to recruit personnel with the appropriate technical or social skills due to labour shortages or the reluctance of British staff to work in a service context.

- Even if it were possible to change the physical environment quickly, hotel organisations are constrained by their own cultures which do not necessarily provide the level of support that high quality service demands (see page 122).

Such cultural constraints may also create recruitment and staff turnover problems.

The first stage in quality management is to determine the level of quality that will satisfy the target market. Berry, Zeithaml and Parasuraman[3] have identified ten determinants of service quality that they believe apply to all services. We agree that they have some value in understanding more about consumer attitudes to hotel service. In no specific order, these determinants are:

- *Reliability*: consistency of performance and dependability, no errors or delay.

- *Responsiveness*: willingness or readiness of employees to provide service.

- *Competence*: knowledge and skill of contact personnel and operational support staff.

- *Access*: approachability and ease of contact.

- *Courtesy*: politeness, friendliness, consideration, tact and respect of service staff.

- *Communication*: informing customers and listening to them.

- *Credibility*: trustworthiness, honesty, believability.

- *Security*: freedom from danger, risk or doubt.

- *Rapport*: understanding the customer's individual needs.

- *Appearance*: the physical evidence of the service, the facilities/personnel equipment.

In the hotel business, there is a tendency to concentrate on those aspects of the operation for which consumer preferences can be easily measured. The major problem facing the hotel operator is identifying what it is that the consumer wants from a hotel. Judging from the grading systems, this is highly oriented towards the tangible aspects of provision. One very good example of this was the English Tourist Board's categories of facilities. This scheme graded:

- accommodation types, such as hotels, guest houses, etc.;

- bedrooms, into six grades;

- services, such as public areas, telephones, porterage, etc.;

- meals, also into six categories.

It was a particularly specific scheme. The requirements for bedrooms include details of minimum floor area for all types of rooms (for example, a single bedroom excluding private bath or shower-room must be not less than 5.60 square metres); minimum bed sizes (for example a double-bed must be no smaller than 1.83×1.22 metres); bed-making daily and linen changed at least weekly or for each new guest; and even the provision of four hangers in the clothes-hanging space for each person.

However, there is further research evidence to suggest that consumers do not evaluate the quality of their stay in a hotel on this basis. Indeed, our brief review of hotel advertising supports the view that hoteliers themselves believe that the less tangible elements such as style, elegance or comfort are what attract customers to hotels. Nightingale's study[4] tends to support this view. The characteristics of quality perceived by guests in his study of businessmen staying in a large city hotel were prioritised as follows:

1. Availability

2. Smooth, fast response

3. Easy to do or use

4. Comfortable, pleasant and relaxing

5. Provision of reasonable facilities

6. Spacious

7. Value for money

8. Adequate choice.

AN APPROACH TO HOTEL QUALITY MANAGEMENT

A fundamental problem facing hotel managers is the static nature of the 'accommodation experience'. The concept of the 'meal experience' was first mooted by Campbell-Smith over twenty years ago. We would argue that an important feature of the meal experience is the extent to which the consumer has control over this experience. Consumers can often choose where to sit, decide what to eat and drink from an extensive menu or wine list, and – in at least one restaurant we know of – decide how much to pay at the end of the meal. In addition to this direct control over their experience, consumers can also indirectly influence aspects of the provision such as speed of service, level of servility and frequency of contact with service staff by their words and actions. If we apply this concept to accommodation, by regarding the time a consumer spends in the hotel as a total experience, we find that most hotel provision is dramatically less dynamic and flexible. For instance, hotel residents all tend to receive very similar experiences to each other, often having minimal control over which room they stay in and the facilities available to them. Hotel residents therefore have much less opportunity to shape and mould the nature of their experience.

The main reason for this is the extent to which their stay is influenced by two factors. The first of these is the tangible, physical characteristics of the hotel we have discussed on page 35. The second factor is the level of contact they have with hotel staff. Much of the meal experience flexibility is derived from the interaction between the server and consumer. In a hotel, the 'pure' accommodation experience has very limited opportunities for customer/staff contact. Essentially this occurs when the customer checks in and when he checks out. Clearly, hotel residents who only sleep in the hotel, without using any of the other facilities of the unit, are rare. In reality the accommodation experience is not 'pure' but includes such things as dining in the restaurant, drinking in the bar, relaxing in the lounge, swimming in the pool, and so on. We can illustrate these two dimensions on a matrix in order to, identify their implications for hotel quality management (see figure 9.2). The first dimension is the tangible and intangible aspects of the experience; the second is the type of contact consumers have with the hotel. Contact with staff we have called 'social contact' and contact with the physical make-up of the unit we have called 'material contact'.

The impression given by this matrix is that each quadrant is equal in importance. This is not the case. We have seen, in both the Berry, Zeithaml and Parasuraman and

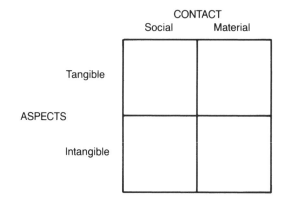

Figure 9.2 *Quality management matrix for hotel operations.*

the Nightingale studies, that the relative importance of these four quadrants is very difficult to measure for certain. However, on the evidence of the Nightingale study, the material/tangible component is much more significant than the material/intangible component. Moreover, from the manager's point of view, the material/tangible component is manifestly more controllable than the material/intangible sector. Likewise, the social/intangible component is more significant than the social/tangible contact. Examples of social/tangible contact are few, for instance porter's carrying luggage and receptionists filling in registration forms for customers. By its very nature social interaction is highly subjective and intangible.

We would argue that effective quality management is concerned with expanding the boundaries of the material/tangible and social/intangible components and reducing the boundaries of the other two components. The basis for this view is that opportunities to manage the social/tangible component are rare and that the capability of managing the material/intangible component is impracticable. We shall examine how this can be done later, but first let us consider what the industry's response has been. In the main, hotel organisations have attempted to suppress the intangible components, both social and material. Thus telephonists respond according to a prescribed script, and computers predetermine the way a member of staff responds to a customer's request. What hotel organisations are trying to avoid is poor service provision due to poor interpersonal skills of staff. They fail to recognise that such interpersonal skills by their very nature must be dynamic, flexible, and responsive to consumer needs. Hotels are impersonal places – residents are given a number, the hotel room is likely to accord with some standard, it contains few personal artifacts, and so on. It is therefore extremely important that social contact is not impersonalised. The distinctive feature of such contact is the ability of staff to respond to any and every need the customer may have, irrespective of whether it relates to the role that member of staff occupies. As the Berry, Zeithaml and Parasuraman study showed, communication, responsiveness, courtesy and rapport are key determinants of service quality.

We have argued that it is possible to move the boundaries of each section of the quadrant. We would go further and argue that the relative size of each section will be determined by the type of establishment and the type of market, and this will affect both the complexity and focus of the management task. In a five-star hotel the level of tangible/material facilities provided will be high both because of the expectations of that grade of establishment by the guest and the requirements of five-star status.

Similarly guests in a five-star establishment expect a high degree of social service contact with staff. In a budget hotel tangible/material facilities will be reduced and social contact between staff and guests will also be acceptable at a lower level.

In this instance it is the complexity of the management task that has altered. In considering a hospital situation, however, it is the focus of management which must alter. Tangible/material aspects of the hospital provision in most NHS hospitals is at a functional level and is seen as a minor consideration; social contact also changes in that a large part of the contact is now of a tangible/social nature. Furthermore, the hotel services manager has little direct influence over the staff engaging in the social contact. It is the intangible/material components of relaxation, comfort and a good night's sleep that assume significant importance and over which we have the least direct control.

There are two basic strategies for managing quality: the 'control' strategy or the 'assurance' strategy. We saw that this concept can also be applied to protecting assets in chapter 5. We propose that quality control is the most appropriate approach to the management of the tangible/material component, often those activities which take place back-of-house. Quality assurance is suitable for the social/intangible component, which tends to be those activities associated with the front-of-house aspect of accommodation provision. The differences between the two will emerge as we discuss each of them in the next two sections.

QUALITY CONTROL IN HOTEL OPERATIONS

A range of models have been proposed with regard to quality management in the catering industry, for instance Wyckoff,[5] Jones[6] and King.[7] However, we are not aware of any research that refers explicitly to quality control of the hotel product, although Nightingale's study included some analysis of this issue. We have therefore selected King's approach, based on the manufacturing model of quality control, since it is fairly typical of these types of strategy.

The model comprises four main stages, as follows:

1. *Design quality level*:
   Define customer requirements:
   - Identify desired quality characteristics.

2. *Set product standards*:
   Design product to meet standards:
   - Drawings
   - Equipment and materials specification
   - Document procedures
   - Plan organisation and training.

3. *Check conformance*:
   Output:
   - Inspecting
   - Quality audit
   - Guest complaint.
   Process:
   - Check employee performance
   - Equipment monitoring.

4. *Correct non-standard output*:
    - Redo or defer sale of rejects
    - Analyse rejects for cause of failure
    - Adjust production process.

We have seen that quality standards are often determined by the grading systems used to categorise hotels. Such standards are further modified by the marketing mix of the particular hotel. A hotel whose the main business is from conferences and the business traveller is therefore likely to provide direct call dialling, work areas within the bedrooms, office services such as telex and fax, and so on. Tourist hotels, on the other hand, incorporate features such as theatre booking services, tourist information services and public areas for people to relax in. There is also a trend to segment the market even further, by providing features aimed at specific market segments. Most notable is Crest Hotels 'Lady Crest' rooms, which have distinctive decor, hair dryers and female toiletries. Another type of segmentation is by income group, whereby hotels usually offer a range of accommodation types at different tariffs, such as standard, de luxe and executive rooms and suites.

The decision to segment the market (which we have discussed in chaper 5), has major implications for quality management. Each market sector has discrete quality standards which must be communicated both to the customer and the staff. One advantage of the concept is that such accommodation can be sold at a premium, for instance Lady Crest rooms are 17 per cent above normal rack rate for single occupancy and 15 per cent above for double occupancy. Another advantage is that the hotel can more closely match the expectations and needs of particular groups of customers. For the manager, however, this creates problems with regard to the complexity and inflexibility of provision. Hotels tend to have a mix of clientele because of the weekly and seasonal demand patterns. But a hotel designed and aimed at business customers from Monday to Friday cannot easily be transformed into a hotel for tourists or pleasure travellers. The transformation implies not simply a change of physical attributes but also a change in the attitude and approach of staff to these two types of customer.

In practice what happens is that the core of the hotel remains the same but the peripherals are changed. That is to say, only relatively minor aspects of provision are modified. For instance, most of the features that make a Lady Crest room distinctive are small, additional items that can be placed into a room if required and can be removed once the female customer has vacated the room.

Once the hotel has determined its market requirements, it can then translate these into definite product specifications in terms of the layout, decor and design of room facilities, equipment and materials to be used in the room and its servicing, ancillary items such as stationery, folders and toiletries, and in a broader context the scale and nature of other facilities and services within the hotel. Furthermore, the operating procedures for the implementation of service provision must also be specified in this approach by detailed standards of performance manuals, detailed training of staff and specific organisational systems. This is illustrated in figure 9.3 which is an example of a standard of performance manual from a large hotel chain.

In this control model of quality management, after designing the quality level and setting product standards, the principal role of the manager is checking on conformance. Two features can be monitored, the actual outcomes and the process or working practices employed. Both can be evaluated internally or by an external auditor. We shall consider the concept of a quality audit on page 158 below, so here we are only

---

Standard Operating Procedure Turndown Service

1) Fold the bedspread toward the front of the bed, approximately half the length of the bed, to expose the upper half of blanket and pillows.

2) Turn only one side of bed down, the side adjacent to the bedside phone. In a DD, both beds will be turned down if room is double occupancy.

    a) Turn back the sheet and blanket approximately half the length and width of the bed on a queen or double size bed.

    b) Half the length and all the width of a twin size bed.

    c) Half the length and one-third the width of a king size bed.

3) Turndown service will include tidying ashtrays and waste baskets, replacing used bathroom terry, and adding soap and guest supplies that may have been used through the day.

4) Turn the radio on an easy listening station and leave the bedside lamp turned on.

5) Leave the general Manager's card and a Godiva mint on the pillow.

6) When turndown service is afforded a guest, it must be continued throughout the guest's stay.

Extra 'frills' and 'niceties' such as the daily newspaper or any other turndown creativity is a property option and is highly encouraged.

Figure 9.3 *Standards of performance for accommodation services in a hotel.*

concerned with how the manager monitors the day-to-day quality performance of the unit.

Outcomes, as we have already discussed, should primarily be evaluated on the basis of consumer satisfaction. But as we shall see there are considerable problems with measuring guest satisfaction. In addition, this approach would argue that so long as the level and standards have been set appropriately, evaluation can be undertaken against these predetermined, absolute criteria. Quality management then tends to become a question of objective measurement of intermediate output, as defined in the last chapter. This means that, with regard to bedrooms from the housekeeping department, it can be carried out by supervisory staff, who on an hourly basis inspect and monitor rooms to ensure they meet the specifications laid down. At the same time as checking on output, supervisors will also be observing the procedures and methods used by their staff to check that they are conforming with the standards laid down. Such standards are not only technical, such as how to make a bed or clean a bath, but behavioural, such as not smoking on duty or playing the radio in guest bedrooms.

The final stage of the control system is to 'correct non-standard output'. This simply means that if a room is not up to the expected standard the maid or supervisor will put it right. If for some reason the room cannot be brought up to standard, perhaps due to inundation by water, vandalism or some other serious defect, then the room will be put 'off' until the necessary work has been carried out to restore it to the level of quality expected. Management should ensure that the reasons for failing to meet the required standards are investigated so that action can be taken to ensure that it does not happen again. Such failures may be due to poor selection of staff, poor on-the-job training, faulty equipment, or simply malpractice by employees. When all staff persistently fail to meet standards, it may be necessary to review the standards of performance criteria originally established and revise these in the light of experience.

The extent to which the hotel industry fits this quality control model we have described is distinctive and remarkable. What we have described is both the theoretical model of quality control *and* actual trade practice. It is usual for housekeepers to check every room every time it is serviced. Even in manufacturing industry, from whence this model of quality control is derived, it is rare for every product to be inspected. In most cases a sample is taken and inspected, or inspection is fully automated. It is difficult to imagine how automation might take the place of personal inspection in hotels, but it is interesting to consider why sampling techniques have not been employed in the industry. The most obvious reason for this is that housekeepers do not trust their staff. It may also be due to the relatively unsophisticated expertise of management in the hotel. There are further problems derived from the relatively high levels of staff turnover and part-time staff amongst room-maids which may necessitate closer supervision than one might expect. However, this reality of tight control and high staff turnover is a sad indictment of recruitment, selection, training and working conditions in many UK hotels.

QUALITY AUDIT

So far we have discussed internal approaches to managing quality in a hotel. An external approach to examining the nature of the service experience in an establishment is to conduct a 'quality audit'. Quality audits can be used either to test hypotheses or substantiate hunches about the organisation's service effectiveness, or they can be used as part of a total quality improvement programme. An audit has been defined[8] as 'an independent evaluation of service quality to determine its fitness for use and conformance to specifications.' As we shall see, such an audit attempts to overcome the problems we have identified above by ensuring objectivity through independence from the organisation and by expert and articulate evaluation of the experience through observation and participation. Prior to any such audit taking place, management and auditor will discuss and agree the objectives, methodology, scheduling and reporting procedures of the study.

In the case of hotels, it is generally accepted[9] that the nature of the service is so complex that an audit cannot be made of the entire service experience. Therefore, it is necessary to establish the objectives of the audit. A commonly used method is Pareto analysis, that is to say every possible problem is listed and then ranked in their order of importance. A second technique, advocated by Wyckoff,[10] is 'fishbone' analysis which helps to identify cause and effect.

Once the objectives are established, the next step is for the auditor to adopt the consumer's frame of reference, that is to say 'adopt the customer's mentality'.[11] This is done by familiarisation with the profile of typical customers in terms of their age, background, occupation, income and so on. From this some judgements can be made concerning their life-style and likely attitudes towards the service provision. Some attempt will also be made to assess the purpose and importance of the service, i.e. overnight stay, to the customer, for instance is the stay for pleasure or business purposes.

The next stage is to conduct the audit itself. There are two main methodologies, both of which are usually used. The first is to observe guests experiencing the service, and the second is to participate as a guest in the experience. Whilst it is possible that the auditor is introduced to employees and his or her role explained, in most cases this is not done. The reasons for this are so that staff do not change their behaviour because they know they are being observed, the auditor experiences the same experience as real customers, and distrust as to the purpose of the exercise is not created. The only disadvantage of this is that the exercise requires a detailed recording of the experience which can involve note-taking, tape-recording, photographs, checklists and chatting to other customers.

Once the observation/participation period is completed a detailed report of the study is written, and an analysis of the findings is made. It is usual to identify each of the contributory factors that lead to guest satisfaction and then to rate them in some way. This can be a rating on a classification scale or a semantic differential scale. The former would grade items along a scale such as excellent, acceptable, moderately acceptable, and so on, often giving a numeric score to each, such as excellent = 1, acceptable = 2, and so on. Another scale can be the better-and-worse-than continuum:

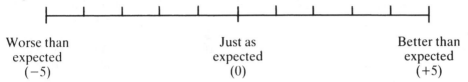

Worse than	Just as	Better than
expected	expected	expected
(−5)	(0)	(+5)

For each of the factors rated the audit would give the basis for any deviation from the best or expected score. For instance, a rating of acceptable with regard to transaction time at a check out might be a result of the average length of time being 30 seconds longer than the expected or laid-down standard length of time.

The *advantages* of quality audits are:

- they are consumer-oriented;

- auditors take a consumer's perspective but can explain themselves to management in a way that management can understand;

- the audit is independent and therefore objective;

- it provides a wealth of detail;

- the data collected is actionable, that is to say management can act to correct below standard performance.

The *disadvantages* are:

- in terms of statistical sampling an audit does not provide any valid evidence of actual guest's level of satisfaction;

- there may be bias on the part of the auditor;

- the auditor's experience, like each other customer's, is unique and may provide misleading evidence;

- an audit can only be carried out infrequently due to its complexity and cost;

- the detail of the audit may result in results that do 'not see the wood for the trees'.

QUALITY ASSURANCE IN HOTEL OPERATIONS

We suggest that this approach is most appropriate for those aspects of provision where there is contact with the customer. However, in view of our comments about the control approach, we would argue that assurance may also have a role to play back-of-house too. As we saw in chapter 3, the essential difference between control and assurance is that the assurance concept is designed to ensure that errors and faults do not occur. This is particularly important where there is face-to-face contact with guests, as badly handled personal interactions are very difficult to correct if they should go wrong. Implicit in the idea is that a premium must be paid is some way to achieve this end.

The whole operational context and management style is likely to be different in a unit that fully adopts quality assurance. This will result in the unit addressing the problems of the social/intangible segment of our matrix (figure 9.2) by allowing staff to personalise their contact with customers. Rather than impose a system upon the operation, 'these new methods give caring workers the tools for self-improvement in delivering service quality – and substantially reduce the need to denigrate service quality by sacrificing customisation, choice, flexibility, and personalised service.'[12] By the operation's very nature, then, stressing as it does customisation and personalisation, there is no *one* specific approach. It is more a question of philosophy than of a system. Merricks and Jones[13] suggest that the principles of this philosophy are:

- imaginative ideas and responses to problems;

- a questioning attitude towards all aspects of the operation;

- a total commitment to quality.

Such principles are fine in theory, but how can they be put into practice? With regard to the business environment, most employees can easily identify what the business is but may have a very wide range of views about the most important aspect of that business. Quality can be brought to the forefront of their thinking by an overt use of the word from the moment of recruitment, right throughout the induction period and during any on-the-job training, as in McDonald's. Or, since this concept may also be consistent with the image the operation wishes to create in the consumer's mind, it can become part of an advertising slogan. This emphasis on one feature of the operation can then become central to the shared value system of the organisation, whereby management praise high quality performance, promotion or bonuses are seen to relate to the quality of work done, the physical resources, such as equipment and work environment, provide the necessary tools to achieve quality and are of high quality themselves, and so on. It will be difficult for management to convince their workforce of the need for quality front-of-house if their changing rooms are filthy, their work clothes ill-fitting, and management do not appear to care about timekeeping, personal appearance and standards.

Both management and staff can therefore help to set standards by behaving as role models, thereby contributing to the cultural climate. This means management and supervisory staff must clearly express opinions and display behaviour that is quality-conscious, and staff who are particularly adept must be seen to be rewarded. Such members of staff become 'heroes' to whom other members of staff can relate and look up to, they make success human and attainable, and potentially they can motivate their fellow workers. This can further be supported by the rites and rituals that arise in any organisation. These might include the manager buying a drink after work for the employee who has been the most quality conscious worker of the week, or the informal presentation of awards to staff during a training session.

As well as these general principles aimed at creating the appropriate climate in which quality can thrive, there is a particular technique that is meant to result in total commitment to the idea – namely the *quality circle*. A quality circle has been described as 'a group of four to ten volunteers working for the same supervisor who meet once a week, for an hour, under the leadership of the supervisor, to identify, analyse and solve their own work-related problems.'[14] The typical features of such circles are that they are entirely voluntary, intensely practical and unbureaucratic. But there is widespread confusion about both the objectives and appropriate format of quality circles in the USA and UK. Originally modelled on circles developed in Japan, certain features of Japanese work ethics and culture do not exist in the West. For instance, Japanese workers are very loyal, expect to work for the same employer for their lifetime, exhibit a group-based work ethic, and are prepared to join in many company organised activities, including quality circles, outside their normal working hours.

On the basis of the Japanese model, it has been proposed that the growth and development of the circles depends entirely on the employees and is not dictated by the organisation. The way in which each circle works should be as follows:

- originate list of problems by brainstorming;
- reject those problems outside own work area;
- select those problems that are possible to solve;
- rank problems in priority order.
- analyse the problem;
- collect relevant data;
- solve problem;
- sell this solution to management.

For this concept to be effective it is essential that some guiding principles are followed. Much of the criticism of quality circles has come from organisations who have implemented the idea without fully adopting these principles.

First, membership of the circle is entirely voluntary. Thus management cannot even set up the first circle, they can only explain the idea to supervisors and workforce and then hope that their staff will take up the idea. Since there is no obligation to return every week, quality circles will only continue if the workforce continue to volunteer.

Secondly, particularly in the early stages, circles should only address themselves to solving problems within their own work area. It is usually the case that poor performance is blamed on other sections of the workforce, but this is not the concern of the members of a quality circle.

Thirdly, the circle itself will determine its mode of operation, although the organisation can provide support with regard to training and expertise in techniques such as brainstorming, data analysis, and so on. Problem-solving requires staff to become experts in a very difficult area of expertise, so that they may also need to be introduced to some of the techniques we have mentioned previously such as Pareto analysis, flow charting, fishbone analysis, and so on.

Fourthly, the circle will only be effective if it is accepted by management and given any information that it thinks it requires to solve problems. Companies and management are often reluctant to divulge information which they regard as confidential, simply because it gives them a psychological edge over others, but 'facts and figures distinguish quality circles from suggestion boxes'.

Finally, the organisation must have a realistic time perspective with regard to how long it will take for the idea and the groups to be effective. It is likely that at least two years are needed before quality circles might start to consider problems at the interface between themselves and other employees. 'Every operator who has reported successful circles . . . has stressed the fact that it has been a long-term growth experience for everybody involved.'[15]

This approach has, however, often had only mixed results. The UK has a very different labour relations and industrial climate to Japan. In particular, by involving employees in a more open and participative style of management, employee expectations may be raised, but frustration may set in when these expectations are not met. Because of this, it may not be practical to think of quality circles as a long-term approach, but one with relatively short-term and specific quality objectives.

The reported benefits of quality circles are numerous. Most importantly they change attitudes within the organisation: staff are better motivated, supervisors gain confidence, problem-solving is more competent, communication at all levels is improved, and there is the creation of a problem-solving rather than blame-shifting ethic. As well as these unquantifiable results, organisations have found that the solutions that circles generate can in some cases save them thousands of pounds per year. And a better motivated work force has resulted in less absenteeism and lower rates of staff turnover.

These reported benefits have also caused some confusion as to the role that circles play. In Japan and as described above, quality circles are all about solving problems and issues broadly related to quality. The 'side effects' of improved work relations are largely taken for granted. In the West, however, quality circles have sometimes been formed with the intention and objectives of improving work relationships. Such objectives should be viewed as possible, but quite separate and distinct from the quality issue. The use of circles to effect such changes at work are in effect using them as a device to modify organisational culture and as such they require even more support, commitment and depth than the QC model described above. In this context, circles should always be viewed as a long-term device since cultural shifts cannot take place in the short term unless very great external forces for change exist. We have discussed the role of culture and its affect on service provision in chapter 7.

Another approach to assuring the quality of service is to adopt 'internal marketing'. Internal marketing recognises the central role that employees make to the effective provision of services. We have examined this in some detail in chapter 7. As Levitt has stated:[16] 'The more people-intensive a product, the more room there is for personal discretion, idiosyncrasy, error, and delay . . . it is an enormous quality control problem.' Jones[17] has argued that: 'Internal marketing tackles this issue by providing a coherent, logical overview of the total service delivery system; facilitating interaction and collaboration between different functions of the organisation; and providing a proactive, rather than reactive, approach to the efficient and effective implementation of new service concept developments.'

This involves recognising that staff, as well as customers, experience the organisation's media advertising. Internal communication with staff should reinforce and build on the message(s) of this advertising. Research has found that well conceived advertising has a positive impact on employees. For instance, the campaign of one American bank about 'person-to-person' banking using bank employees to explain the idea resulted in 90 per cent recall by employees, over 80 per cent agreeing that the advertisement set a job performance standard for them to follow, and nearly 75 per cent stating that they had become more concerned with customer care. The same impact of advertising has also been seen in airline organisations, railways, travel and hotel companies. Similarly, approaches that increase sales such as sales promotions can equally be applied to staff. For instance, just as it is possible to 'reward' loyal customers with gold charge cards, it is possible to reward loyal staff with a badge or insignia of 'rank'.

The recognition of staff as a secondary market accords with the idea of considering staff as 'secondary' consumers, specifically those in contact with the customer. Usually, customer contact staff depend in some way on the support of back-of-house resources, which might be either technical or labour-based. For instance, the hotel receptionist depends on the housekeeping staff. By developing the idea of front-of-house staff being 'customers', back-of-house staff are encouraged to participate more in the role of hotel-keeping and provide higher levels of support to colleagues.

MANAGING CUSTOMER PERCEPTIONS

We have identified the fact that quality is in 'the eye of the beholder'. It is the customer's perception of reality, rather than reality itself, that is important. Capoor[18] captures this important point by providing an alternative view of service provision which divides service provision into three components:

1. *core process*: the tangible aspects;

2. *interactive process*: the infinite variations derived in partnership with customers;

3. *customer component*: infinite needs satisfied and received by customers.

So far we have concentrated on how the hotel manager manages the quality of the first two of these components. This is because it is extremely difficult to manage the customer component, their perceptions. But we know that quality in services is made up of determinants that are perceptual rather than concrete, such aspects as 'credibility', 'rapport', and 'freedom of choice'.

The issue of managing customer perception is largely that of marketing the service effectively. There are at least four potential causes of a breakdown in quality perception. First, management may not correctly interpret customers' needs and expectations. Secondly, even if these are correctly interpreted, their translation into service quality specifications may be imperfect, so that even if the service is delivered to these standards, customers will not be satisfied. Thirdly, the external communication of the service, through advertising, merchandising and so on, may give a false impression to the customer. And finally, the customer's perception of the actual service may be different to what they thought they wanted.

We are primarily concerned here with the ongoing management of quality. The first and second perceptual 'gaps' highlighted above derive largely from market research and new product development, which are outside the scope of this text. They are, however, dealt with in some depth in *Hotel and Food Service Marketing*.[19]

With regard to the effective ongoing marketing of the hotel and its services, and the role of this in the customer's perception of quality, the main strategy service organisations have adopted has been to make the intangibles tangible. There are a variety of ways in which intangible services, which are perceived as more risky by consumers, can be made more tangible. First, television is more powerful than any other medium since it enables the actual act of service and happy customers to be portrayed. Secondly, since this media is not always affordable or appropriate, concrete and easily identifiable logos help to support the advertising. A good example is Legal and General's umbrella, and Embassy Hotels' crown. Thirdly, personalities with the appropriate image can be featured in both print and television advertising, or as voice-overs on radio or television. Both logos and personalities should also ensure continuity. This is particularly important in services as customers need continual reassurance that the service is as good as it has always been. McDonald's are particularly good at this. Their television advertising may be promoting some specific aspect of the business, but the music, logo, images and personalities are always consistent. Fourthly, concrete images can be structured to convey tangible clues as to the nature of the service. For instance, Thistle Hotels recently ran a campaign based on actual examples of the individuality and up-market nature of their units.

The Thistle example also illustrates an important feature of service advertising, namely never promise something that cannot be delivered. In the Thistle case, one advertisement illustrated the four-poster bed in a certain room. For many weeks after the advertisement was run in the national press, that hotel had to refuse customers specifically requesting to reserve the featured room. Much worse than this, is the advertising claim that promises a level of service that cannot be met.

As well as making intangibles more tangible in marketing, a hotel can and may have to apply the same idea to its actual service provision. For instance, customers may be concerned about the health and hygiene aspect of their hotel stay. The cling-film wrapping of toilet seats and individual sealing of drinking glasses provide concrete evidence of the cleanliness of the unit. By doing these two things, customers are reassured about the cleanliness of all items and parts of the hotel. Another aspect of service may be its speed. One hotel that experienced customer complaints that service was slow found that in fact service was not slow at all. The hotel therefore provided guests with evidence of this fact by using an old-fashioned egg-timer (the kind that lets sand trickle through from one glass container to another). Each customer was escorted to a table by the restaurant supervisor, who placed the egg-timer on the table. The customer was told that it took one minute for the sand to run through and, if by that time, the waiter had not come to take the order, then the meal would be free of charge.

MEASURING GUEST SATISFACTION

Following on from new product development and marketing, it is clear that customer's perceptions need to be analysed on an ongoing basis. Guest satisfaction may be monitored in three main ways: unsolicited complaints and compliments, comment cards and customer surveys. Of these, the first two only represent an active segment of all customers, i.e. those prepared to comment verbally or in writing. A customer survey, however, obtains opinions from a much broader range of customers and as such is preferable as a means of ensuring quality management has been effective.

Using unsolicited complaints and compliments is not a particularly sound way of measuring satisfaction for a variety of reasons. They can be expressed either at the time the customer is experiencing the service or afterwards, usually through a complaint letter. In fact one survey found that 60 per cent of all written complainants had already expressed their complaint in person at the time.[20] It is unlikely that management will keep any valid record of such verbal complaints, simply because the recording of them would be impractical, so that it is usually written complaints that form the basis of evaluation. Such complaints ignore the customers who are only moderately dissatisfied, maybe enough not to use the establishment again but not so annoyed as to write to complain. The ratio of complaints to compliments received is often used as a measure of the quality of management. However, the same research showed that, using both letters and comment cards, actual complaints and compliments received did not reflect the actual ratio of happy and dissatisfied customers. One in three compliments were expressed but only two in seven complaints, so an operation that had approximately an equal number of complaints and compliments would, in fact, have more dissatisfied customers than satisfied ones.

Comment cards have also come in for a considerable amount of criticism. Lewis and Pizam[21] have described most of them as meaningless, unreliable, product-oriented and statistically not valid. Typical faults included asking customers to rate rooms on a scale such as excellent, good, fair, poor. In this instance, whilst a rating of poor will clearly indicate dissatisfaction, management are unable to identify the exact nature of the problem. Another format is to ask yes/no questions such as: 'Was your room properly prepared?' In this case it is easy to see that a customer might answer yes to this question, even if he or she did not actually like the room. A slightly more effective means of asking customers for their opinion is to ask if the provision met their expectations or not. At least here, there is an attempt to match service with customers' wants. Once again, however, a respondent who replies that the service did not meet expectations could mean that, whilst it was not as good as expected, it was still satisfactory.

Lewis and Pizam have identified the factors that a satisfaction index should achieve. It should:

- measure the dominant trends in consumer satisfaction;
- provide straightforward information;
- not be too long to encourage customers to respond;
- tell the organisation if the guest will return or not;
- meet the specific needs of an operation;
- be easy to analyse, so that prompt action can be taken.

In order to do this they suggest the following methodology. First, detailed interviews are conducted with customers of a business to discover which variables were important in creating satisfaction or dissatisfaction. This potentially long list of variables is then factor analysed to arrive at a smaller number of main factors or dimensions, so that the final survey is not too long. In the event that a particular dimension is found to be rated badly, it can be examined in more detail by separating out the original variables to investigate the exact nature of the problem in a subsequent survey. The most important step is then to use regression analysis in order to weight each of the dimensions according to their importance in contributing to an overall level of satisfaction, for example in a hotel bedroom layout might have a weighting of 0.5, whilst the bed size might have a weighting of 0.1. The significance of this weighting is seen when guests are asked to rate the dimensions on a five-point scale, as illustrated in table 9.1.

Table 9.1 illustrates the importance of weighting each factor. Both example A and B have a total rating of 15, representing a satisfaction level of 60 per cent. However, after each factor is weighted, in example A the customer has a satisfaction level of 80 per cent because the most important factors are rated highly, whereas in example B

Table 9.1 *Hypothetical Satisfaction Index for a Hotel Bedroom.*

Example A

Factor	Weight	Rating 1 to 5	Possible	Weighted Rating	Possible
Room layout	0.5	5	5	2.5	2.5
Room size	0.2	4	5	0.8	1.0
Executive rooms	0.15	3	5	0.45	0.75
Bed size	0.1	2	5	0.2	0.5
Room decor	0.05	1	5	0.05	0.25
	1	15	25	4	5
Satisfaction level		60%		80%	

Example B

Factor	Weight	Rating 1 to 5	Possible	Weighted Rating	Possible
Room layout	0.5	1	5	0.5	2.5
Room size	0.2	2	5	0.4	1.0
Executive rooms	0.15	3	5	0.45	0.75
Bed size	0.1	4	5	0.4	0.5
Room decor	0.05	5	5	0.25	0.25
	1	15	25	2	5
Satisfaction level		60%		40%	

Adapted from Lewis and Pizam[21]

the customer's satisfaction is only 40 per cent since the most important factors are rated poorly.

Whilst it is admitted that this methodology provides both reliability and validity, it does require a detailed survey of the particular operation to be made in order to establish the weighted factors, which to a certain extent counteracts the ease of administration and analysis that the method affords. The detailed preliminary survey can only be administered once in several years, and there must be concern as to how long the factors identified, and in particular their weighting, will remain valid over such a long period of time in what is recognised to be a highly dynamic market.

SUMMARY

However good a quality management system, it is inevitable that some customers will complain. As well as monitoring the level of complaint for feedback purposes it is important to take action to resolve the complaint as soon as possible. Whilst the nature of the hotel operation does present a whole host of problems that we have discussed in this chapter, to a certain extent these characteristics make complaint resolution somewhat easier than in other businesses. First, it may be possible to put things right straight away; face-to-face contact enables an apology to be offered, and if need be, some form of reparation, such as no charge for an item or some form of discount. Thus it may be possible to extinguish dissatisfaction before the customer has the opportunity to complain to others. Indeed, swift and efficient response can actually reinforce satisfaction and loyalty. In particular, customers who complain need to be convinced that management have taken action to ensure that the cause of the complaint has been removed, not only from their point of view but for ever. Dissatisfaction can often be aggravated by a response that suggests a standard reply, without any action to resolve the cause for the original complaint.

In this chapter we have identified the importance of quality to the hotel operation, examined the meaning of quality and the problem of defining quality standards for the hotel industry. We suggested that approaches to hotel quality management can be seen as a matrix with a dimension relating to the level of tangible provision and a dimension relating to the type of contact the customer has in the unit. For those material/tangible components, typically back-of-house, we identified that the industry has traditionally adopted a quality control system approach. We went on to advocate for the social/intangible component the adoption of a quality assurance approach including the use of quality circles to involve staff in quality management. We also explained the role of quality audits in providing an external check on a hotel's quality performance. Essentially our analysis suggests that the material/intangible component is outside the direct control of management, but is affected by effective marketing and new product development. By implementing quality control and assurance techniques, the manager can influence customer satisfaction which should be measured on a regular basis.

REFERENCES

1. British Standards Institute, BSI 4778: BSI Handbook 22: 1983.

2. Hart, C. W. L., and Casserly, G. D., 'Quality: a brand-new, time-tested strategy', *Cornell HRA Quarterly*, pp. 52–63 November 1985.

3. Berry, L. L., Zeithaml, V. A., and Parasuraman, A., 'Quality counts in services, too', *Business Horizons* vol. 28. no. 3, pp. 44–52, May/June 1985.

4. Nightingale, M., 'The hospitality industry: defining quality for a quality assurance programme – a study of perceptions', *Service Industries Journal* vol. 5, no. 1, pp. 9–22, 1985.

5. Wyckoff, D. D., 'New tools for achieving service quality', *Cornell HRA Quarterly*, pp. 78–91, November 1984.

6. Jones, P., 'The restaurant – a place for quality control and product maintenance?' *International Journal of Hospitality Management* vol. 2, no. 2, pp. 93–100, 1983.

7. King, C. A., 'Service-oriented quality control', *Cornell HRA Quarterly*, pp. 92–98, November 1984.

8. Juran, J. M., and Gryna, F. M., *Quality Planning and Analysis*, McGraw Hill, 1980.

9. Haywood, K. M., 'Assessing the quality of hospitality services', *International Journal of Hospitality Management* vol. 2, no. 4, pp. 165–177, 1983.

10. Wyckoff, D. D., *op. cit.*

11. Haywood, K. M., *op. cit.*

12. Jones, P., *op. cit.*

13. Merricks, P., and Jones, P. L. M., *The Management of Catering Operations*, Holt, Rinehart and Winston (Cassell) 1986.

14. Robson, M., *Quality Circles: A Practical Guide*, Gower, 1983.

15. Faulkner, E., 'Will quality circles work in American foodservice operations?', *Restaurants and Institutions*, September 1983.

16. Levitt, T., 'Marketing intangible products and product intangibles', *Harvard Business Review*, pp. 94–102, May/June 1981.

17. Jones, P. L. M., 'Internal marketing', *International Journal of Hospitality Management* vol. 5, no. 4, pp. 201–204, 1986.

18. Capoor, R., 'Strategic planning', *Restaurant Business*, pp. 198–202, May 1981.

19. Buttle, F., *Hotel and Food Service Marketing*, Holt, Rinehart and Winston (Cassell), 1986.

20. Lewis, R. C., 'When guests complain', *Cornell HRA Quarterly*, pp. 23–32, August 1983.

21. Lewis, R. C., and Pizam, A., 'The measurement of guest satisfaction', in Pizam, A., Lewis, R. C., and Manning, P. (eds), *The Practice of Hospitality Management* AVI Publishing, pp. 189–201, 1982.

10 Managing the Key Result Areas

INTRODUCTION

This text has approached hotel management in a distinctive and specific way. We have proposed that the most effective and relevant approach is based around the concept of key result areas and we have identified in the last seven chapters ideas, techniques and systems that enable the manager to be successful in each of these areas. But as we identified in figure 2.5, a fundamental feature of our model of hotel management is the integrative nature of these key result areas. This chapter therefore has three main objectives: first, to identify and explain the extent to which our model hotel manager is likely to be different from the traditional hotel manager; secondly, to investigate the implications of applying the concept of key result areas to a typical hotel unit and to a typical hotel organisation; and finally, we shall attempt to illustrate how a hotel manager working within the guidelines of this text should behave and act in order to implement the approach successfully.

Before meeting these objectives it is important to state that we are not proposing a total revolution. Indeed it could be argued by directors and managers of hotel companies that their business success indicates that there is no need to change anything in terms of management approach and style. The fantastic growth rate of chains such as Mount Charlotte and Queens Moat Houses, the acquisition of Hilton International by Ladbrokes, the world-wide pre-eminence of Trusthouse Forte, suggests that British hotel managers are successful and effective. However, this rosy picture is clouded by high levels of management turnover within the industry, a shortage of hotel rooms which makes London one of the most expensive places in the world to stay, frequent organisational restructuring within hotel firms, a sense of frustration and antipathy between hospitality practitioners and educators, and a sense of 'we could do better' amongst certain key individuals and major organisations. Venison[1] is an excellent example of a highly talented and effective manager who attempts to reconcile his own personal approach to management with both management theory and industry practice. Commonwealth Holiday Inns of Canada are an example of an organisation which is also seeking through research, investigation and innovation to improve upon its present level of success.

We believe that this text contributes to the search for better ways of doing things in two main ways. First, it takes the body of knowledge that already exists in its traditional form and restructures it in a framework based around key result areas that facilitate and encourage effective hotel management. It does this by focusing on the issues that lead to success rather than concentrating on simple techniques and approaches divorced from the context in which they are to be applied. Secondly, the text adds to the body of knowledge a whole range of developing ideas and concepts derived from research into service industries and suggests how these may be applied to the hotel context.

COMPARING THE TRADITIONAL AND KEY RESULT MODELS

The traditional model of hotel management has certain key features. These include power relationships, organisation structure, performance measurement, a functional perspective and the aims of the organisation. These are usually quite clearly expressed either extrinsically through policy statements, company reports, internal memoranda, and so on, or intrinsically through the behaviour of managers and staff, customer satisfaction levels and market research. All too often, however, these five features are internally inconsistent with each other and give rise to conflict. Power is used by managers on the basis of their position and authority; organisation structures are hierarchical, rigid and prescribed; managers concentrate on their own departmental or functional area with little consideration for the total unit; management performance is measured purely in financial terms; and the aims and objectives of the organisation are also largely specifically expressed in terms of financial performance and only vaguely expressed in terms of customer and employee satisfaction.

These five factors combine to produce an organisational culture which may be role-, task- or power-oriented as discussed in chapter 7 but which has an inappropriate service climate that fails to reconcile the needs and wants of the organisation, the consumer and the employees. Evidence of this is found in nearly every annual report of British hotel companies, in the written job descriptions of hotel managers, in the levels of staff turnover in the industry, in the levels of dissatisfaction expressed by hotel customers in market research surveys, in customers' lack of company loyalty, in the stress induced by excessively long hours worked by hotel management staff, in the number of job vacancies advertised every week in the *Caterer and Hotelkeeper*, in the concern expressed by hotel management students, in the sometimes contentious dialogue and debate between hoteliers expressed in the media, in the lack of chain hotels in the major UK hotel guide books, and in the poor image the industry has as an employer.

The approach to hotel management based on key result areas challenges many of these traditional and established practices. First, by presenting management as the integration of seven major areas of focus it demands that tasks and activities are not placed in discrete functional boxes. It follows that management must work more closely together as a team, which will have inevitable consequences for the distribution of power within the organisation. Secondly, there is an extremely strong emphasis on the role of the consumer in terms of being effective in the hotel context, and an equally strong emphasis on the importance of employees. This relegates the product-oriented financially focused approach to a less significant part of the manager's job. We have argued that performance measurement with regard to customers and employees cannot and should not always be expressed in terms of money. Thirdly, this emphasis on people results in a management style and service orientation that radically alters the relationship of all employees operating at unit level, management and staff alike. A proactive and diligent team work to create a climate of trust between themselves and their staff, aimed at meeting objectives and designed to meet both consumer and organisational needs. The focus of the model is on quality which underpins all of the activities undertaken by managers and staff. Such a focus on the quality of the experience by all participants in the service encounter creates a totally new perspective on what hotel management is all about.

THE FUTURE OF HOTEL MANAGEMENT

We would argue that a new approach to hotel management is required in view of the trends and developments taking place in the hotel industry, now and in the future. One major and significant development is the increased emphasis on catering for specific market segments. There has been a substantial increase in the number of hotel groups offering two or three different services aimed at different levels of the market. For example, Holiday Inns, as well as offering their standard product, now offer a budget hotel chain, branded as Hampton Inns, and an up-market chain, branded as Crowne Plaza. In addition, Holiday Inns have also developed all-suite concepts at both economy and luxury levels.

This market differentiation requires management to have a clear understanding of customers and the typical and specific needs of the market segment they are serving. This is made even more complicated by another current trend, the growth of product differentiation within each unit, as typified by the executive floors and ladies' rooms. A clear understanding of what is meant by quality, and defined in chapter 9, is fundamental to this process, but there are clearly implications for all of the key result areas we have identified.

A second major trend is the increasing use and sophistication of computer technology to provide management information. From a slow start to the adoption of this technology the hotel industry has now become heavily reliant on the systems to provide central reservations, front-office and billing administration, and financial and management accounting. In the near future, many hotel companies will have a direct financial link between the unit and head office; financial control information and operating statistics will be directly and immediately available to senior management. It will also be possible to link the guest directly into the system so enabling information about guest satisfaction also to be immediately accessible. If the traditional and existing management approaches were to continue in the context of this information technology explosion, it would seem likely that unit management would become emasculated, rigid hierarchical control would be imposed, and the quality of service would tend towards highly task-oriented, impersonal activity. This may be satisfactory if demand exceeds supply, as has been the case in the past, but this situation may radically change over the next few years.

There seems to be some evidence that the hotel industry is likely to become very much more competitive. Accor Hotels plan to build 30 new hotels in the UK between 1987 and the end of 1989. CHIC have plans to open three Holiday Inns and ten budget hotels in the same period. Trusthouse Forte are rapidly expanding their chain of budget hotels based around their Little Chef operations and the newly acquired Happy Eater chain. Several of the major brewing organisations are investigating the potential of letting accommodation in their larger licensed premises. For instance,

Invicta Inns in Kent and Sussex are significantly investing in their properties in this way.

This increasing competitiveness must increase the need for hotel managers to have a market- and customer-oriented approach. The importance of building customer loyalty in chain operations that have achieved geographic coverage of the UK will depend on the continued excellence of performance by the staff operating in each of the hotels. Whereas previously it was enough to measure a hotel's performance in terms of relatively simple financial targets based on previous years' performances, this rapidly expanding and dynamic marketplace, will require more sophisticated measures of performance. The information technology on site will provide sophisticated analysis, but it will require sophisticated managers to implement appropriate strategies at unit level appropriate for the specific locale, market, and level of competition for each of the chain's hotels. Whereas in the past, organisations may have instituted company-wide quality improvement programmes or sales improvement drives, these may and should become implemented at unit level, drawing on the expertise and resources of head office.

A fourth factor is the concentration occurring in the industry, so that there are many more large-scale organisations emerging. The increasing scale of operations has attracted a great deal of interest and attention from significant parties outside the industry, notably financiers, investors and government. With the shift in the UK towards a service-based economy, more and more attention is being given to the financial and business performance of hotel firms. Whilst this attention may in the short term be focused on those firms with a good past record, analysts are also concerned with future prospects and on investing in those firms which appear to have the appropriate strategy and expertise for the future. There is also outside interest in the industry by other bodies such as trades unions and consumer groups that are also looking to the future and recognising the growing importance of the hotel industry.

All of these external pressures demand that firms should develop the skills and expertise of their managers in the context of the 1990s. Large-scale organisations cannot be seen to have managers who are bad employers, with shortsighted and poor operators who lack initiative, so perpetuating the old image of the hotelkeeper as little more than an up-market pub landlord. There is also a need by such organisations to keep their best managers and not lose them to their competitors. Whereas in the past, perhaps only Trusthouse Forte could offer a clear career path, now many more companies have a range of opportunities for development. Management loyalty, as well as customer loyalty, is likely to become a major issue in the 1990s.

GETTING THERE FROM HERE

At the World Hospitality Congress in Boston in March 1987 the recurring theme of the chief executives of major hotel companies in their addresses to the delegates was the idea that the one certain thing that we know about the future is change. The environment in which hotelkeeping takes place and the nature of hotelkeeping itself is increasingly more dynamic. We have identified some of these trends above, and also suggested that the key result approach to hotelkeeping is the most effective way of dealing with the demands of the next decade. But given that few, if any, hoteliers and hotel companies are looking at the work in this way, and accepting that the traditional model of the industry is the norm, how do we propose that managers and organisations transform themselves?

Major transformational change is possible and is becoming more prevalent in many industries in the UK as they all adjust to the late-twentieth-century economic realities. In many respects, despite world-wide recession, hotel companies have been insulated from this. But such well-known British organisations such as British Airways, British Rail and Jaguar cars have all carried out major transformations. There are potentially five areas that are probably all needed to shift hotel organisations into the mode of the future. These are:

1. organisational design;

2. management development;

3. culture and climate;

4. performance measurement;

5. management information systems.

The idea of key result areas questions the typical organisational structure of the hotel, which broadly speaking comprises a general manager with assistant managers responsible for the functional areas such as food and beverage, rooms division, personnel, and sales and marketing. As we saw in chapter 2 when looking at the Hales and Nightingale study,[2] these specialists are usually designated a number of tasks aimed at achieving specific results in their areas of expertise. But most of the key result areas we have identified in broad terms cannot clearly be assigned to any one of these functional areas alone. For instance, managing demand and supply is equally the responsibility of the rooms division manager as much as the sales manager, just as improving employee performance depends on the operational managers and the personnel manager working in close co-operation.

Does this mean that hotels must totally rethink the management structure in their units? A potentially radical solution would be to discard completely the traditional model and to appoint three assistant managers each with responsibility for one of the primary key result areas, i.e. assets, employees and customers. Within this context it would be possible to assign clear areas of responsibility and to set appropriate objectives. It would also be possible to identify how these managers could jointly collaborate on managing the performance of each of the secondary key result areas, i.e. productivity, service and income. Finally it is clear that responsibility and achievement of results in terms of the quality of performance in the unit would be in the hands of all three managers.

The role of the general manager within this context would be to ensure that effective collaboration and teamwork were achieved and to take a strategic and objective overview of performance targets in each key result area. Implicit in this radical structure is the idea that if managers are managing key result areas and dealing with the issues we have identified, then the role of heads of department and supervisory management personnel is to ensure the effective hour-by-hour operation of the unit.

Such a radical alternative in terms of approach must of necessity require a great deal of management development. It requires hotel management educators, hotel management development executives and all those concerned with the nature of management in their organisation to rethink their whole approach. It is regrettably extremely unlikely that any organisation will be brave enough (or foolhardy enough) to implement this radical alternative. It is, however, quite possible to envisage organisations taking the idea of key result areas and, within the context of existing or slightly modified structures, developing their management personnel in such a way that they begin to think about the world in the way we have outlined. This more realistic view of how managers might manage in the future would still demand a great deal of support and development in terms of existing and future management personnel.

A particular area of management development will be to focus on achieving results through people. Although hotel management degree and diploma courses have paid lip-service to the idea that graduates will be skilled in people management, all too often the courses themselves have been preoccupied with technology systems and hardware. Likewise, in-house management development programmes tend to be preoccupied with the procedural dimensions of hotel management. The increasing use of technology will involve considerable development needs, but it is important that this development sees technology as a means to an end rather than an end in itself.

A third strand in the implementation of the concept of key result areas depends upon the will and ability of senior executives to create the appropriate organisational culture. We have shown, particularly in chapters 4 and 7, how at unit level the appropriate culture is essential to effective performance. In the same way the application and development of key result areas should be viewed as the adoption of a specific philosophical orientation to how business should be conducted in the hotel industry.

As well as the informal context of culture, a further means of promoting key result areas would be the creation and development of appropriate policies and performance measures, such as have been outlined as appropriate for each of the key result areas we have examined. Depending on the nature and approach of the existing hotel organisation, this need not entail a major rethink but rather a reordering of priorities and a reworking of existing documentation and procedures. The formal restructuring cannot and will not be successful without the successful implementation of the shift in the organisational culture described above.

It is not possible to be too prescriptive as to the exact nature of these policies and performance measures. A feature of our model is the idea that there is a potentially unique set of techniqes, systems, procedures and measures for each hotel organisation depending upon its size, market, geographical spread, expertise, strategic objectives and so on. Assuming a hotel organisation is currently relatively successful it is likely to have encapsulated many of these already, but it will need to rethink them in the context of key result areas.

We have already indicated that information technology will be a major vehicle for providing the level of sophistication at the unit level that will be necessary to underpin this approach. For instance, it will not be possible to adopt and implement the ARGE approach to capacity management without up-to-date software packages running on appropriate hardware.

UNIT MANAGEMENT BEHAVIOUR

How will managers behave and act on a day-to-day basis in the context of our modified organisation? Will they continue to work fifteen hour days, embroiling themselves in the everyday interactions of their operations, spending a great deal of their time overseeing and participating in the actual service experience? Clearly the answer to this question is *no*! This cannot be a situation that it is desirable to perpetuate. After nearly one hundred years of hotelkeeping this situation must surely change, especially as the conditions of service of hospitality managers in other sectors such as contract catering are becoming increasingly attractive. In any case it is totally contrary to the concepts of key result areas that managers should behave in this manner. It is our hope that if they apply the ideas and approaches developed here concerning improving employee performance, managing the service encounter and managing quality then they will not need to continue in this manner. Indeed, if they did so, this would be counterproductive to the successful implementation of our proposed strategies, as it would undermine the climate of trust that is fundamental to much of our approach. This does not mean to say that managers will not have a high profile in the unit but that they will need to be far more selective in terms of when they are seen, who they are seen by and what they are seen to do than at present. The ideas advanced by Venison[3] of being in the appropriate place at the appropriate time can clearly be seen to fit with the ideas developed earlier in the text, for instance with regard to providing a role model for staff to follow, focusing attention on particular issues, and so on.

There are already many examples of good practice adopted outside of policy statements that fit with our proposals: the unit manager that replies in person and in detail to any letter of complaint or compliment received by the unit; the front-office manager who will greet in person all arriving customers at a specified time during his shift.

A second feature of management behaviour will be a highly proactive approach to problem-solving and performance improvement in the unit. Whilst recognising that people are the key to improving performance, the future manager will recognise that information is the key to identifying what needs to be done. Such information will be derived, not just from the formal management information systems based on computer technology, but also from sensitivity and awareness of the communication signals generated by customers and staff.

SUMMARY

You may have noticed that the approach we have taken in this chapter has been rather different to the rest of the book. Through the rest of the chapters we have tried to take a reasoned approach supported where possible by research evidence or by industry example. In this chapter we have tried to take the model to its ultimate conclusion; it is our flight of fancy but with a serious purpose.

It would have been possible to write this book without including chapter 2. Each chapter stands in its own right as a collection of approaches, techniques and ideas that can be applied to the operation of a hotel to solve specific problems in specific areas. A hotel manager concerned about one aspect of his or her operation could take one single chapter and find some helpful guidance. However, we feel that the nature of hotel operations is such that it needs a co-ordinated and integrated approach and that the key result model therefore should be applied to the operation in an integrated way. The key result model provides the integrating framework, a conceptual approach to the problems encountered in hotel management, which we feel is valid within the emerging context of hotel operations outlined above. It is, however, a different way of looking at the hotel world, although some aspects of it may be familiar; it is a theoretical alternative to established practice. The implementation of such a model questions the traditions of the hotel industry; it provides a challenge to the established order.

It must be realised, however, that there is limited evidence to support the case we make. It is based on our experience both as managers and as educators and fulfills one of the reasons for writing a book of this nature. It is relatively easy to write a text book which provides a prescriptive approach, giving the correct way to prepare hotel accounts, serve caviar or adopt the appropriate leadership style; we hope that a text book should also be about what *could* be done, how things *might* work. This then is our discussion document, our way of looking at the world, our attempt to stimulate a debate which we believe the industry needs to consider. It is, however, up to individual readers to develop their own internally consistent framework. Readers will take their present views of hotel operations and compare them with our model. There will be areas of agreement and areas of conflict, but from this there should be a synergy of approach which works for readers in their own circumstances to meet their own objectives. It should provide the opportunity for readers to investigate their own perceptions and understandings of how hotels can be managed to bring about the successful hotel operation which is the ultimate goal of us all.

REFERENCES

1. Venison, P., *Managing Hotels*, Heinemann, 1983.

2. Hales, C., and Nightingale, M., 'What are unit managers supposed to do? A contingent methodology for investigating managerial role requirements', *International Journal of Hospitality Management* vol. 5, no. 1, pp. 3–11, 1986.

3. Venison, P., *op. cit.*

Index

Note: All references are to hotel management and UK, except where otherwise indicated.